CBEST® CALIFORNIA BASIC EDUCATIONAL SKILLS TEST™

D0125216

Shannon Grey, Ed.D.
Princeton University
Princeton, New Jersey

Kathryn Porter, Ph.D.
Saint Mary's College of California
Moraga, California

Research & Education Association
www.rea.com

Research & Education Association
61 Ethel Road West
Piscataway, New Jersey 08854
E-mail: info@rea.com

CBEST (California Basic Educational Skills Test) with Online Practice Tests, 7th Edition

Published 2017

Printed in the United States of America

Library of Congress Control Number 2010931552

ISBN-13: 978-0-7386-0784-9
ISBN-10: 0-7386-0784-3

For all references in this book, California Basic Educational Skills Test™ and CBEST® are trademarks, in the U.S. and/or other countries, of the California Commission on Teacher Credentialing and Pearson Education, Inc., or its affiliates.

The competencies presented in this book were created and implemented by the California Commission on Teacher Credentialing and Pearson Education, Inc., or its affiliate(s).

Cover image: Image Source/Getty Images

About REA

Founded in 1959, Research & Education Association (REA) is dedicated to publishing the finest and most effective educational materials—including study guides and test preps—for students of all ages.

Today, REA's wide-ranging catalog is a leading resource for students, teachers, and other professionals. Visit *www.rea.com* to see a complete listing of all our titles.

Acknowledgments

We would like to thank Larry Kling, Vice President, Editorial, for his overall direction; Pam Weston, Publisher, for setting the quality standards for production integrity and managing the publication to completion; John Cording, Vice President, Technology, for coordinating the design and development of the REA Study Center; and Diane Goldschmidt, Senior Editor, for editorial review.

We also gratefully acknowledge Renee Kusch for technical editing; Caragraphics, for typesetting; and Terry Casey for indexing the manuscript.

About the Authors

Dr. Shannon Grey has had a successful career in education for twenty-four years. She graduated with honors with a B.S. in Early Childhood Development from New York University. Dr. Grey received her Masters of Education from Rutgers, The State University of New Jersey's Graduate School of Education, with a specialization in Elementary Language Arts. She earned her doctorate of education from Rutgers in the area of Sociological and Philosophical Foundations of Education, specializing in Curriculum Theory and Development.

Dr. Grey taught elementary school for thirteen years in highly acclaimed public schools. During her time as a teacher she served as a mentor for novice educators, a staff developer, and the chairperson of several school-based and district-wide committees. Dr. Grey was also the co-creator of a summer institute aimed at instructing students in the areas of language arts and mathematics. She has contributed to several REA publications. As a faculty lecturer, she has taught classes in teacher education at Rutgers University, and has taught and supervised student teachers for Princeton University's Program in Teacher Preparation.

Dr. Kathryn F. Porter is Professor of Mathematics at Saint Mary's College of California where she has held various positions including the Coordinator of the Mathematics Preparation Program for future secondary mathematics teachers, the Chair of the Department of Mathematics and Computer Science, the Director of the Liberal and Civic Studies Program, and is currently the Director of Mathematics Readiness. Dr. Porter earned her Ph.D. and M.S. in Mathematics at the University of Delaware and her B.S. in Secondary Education and Mathematics at Slippery Rock University. Professor Porter has written many research articles in the mathematical area of Topology and has served on numerous committees related to mathematics, teaching, and governance. Professor Porter is one of the founders of the highly regarded *Teachers for Tomorrow* program at Saint Mary's College, and has advised future elementary school teachers as well as future secondary mathematics teachers throughout her twenty years at Saint Mary's College.

Contents

The Diagnostic Test is also available online at *www.rea.com/studycenter*

CONTENTS

Studying for the Test

It is never too early to start studying for the CBEST. The earlier you begin, the more time you will have to sharpen your skills. Do not procrastinate. Cramming is not an effective way to study, since it does not allow you the time needed to learn the test material.

When you take REA's practice tests, simulate the conditions of the actual test as closely as possible. Turn your television and radio off, and go to a quiet place free from distraction. Read each question carefully, consider all answer choices, and pace yourself.

As you complete each test, review your performance, study the diagnostic feedback, and review the explanations to the questions you answered incorrectly. But don't overdo it. Take one problem area at a time; review it until you are confident that you understand the material. This strategy will help raise your score.

Keep track of your scores. By doing so, you will be able to gauge your progress and discover your strengths and weaknesses. Take notes on material you will want to go over again. Making notecards or flashcards to record information for future review is a good way to study and keep the information at your fingertips.

Study Schedule

There are many different ways to prepare for the CBEST. The method that is best for you depends on how much time you have to study and how familiar you are with the subject matter. To achieve the highest score possible, you need a study system customized to fit you: your schedule, your learning style, and your current level of knowledge. This book and its accompanying online practice tests provide the tools that allow you to customize your study and will get you ready to pass the exam!

Study Plan: 6 Weeks till Test Day

Week	Activities
1	Read the introduction to this book. This section introduces you to the format of the exam. Be sure you understand the format of the CBEST and know exactly what is tested on the exam. Take the Diagnostic Test in the book or online at the REA Study Center (*www.rea.com/studycenter*). Your detailed score report will identify the topics where you need to focus your study.
2	Study Chapter 3, the Reading Skills Review, and complete the practice questions at the end of the chapter. Give yourself time to review any areas in which you feel you need improvement and take notes on the sections you need to study most. After reviewing this section completely, retake only the section that covers reading skills on the Diagnostic Test to see how your score improves.
3	Study Chapter 4, the Mathematics Review, and complete the practice questions at the end of the chapter. If you missed a lot of questions in one section (algebra, for example), go back and re-read the algebra section of the review and check your answers for each drill question that you answered incorrectly. Retake the math section of the Diagnostic Test and note any improvement.
4	Study Chapter 5, the Writing Review. Focus on the topics and writing examples provided, and make sure you understand how the essays will be graded. Now is also a good time to review any supplemental materials (such as a writing and/or grammar handbook) that will aid you in writing clearer, better focused essays. Try a few practice essays on your own and ask a coworker, spouse, or friend to give you feedback.
5	Take Practice Test 1 in the book or online at the REA Study Center (*www.rea.com/studycenter*). You may take all three sections in one sitting, or take them on different days. Be sure to time yourself as you complete each subtest. Review the explanations for the questions you answered incorrectly. After you've finished the exam, go back and study the detailed explanations of answers to any questions you answered incorrectly.
6	Take Practice Test 2 in the book or online at the REA Study Center (*www.rea.com/studycenter*). Review the explanations for the questions you answered incorrectly. Return to the review chapters in this book to study any topics you are still struggling with. If you have time, you may want to retake sections of the exams.

Good luck on the CBEST!

Introduction

How to Prepare for and Do Your Best on the CBEST

By reviewing and studying this book, you can achieve a top score on the California Basic Educational Skills Test, or CBEST. The CBEST assesses knowledge that you have gained throughout your academic career. Most of the knowledge tested by the CBEST is covered in your college or university teacher preparation programs or through other classes. While the test does not ascertain aspects of teaching such as dedication, rapport with students, and motivation, it does assess basic skills relevant to the teaching profession.

We at REA believe the best way to prep for the CBEST is to replicate the complete CBEST test-taking experience. Toward that end, we provide three full-length exams that accurately reflect the CBEST in terms of format, content, and degree of difficulty. Our practice exams mirror the latest CBEST test forms and include every type of question that you can expect to encounter when you sit for the exam. Following each of our practice exams is an answer key complete with detailed explanations and solutions. Designed specifically to clarify the material for the student, the explanations not only provide the correct answers, but also explain why the answer to a particular question is indeed the best choice. By completing all three practice exams and studying the explanations that follow, you will flesh out your strengths and weaknesses. This in turn will allow you to concentrate progressively on attacking the sections of the exam you find to be toughest.

About REA's Test Experts

To aid us in meeting our objective of providing you with the best possible study guide for the CBEST, REA's test experts have carefully prepared our topical reviews and practice exams. Our authors come armed with specific knowledge of the CBEST. They have thoroughly examined and researched the mechanics of the CBEST to ensure that our model tests accurately depict the exam and appropriately challenge the student. Our experts are highly regarded in the educational community. They have an in-depth knowledge of the subjects presented in the book, and provide accurate questions that will help you best prepare for the exam. Each question is clearly explained in order to help you achieve a top score on the CBEST.

About the CBEST

The state of California specifies that teacher candidates seeking a credential, certificate, or permit to work in California's public schools "must demonstrate basic skills proficiency." The CBEST is the most commonly used method by which teacher candidates meet this requirement. The CBEST may be used:

- As a step toward earning a teaching credential

- To allow for employment as a substitute teacher

- For other purposes such as earning services credentials

To determine whether you should take the CBEST, consult your teacher preparation program or contact the school district where you would like to be work. For questions on CBEST policies, contact the California Commission on Teacher Credentialing:

California Commission on Teacher Credentialing
Attention: CBEST Project Officer
1900 Capitol Ave.
Sacramento, CA 95811-4213
Phone: (916) 322-4974
Website: *www.ctc.ca.gov*

The CBEST is offered as a computer-based test or a paper-based test. Computer testing is offered year-round, Monday through Saturday by appointment only. The paper-based CBEST exam is offered five times a year: in September, December, February, April, and

July. The test is administered by Pearson Education, Inc., under the direction of the CBEST Program. Questions regarding registration procedures for the CBEST can be referred to:

CBEST Program
Evaluation Systems
Pearson Education, Inc.
P.O. Box 340880
Sacramento, CA 95834-0880
Phone: (916) 928-4001 or (800) 262-5080
TTY: (916) 928-4191
Website: *www.ctcexams.nesinc.com*

The CBEST is also accepted in six other states: Alaska, Delaware, Nebraska, Nevada, Oregon, and Washington. Be sure to check for updates on your options with your education program or your state's teacher credentialing agency.

The exam tests reading skills (critical analysis and evaluation and comprehension and research skills), mathematics skills (estimation, measurement, and statistical principles, computation and problem solving, and numerical and graphic relationships), and writing skills (insight into a subject, writing for a specific audience, clarity, consistency of point of view, strength and logic of supporting information, and overall mechanics, spelling, and usage). The CBEST consists of multiple-choice questions and two essay questions. Each multiple-choice question presents five choices (A through E). Examinees are given four hours to take the test. You can divide this time in any way you wish among the three sections.

The test's three sections look like this:

1. **Reading Section:** This section contains 50 multiple-choice questions based on original passages of between 100 and 200 words. In some cases, however, these passages may be short statements of not more than one or two sentences.

2. **Mathematics Section:** This section contains 50 multiple-choice questions. These questions come from three broad categories: arithmetic, algebra, and measurement and geometry. Within these categories, the following types of problems will be tested:

   • Processes Used in Problem Solving—For example, identifying an operation needed to solve a problem or changing a verbal problem into one using math symbols.

   • Solution of Applied Problems—For example, answering word problems including arithmetic, percent, ratio and proportion, algebra, elementary geometry, and elementary statistics.

- Mathematical Concepts and Relationships—For example, recognizing the definitions of certain terms (such as percent) and relationships shown by graphs.

All of these categories require knowledge of arithmetic, algebra, and measurement and geometry.

3. **Writing Section:** This section contains two essay questions. You must write on both topics. One topic requires you to analyze a given situation, the other asks you to write about a personal experience.

Following this introduction are test strategies, examples, and suggested study techniques, all of which will help you properly prepare for the CBEST.

About This Book + Online Prep

About the Review

This book offers three topical reviews that correspond to the subject areas you will find on the exam. These include Reading Skills, Mathematics, and Writing. Supplementing your studies with our review will provide focus and structure and will allow you to choose a particular subject or subtopic to study. The reviews are set up to give you exactly what you need to do well on the exam.

Reading Skills Review

In this review you will be taught to recognize literal, inferential, and critical comprehension questions. We give general strategies for answering reading comprehension questions and then give you ample opportunity to practice these strategies on sample questions.

Mathematics Review

The Mathematics Review offers three mini-reviews on the following topics:

- **Basic Mathematical Concepts**, including integers, prime and composite numbers, odd and even numbers, place value, powers and roots of whole numbers, addition, subtraction, multiplication, and division of integers, common fractions, decimal fractions, percents, and elementary statistics.

- **Algebra**, including algebraic expressions, simplifying algebraic expressions, factoring, solving linear equations, solving inequalities, evaluating formulas, elementary probability, and algebra word problems.

- **Geometry and Measurement**, including perimeter and area of rectangles, squares and triangles, circumference and area of circles, volume of cubes and rectangular solids, angle measure, properties of triangles, the Pythagorean Theorem, properties of parallel and perpendicular lines, coordinate geometry, graphs, and the metric system.

You can read a full review on each topic and then practice your skills with the exercises at the end of the chapter.

Writing Review

The Writing Review focuses specifically on essay writing for the CBEST. You will learn about the types of topics you can expect to see on the CBEST. In addition, you will learn how the essay grade is determined to help you sharpen your writing ability and improve your score.

About Our Practice Tests

REA's three full-length practice tests for the CBEST are offered both in the book and online at the REA Study Center (*www.rea.com/studycenter*). The CBEST is given in paper- and computer-based formats, and our tests will help you prepare for either version of the exam.

Our CBEST practice tests include:

- **1 Full-Length Diagnostic Test**—Before you review with the book, take our diagnostic test. Your score report will pinpoint the topics for which you need the most review, to help focus your study.

- **2 Full-Length Practice Tests**—These practice tests give you a complete picture of your strengths and weaknesses. After you've studied the review, test what you've learned by taking the first practice exam. Review your answers, then go back and study any topics you missed. Take the second practice test to ensure you've mastered the material and are ready for test day.

If you're taking the computer-based exam, we recommend that you take our online practice tests at the REA Study Center (*www.rea.com/studycenter*).

These practice exams simulate the computer-based format of the CBEST and come with:

- **Automatic scoring**—Find out how you did on your test, instantly.

- **Diagnostic score reports**—Pinpoint areas where you need to improve, so you can focus on the topics that challenge you the most.

- **On-screen detailed answer explanations**—See why the correct response option is right, and learn why the other answer choices are incorrect. Our solutions carry you every step of the way, so you'll never be left wondering how to get the answer.

- **Timed testing**—Learn to manage your time as you practice, so you'll feel confident on test day.

To achieve the best results, we recommend you take the diagnostic test and both practice tests. Remember, the more you practice, the more comfortable you will be with the material tested on the CBEST—helping you to score higher!

Scoring the Exam

The Reading and Mathematics sections in the CBEST are scored the same way: raw scores are determined by adding together all the correct answers without deducting points for incorrect answers.

The Writing section is scored a different way. Each of your essays will be scored by two readers. The criteria by which the readers must grade your work are determined before the reading process begins, and the readers are thoroughly trained to grade using only these criteria. The readers are college professors from public and private institutions in California, as well as elementary and secondary school English teachers.

The two readers will assess each of your essays independently. Each will assign a score from 1 to 4, with 4 being the highest:

4 = Pass
3 = Marginal Pass
2 = Marginal Fail
1 = Fail

The four scores are added, yielding a raw section score that can range from a high of 16 to a low of four.

Every CBEST test form is designed to measure the same cluster of basic skills. Nonetheless, the fact that each CBEST test form may have different questions—with varying degrees of difficulty—makes it necessary to convert the raw scores to a scale that adjusts for those variations. The scaled scores run from a low of 20 to a high of 80 for each of the test's three sections.

Attaining a passing score on the CBEST is not just a matter of achieving a minimal overall score, but of doing so on *each section* separately. The scaled passing score on each section is 41, which means that a total score of 123 is required for passing status. While it is possible to pass the CBEST with a scaled score as low as 37 on one or two sections, examinees *cannot pass* the CBEST if they score *below 37* on any one section, no matter how high their total score may be.

Scoring Rule of Thumb: If you correctly answer roughly 70 percent of the items on each section of the test (i.e., Reading, Mathematics, Writing), you will receive a passing grade for the whole test. It should be noted that the actual raw passing score could vary a point or two each time the test is given because different forms of the test may be administered.

Test-Taking Tips to Boost Your Score

1. Guess Away

One of the most frequently asked questions about the CBEST test is: Can I guess? The answer: absolutely! There is no penalty for guessing on the test. That means that if you guess incorrectly, you will not lose any points, but if you guess correctly, you will gain points. Thus, while it's fine to guess, it's important to guess smartly. Be sure, for example, to use the process of elimination (see Strategy No. 2). Your score is based strictly on the number of correct answers. So answer all questions and take your best guess when you don't know the answer.

2. Process of Elimination

Process of elimination is one of the most important test-taking strategies at your disposal. Process of elimination means looking at the choices and eliminating the ones you know are wrong, including answers that are partially wrong. Your odds of getting the right answer increase from the moment you're able to get rid of a wrong choice.

3. All in

Review all the response options. Just because you believe you've found the correct answer—it's still worth looking at each choice so you don't mistakenly jump to any conclusions. If you are asked to choose the best answer, be sure your first answer is really the best one.

4. Use Choices to Confirm Your Answer

The great thing about multiple-choice questions is that the answer has to be staring back at you. Have an answer in mind and use the choices to *confirm* it. For the math section, you can work the problem and find the match among the choices, or you may want to try the opposite: *backsolving*—that is, working backwards—from the choices given.

5. Watch the Clock

Among the most vital point-saving skills is active time management. Make sure you stay on top of how much time you have left and never spend too much time on any one question. Treat each one as if it's the one that will put you over the top. You never know, it just might.

6. Read, Read, Read

It's important to read through all the multiple-choice options. Even if you believe answer choice A is correct, you can misread a question or response option if you're rushing to get through the test. While it is important not to linger on a question, it is also crucial to avoid giving a question short shrift. Slow down, calm down, read all the choices. Verify that your choice is the best one.

7. Take Notes

If you are taking the computer-based version of the test, the test center will provide you with a pen and erasable sheets. Make sure you get these sheets. Use them just like scratch paper to make notes as you work your way toward the answer(s).

8. Isolate Limiters

Pay attention to any limiters in a multiple-choice question stem. These are words such as *initial, best, most* (as in *most appropriate* or *most likely*), *not, least, except, required,* or *necessary.* Especially watch for negative words, such as "Choose the answer that is *not* true." When you select your answer, double-check yourself by asking how the response fits the limitations established by the stem. Think of the stem as a puzzle piece that perfectly fits only the response option(s) that contain(s) the correct answer. Let it guide you.

9. Choice of the Day

What if you are truly stumped and can't use the process of elimination? It's time to pick a fallback answer. On the day of the test, choose the position of the answer (e.g., the third of the four choices) that you will pick for any question you cannot smartly guess. According to the laws of probability, you have a higher chance of getting an answer right if you stick to one chosen position for the answer choice when you have to guess an answer instead of randomly picking one.

10. Confirm Your Click

In the digital age, many of us are used to rapid-clicking, be it in the course of emailing or gaming. If you are taking the computer-based version of the exam, look at the screen to be sure to see that your mouse-click is acknowledged. If your answer doesn't register, you won't get credit. However, if you want to mark it for review so you can return later, that's your call. Before you click "Submit," use the test's review screen to see whether you inadvertently skipped any questions.

11. Creature of Habit? No Worries

We are all creatures of habit. It's therefore best to follow a familiar pattern of study. Do what's comfortable for you. Set a time and place each day to study for this test. Whether it is 30 minutes at the library or an hour in a secluded corner of your local coffee shop, commit yourself as best you can to this schedule every day. Find quiet places where it is less crowded, as constant background noise can distract you. Don't study one subject for too long, either. Take an occasional breather and treat yourself to a healthy snack or some quick exercise. After your short break—5 or 10 minutes can do the trick—return to what you were studying or start a new section.

12. B-r-e-a-t-h-e

What's the worst that can happen when you take a test? You may have an off day, and despite your best efforts, you may not pass. Well, the good news is that a test can be retaken. In fact, you may already be doing this—this book is every bit for you as it is for first-timers. Fortunately, the CBEST test is something you can study and prepare for, and in some ways to a greater extent than other tests you may have taken.

Section 1: Reading

#						#						#					
1.	**A**	B	C	D	E	21.	**A**	B	C	D	**E**	41.	A	B	C	D	E
2.	A	B	C	**D**	E	22.	A	B	**C**	D	E	42.	**A**	B	C	D	E
3.	A	B	C	D	E	23.	A	**B**	C	D	E	43.	A	B	C	D	E
4.	**A**	**B**	C	D	E	24.	A	B	**C**	D	E	44.	A	B	C	D	**E**
5.	**A**	B	C	D	E	25.	A	B	C	**D**	E	45.	**A**	B	C	D	**E**
6.	**A**	B	C	D	E	26.	A	B	C	D	**E**	46.	A	B	C	D	**E**
7.	A	B	**C**	D	E	27.	**A**	B	C	D	E	47.	**A**	B	C	D	E
8.	A	B	**C**	D	E	28.	**A**	B	C	D	E	48.	A	**B**	C	D	E
9.	A	B	**C**	D	E	29.	A	B	C	D	**E**	49.	A	**B**	C	D	E
10.	A	**B**	C	D	E	30.	**A**	**B**	C	D	E	50.	A	B	**C**	D	E
11.	A	B	C	D	**E**	31.	A	B	**C**	D	E						
12.	A	B	C	**D**	E	32.	A	B	**C**	D	E						
13.	A	B	C	**D**	E	33.	A	B	C	D	**E**						
14.	A	**B**	C	D	E	34.	**A**	B	C	D	E						
15.	A	B	**C**	D	E	35.	A	B	**C**	D	E						
16.	A	**B**	**C**	D	E	36.	**A**	B	**C**	D	E						
17.	A	B	**C**	D	E	37.	**A**	B	C	D	E						
18.	**A**	B	**C**	D	E	38.	A	B	**C**	D	E						
19.	A	B	**C**	D	E	39.	A	B	C	D	**E**						
20.	A	**B**	C	D	E	40.	**A**	B	C	D	**E**						

Diagnostic Test

CBEST

This test is also offered online at the REA Study Center (*www.rea.com/studycenter*). We highly recommend that you take the computerized version of the exam to simulate test-day conditions and to receive these added benefits:

- **Timed testing conditions**—Gauge how much time you can spend on each question.

- **Automatic scoring**—Find out how you did on the test, instantly.

- **On-screen detailed explanations of answers**—Learn not just the correct answers, but also why the other answer choices are incorrect.

- **Diagnostic score reports**—Pinpoint where you're strongest and where you need to focus your study.

DIAGNOSTIC TEST

Section 1: Reading

DIRECTIONS: One or more questions follow each statement or passage in this test. The question(s) are based on the content of the passage. After you have read a statement or passage, select the best answer to each question from among the five possible choices. Your answers to the questions should be based on the stated (literal) or implied (inferential) information given in the statement or passage. Mark all answers on your answer sheet. Note: You will encounter some passages with numbered sentences, blank spaces, or underscored words and phrases. These cues are provided on the CBEST for your reference in answering the questions that follow the relevant passages.

Questions 1–5 refer to the following passage:

[1]Spa water quality is maintained by a filter to ensure cleanliness and clarity. [2]Wastes such as perspiration, hairspray, and lotions that cannot be removed by the spa filter can be controlled by shock treatment or super chlorination every other week. [3]Although the filter traps most of the solid material to control bacteria and algae and to oxidize any organic material, the addition of disinfectants such as bromine or chlorine is necessary.

[4]As all water solutions have a pH which controls corrosion, proper pH balance is also necessary. [5]Based on a 14-point scale, the pH measurement determines if the water is acid or alkaline. [6]High pH (above 7.6) reduces sanitizer efficiency, clouds water, promotes scale formation on surfaces and equipment, and interferes with filter operation. [7]Low pH (below 7.2) is equally damaging, causing equipment corrosion, water which is irritating, and rapid sanitizer dissipation. [8](When pH is high, add a pH decreaser such as sodium bisulphate [e.g., Spa Down]; when pH is low, add a pH increaser such as sodium bicarbonate [e.g., Spa Up].)

[9]The recommended operating temperature of a spa (98°–104°) is a fertile environment for the growth of bacteria and viruses. [10] This growth is prevented when appropriate sanitizer levels are continuously monitored. [11]Maintaining a proper bromine level of 3.0 to 5.0 parts per million (ppm) or a chlorine level of 1.0–2.0 ppm can also control bacteria. [12]As bromine

tablets should not be added directly to the water, a bromine floater will properly dispense the tablets. [13]Should chlorine be the chosen sanitizer, a granular form is recommended, as liquid chlorine or tablets are too harsh for the spa.

1.   Although proper chemical and temperature maintenance of spa water is necessary, the most important condition to monitor is preventing

    (A.)   growth of bacteria and virus.

    B.   equipment corrosion.

    C.   soap build-up.

    D.   scale formation.

    E.   cloudy water.

2.   The ideal operating temperature of a spa is

    A.   above 105°.

    B.   3.0 to 5.0.

    C.   7.2 to 7.6.

    (D.)   98° to 104°.

    E.   1.0 to 2.0.

3.   The primary purpose of the passage is to

    A.   relate how spa maintenance can negate the enjoyment of the spa experience.

    B.   provide evidence that spas are not as practical as swimming pools.

    C.   suggest that spa maintenance is expensive and time-consuming.

    (D.)   explain the importance of proper spa maintenance.

    E.   instruct you on how to care for your spa.

4. Which of these numbered sentences directly states why the use of disinfectant is necessary in the spa?

    A. Sentence 3
    B. Sentence 9
    C. Sentence 7
    D. Sentence 11
    E. Sentence 1

5. Which chemical should one avoid when maintaining a spa?

    A. Liquid chlorine
    B. Bromine
    C. Sodium bisulfate
    D. Baking soda
    E. All forms of chlorine

Questions 6–10 refer to the following chart:

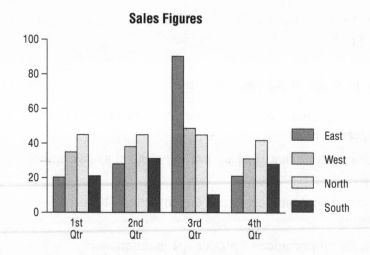

The four divisions of Company X (North, West, South, and East) are represented in the graph by region. The numbers along the left-hand side represent profits from sales in thousands of dollars, while the numbers along the bottom represent the company's fiscal year divided into quarters.

6.   Which region shows the most consistent sales figures for the fiscal year?

   A.   North
   B.   East
   C.   West
   D.   None of the divisions show consistent sales figures.
   E.   Except for one spike in the third quarter, they are all about the same.

7.   Which region shows the greatest profit in one quarter?

   A.   South
   B.   West
   C.   East
   D.   North
   E.   Since it's the same company, all profits are equal.

8.   Which division has the overall lowest sales figures for one quarter?

   A.   West
   B.   North
   C.   South
   D.   East
   E.   None, they all show a profit.

9.   Which two divisions made just over $40,000 in one quarter?

   A.   East and West in the second quarter
   B.   North and South in the first quarter
   C.   North and West in the third quarter
   D.   South and East in the fourth quarter
   E.   South and West in the third quarter

10. Which region shows the most profits for the fiscal year?

    A. East
    B. North
    C. West
    D. South
    E. None of the above

Questions 11–14 refer to the following passage:

Learning to communicate well is very important. _____ communicate articulately, one must understand the meaning embedded in the language. _____ , one must understand a word's connotations (implied meanings) and denotations (literal meanings) in order to communicate clearly. Obviously, articulate communication in the classroom is essential. By being positive role models, teachers can help students develop the skills necessary to put their thoughts and feelings into words. Without <u>articulate</u> communication skills, an individual's thoughts, words, and feelings appear random, confused, and, ultimately, insignificant.

Learning theorists emphasize specific components of learning; behaviorists stress behavior in learning; humanists stress the affective in learning; cognitivists stress cognition in learning. All three of these components occur simultaneously and cannot be separated from each other in the learning process. In 1957, Festinger referred to dissonance as the lack of harmony between what one does (behavior) and what one believes (attitude). Attempts to separate the components of learning either knowingly or unknowingly create dissonances wherein language, thought, feeling, and behavior become diminished of their authenticity. _____ , ideas and concepts lose their content and vitality, and the manipulation and politics of communication assume prominence.

11. Which of the following best describes the author's attitude toward the subject discussed?

    A. A blatant disregard
    B. A moral indignation
    C. Passive resignation
    D. An emotional response
    E. An informed concern

12. The primary purpose of the passage is to

    A.   stress the importance of higher education.

    B.   explain the criteria for learning theories.

    C.   assure teachers that articulate communication is required in the classroom.

    D.   discuss the relationship between learning and communication, and the role of both in the classroom.

    E.   explain the different types of theorists and how they view the classroom differently.

13. What is the most accurate and complete definition of the term <u>articulate</u> as used in the passage?

    A.   Talkative

    B.   Enunciate clearly

    C.   Little

    D.   Important

    E.   Lucid and well-spoken

14. Which of the grouped words or phrases, if inserted in order into the passage's blank lines, would address the logical sequencing of the narrative?

    A.   For example, to; Consequently; Nonetheless

    B.   In order to; That is; As a result

    C.   Thus, to; Moreover; Consequently

    D.   Surprisingly; Thus; Initially

    E.   Ironically; That is; Finally

Use the table of contents below from an education textbook to answer the three questions that follow.

Contents

15. In which part of the book would information about issues facing city schools most likely be found?

    A.   Preface

    B.   Introduction

    C.   Chapter One

    D.   Chapter Two

    E.   Chapter Three

16. A reader is looking to find out about how and/or why the author wrote the book. The reader could probably find this information by looking in which of the following sections of the book?

    A. Title Page

    B. Preface

    C. Introduction

    D. Chapter One

    E. Chapter Two

17. In which part of the book would a reader most readily find information on John Dewey?

    A. Introduction

    B. The Achievement Gap

    C. Prominent Philosophers of Education

    D. Branches of Philosophy

    E. Schools and the Family

Questions 18 and 19 refer to the following passage:

> A major problem with reading/language arts instruction is that practice assignments from workbooks often provide short, segmented activities that do not really resemble the true act of reading. Perhaps more than any computer application, word processing is capable of addressing these issues.

18. The author suggests that a major benefit of computers in reading/language arts instruction is

    A. that the reading act may be more closely resembled.

    B. that short, segmented assignments will be eliminated.

    C. that the issues in reading/language arts instruction will be addressed.

    D. that computer application will be limited to word-processing functions.

    E. that reading practice will be eliminated.

19. The way in which a word-processing program is capable of resembling the "true act of reading" is

    A.   clearly detailed.

    B.   highly desirable to educators.

    C.   unstated.

    D.   suggested as curriculum.

    E.   more accessible, as computers are less expensive.

Questions 20–22 refer to the following passage:

In view of the current emphasis on literature-based reading instruction, a greater understanding by teachers of variance in cultural, language, and story components should assist in narrowing the gap between reader and text and improve reading comprehension. Classroom teachers should begin with students' meanings and intentions about stories before moving students to the commonalities of story meaning based on common background and culture. With teacher guidance, students should develop a fuller understanding of how complex narratives are when they are generating stories as well as when they are reading stories.

20. Who is the intended audience for the passage?

    A.   Parents with young children just entering school

    B.   English teachers using literature-based curriculum

    C.   Administrators who develop school curriculum

    D.   Teachers with multicultural classroom populations

    E.   Students of language and literature

21. Where does the passage suggest that meaning begins?

    A.   In culture, language, and story components

    B.   In comprehension

    C.   In students' stories

    D.   In the teacher's mind

    E.   In students and narratives

22. What is meant by the phrase "variance in culture"?

   A. Different types of stories
   B. Different types of writing techniques
   C. Difference in heritage
   D. Difference in school locations
   E. Difference in educational levels

Questions 23–25 refer to the following passage:

> To define Jonathan Edwards as a representative of the Colonial period in American Literature (1607–1765) requires a brief definition of that era's key ideologies. In the midst of a continuing conflict between advancing scientific frontiers and diversifying religious exegetical interpretations came advances in technology, industrialization, and colonial expansion. Reason and enlightenment were the maxims of the day. For the sake of this argument, the term Colonialism will refer to a direct conquest and control of another's land, culture, heritage, government, and so on. Imperialism will denote the ideology of globalization of capitalist productions. Romanticism, with reference to both these issues, will suggest a form of diluted or tranquilized representation, which thereby makes the horrific realities of these colonial practices gentler to endure, both for the oppressor as well as the oppressed.

23. What does the author mean by Romanticism?

   A. He is in love with his subject matter.
   B. It is a form of stylized representation.
   C. It is a form of make-believe or sentimental drivel.
   D. It is a literary period famous for poetry.
   E. It is a time when people were free to express their feelings.

24. The main idea of the passage is

   A. to introduce Jonathan Edwards.
   B. to present the turmoil of the Colonial period.
   C. to define terminology and philosophy.
   D. to comment on the evils of colonial practices.
   E. to endorse colonial expansion.

25. Which of the following is the most complete and accurate definition of the term <u>Colonialism</u> as used in the passage?

    A. A settlement, homestead, or community in the wilderness

    B. A pioneer

    C. Migrating from one place to another

    (D.) Acquisition and occupation of another's territory, culture, ancestry, etc.

    E. Pilgrim settlements in the New World

Questions 26–29 refer to the following passage:

_____ . This theme has been traced through the following significant occurrences in education: Benjamin Franklin's advocacy in 1749 for a more useful type of education; Horace Mann's zealous proposals in the 1830s espousing the tax-supported public school; John Dewey's early twentieth-century attack on traditional schools for not developing the child effectively for his or her role in society; the post-Sputnik pressure for academic rigor; the prolific criticism and accountability pressures of the 1970s; and the ensuing disillusionment and continued criticism of schools through the turn of the millennium. Indeed, the waves of criticism about American education have reflected currents of social dissatisfaction for any given period of this country's history.

As dynamics for change in the social order result in demands for change in the American educational system, so, in turn, insistence has developed for revision of teacher education (witness the more recent Holmes report [1986]). Historically, the education of American teachers has reflected evolving attitudes about public education. With slight modification, the teacher education pattern established following the demise of the normal school during the early 1900s has persisted in most teacher preparation programs. The pattern has been one requiring certain academic and professional (educational) courses, often resulting in teachers prone to teach as they had been taught.

26. The author of this passage would probably agree with which of the following statements?

   A. Teacher education courses tend to have no real value.

   B. Social pressures should cause change in the American school system.

   C. Teacher education programs have changed greatly since normal schools were eliminated.

   D. Critics of American education have strong lobbies and political interests.

   E. Teachers' teaching methods tend to reflect what they have learned in their academic and professional courses.

27. Which sentence, when inserted into the blank line, would best present the main idea of the passage?

   A. Seldom has the American school system not been the target of demands for change to meet the social priorities of our times.

   B. Times have been tough lately for the nation's schools.

   C. Teachers' unions have expressed growing concern over the widespread use of so-called high-stakes testing.

   D. Teaching is not the easiest profession.

   E. America's public schools are under siege.

28. One possible sequence of significant occurrences in education noted in the passage is

   A. Mann's tax-supported public schools, post-Sputnik pressures for academic rigor, and the Holmes report.

   B. Franklin's more useful type of education, Dewey's educating children for their role in society, and Mann's tax-supported public schools.

   C. Mann's tax-supported public schools, the Holmes report, and post-Sputnik pressures for academic rigor.

   D. Franklin's more useful type of education, the Holmes report, and accountability pressures of the 1970s.

   E. Mann's tax-supported public schools, accountability pressures of the 1970s, and the post-Sputnik pressures for academic rigor.

29. Which of the following statements implies dissatisfaction with the preparation teachers receive in the United States?

   A. Demands for change in the educational system lead to change in the teacher education programs.

   B. Teacher education requires certain academic and professional education courses.

   C. The education of American teachers reflects the evolving attitudes about public education.

   D. Teachers, like pilots, need renewal training every four years.

   E. Teacher education has changed very little since the days of Benjamin Franklin, while teachers tend to teach as they were taught.

Questions 30–33 refer to the following passage:

HAWK ON A FRESHLY PLOWED FIELD

My lord of the Field, Proudly perched on the sod,
You eye with disdain
And mutter with wings
As steadily each furrow I tractor-plod.

"Intruder!" you glare, firmly standing your ground,
Proclaim this fief yours
By Nature so willed—
Yet bound to the air on my very next round.

You hover and soar, skimming close by the earth,
Distract me from work
To brood there with you
Of changes that Man wrought you land—for his worth.

In medieval days, lords were god over all:
Their word was law.
Yet here is this hawk
A ruler displaced—Man and Season forestall.

My Lord of the Field, from sight you have flown
For purpose untold,
When brave, you return
And perch once again, still liege-lord—but Alone.

Jacqueline K. Hultquist (1952)

30. Which of the following definitions is the most complete and accurate in defining the term <u>liege-lord</u> as used in the passage?

    (A.) Landlord

    B. King

    C. Proprietor

    D. Hawk

    E. Entertainer

31. What seems to be the author's disposition toward the hawk?

    A. Whimsical

    B. Imaginary

    (C.) Pensive

    D. Contemptible

    E. Apprehensive

32. How does the hawk observe, according to the narrator?

    A. Contentedly

    B. Admiringly

    (C.) Contemptuously

    D. Adoringly

    E. Complacently

33. Which is the most complete and accurate definition of the term <u>medieval</u> as it is used in the passage?

    A. Archaic

    B. Feudal

    C. Heroic

    D. Antebellum

    (E.) Olden

Questions 34–37 refer to the following passage:

Reduced to its simplest form, a political system is really no more than a device enabling groups of people to live together in a more or less orderly society. As they have developed, political systems generally have fallen into the broad categories of those which do not offer direct subject participation in the decision-making process, and those which allow citizen participation—in form, if not in actual effectiveness.

Let us consider, however, the type of political system that is classified as the modern democracy in a complex society. Such a democracy is defined by Lipset (1963) as "a political system which supplies regular constitutional opportunities for changing the governing officials, and a social mechanism which permits the largest possible part of the population to influence major decisions by choosing among alternative contenders for political office."

Proceeding from another concept (that of Easton and Dennis), a political system is one of inputs, conversion, and outputs by which the wants of a society are transformed into binding decisions. Easton and Dennis (1967) observed: "To sustain a <u>conversion</u> process of this sort, a society must provide a relatively stable context of political interaction, as a set of general rules of participating in all parts of the political process." As a rule, this interaction evolves around the settling of differences (satisfying wants or demands) involving the elements of a "political regime," which consists of minimal general goal constraints, norms governing behavior, and structures of authority for the input-output function.

In order to persist, a political system would seem to need minimal support for the political regime. To insure the maintenance of such a support is the function of political socialization, a process varying according to political systems but toward the end of indoctrinating the members to the respective political system. Again, Easton and Dennis's observation was, "To the extent that the maturing members absorb and become attached to the overarching goals of the system and its basic norms and come to approve its structure of authority as legitimate, we can say that they are learning to contribute support to the regime." The desired political norm (an expectation about the way people will behave) is that referred to as a political efficacy—a feeling that one's action can have an impact on government.

Adapted from Easton, B. and J. Dennis, "The Child's Acquisition of Regime Norms: Political Efficacy," American Political Science Review, March 1967.

34. According to the passage, political efficacy is

    A. most likely to be found where citizen participation is encouraged.

    B. most likely to be found where little direct citizen participation is offered.

    C. in an expanding concept of political efficiency.

    D. in a diminishing concept of political efficiency.

    E. in a figurehead of political system.

35. Political socialization is a process that

    A. occurs only in democracies.

    B. occurs only in totalitarian regimes.

    C. occurs in any type of political system.

    D. occurs less frequently in recent years.

    E. occurs when members reject the goals of the system.

36. As used in the passage, which of the following is the most complete and accurate definition of the term <u>conversion</u>?

    A. Transformation

    B. Changeover

    C. Growth

    D. Resolution

    E. Passing

37. The major distinction between the concepts of Easton and Dennis as opposed to the concepts of Lipset is

   A. that the concepts of Easton and Dennis are based on the wants of a society, whereas Lipset's concepts are based on change of governing officials.

   B. that Easton and Dennis's concepts are based on arbitrary decisions, whereas Lipset's concepts are based on influencing major decisions.

   C. that Easton and Dennis's concepts must have a set of general rules, whereas Lipset's concepts provide for irregular constitutional opportunities.

   D. that Easton and Dennis's concepts have no inputs, conversion, and outputs, whereas Lipset's concepts allow for no regular constitutional opportunities.

   E. that Easton and Dennis's concepts evolve around the settling of differences, whereas Lipset's concepts permit the largest conflict possible.

Questions 38–41 refer to the following passage:

Because Western European historicism constructs a worldview in its own imaginary image, marginal authors such as María Amparo Ruiz de Burton must reclaim or redefine a non-Eurocentric voice in order not only to be heard, but to reenter mainstream society by reestablishing an ethnic identity. One of the ways of recognizing the influence of Western imperialism is by "acknowledging how effectively it naturalizes its own [imperially constructed] history, how it claims precedence for its own culture by identifying culture with nature," and thus assimilates or eradicates indigenous narrative voice (Deane, 357). One such example would be the attempted eradication of the Native American Indian from the social consciousness by speaking of their culture in the past tense, thus implying an extinction process of natural selection. The continuity of this same narrative ideology proposed by Deane (1995) is reflected and reconstituted in Homi Bhabha's DissemiNation (1990) assertion that, "turning Territory into Tradition provides marginal voices [or minority discourse] a place from which to speak" (Bhabha, 300).

38. What does <u>Western European historicism constructs a worldview in its own imaginary image</u> mean?

    A.   Western European historicism is literal and should be understood as such.

    B.   Western European historicism is precise and careful to record facts just as they happened.

    C.   Western European historicism is malleable and periodically adjusted to fit the socioeconomic climate.

    D.   Western European historicism is erroneous and the rest of the world is correct.

    E.   Western European historicism is accurate and the rest of the world is miscalculated.

39. What does the author mean by a <u>non-Eurocentric voice</u>?

    A.   Someone from Europe who cannot speak English

    B.   Someone who is born in Europe and moves to America

    C.   Someone from America who moves to Europe

    D.   Someone from America who cannot speak European

    E.   Someone whose worldview is not filtered through the lens of Western European cultural touchstones

40. What does the author mean by the phrase <u>eradicates indigenous narrative voice</u>?

    A.   The obliteration of traditional native beliefs

    B.   People who cannot speak for themselves

    C.   People who live in a certain region speak their own language

    D.   The creation of native narrative stories

    E.   The removal of one character from a narrative and the replacement of another

41. Which of the following best describes the author's attitude toward the subject discussed?

    A. Morally outraged
    B. Flippant and sarcastic
    C. Frustrated and angry
    D. Informed and involved
    E. Righteously angry and austere

Questions 42–44 refer to the following passage:

Beginning readers, and those who are experiencing difficulty with reading, benefit from assisted reading. During assisted reading, the teacher orally reads a passage with a student or students. The teacher fades in and out of the reading act. For example, the teacher lets his or her voice drop to a whisper when students are reading on their own at an acceptable rate and lets his/her voice rise to say the words clearly when the students are having difficulty.

Assisted reading will help students who are threatened by print read word-by-word, or rely on grapho-phonemic cues. These students are stuck on individual language units, which can be as small as a single letter or as large as a phrase or a sentence. As Frank Smith (1977) and other reading educators have noted, speeding up reading, not slowing it down, helps the reader make sense of a passage. This strategy allows students to concentrate on meaning, as the short-term memory is not overloaded by focusing on small language units. As the name implies, assisted reading lets the reader move along without being responsible for every language unit; the pressure is taken off the student. Consequently, when the reading act is sped up, it sounds more like language, and students can begin to integrate the cueing system of semantics and syntax along with grapho-phonemics.

42. As a strategy, assisted reading is best for

   A. beginning readers who are relying on grapho-phonemic cues.
   B. learning disabled readers who are experiencing neurological deficits.
   C. beginning readers who are relying on phono-graphic cues.
   D. remedial readers who are experiencing difficulty with silent reading.
   E. beginning readers who are experiencing difficulties with silent reading.

43. Language units as presented in the passage refer to

   A. individual letters, syllables, or phrases.
   B. individual letters, syllables, or sentences.
   C. individual letters, phrases, or paragraphs.
   D. individual letters, phrases, or sentences.
   E. individual letters, sentences, or paragraphs.

44. According to the passage, to make sense of a passage a reader must

   A. focus on small language units.
   B. overload short-term memory.
   C. slow down when reading.
   D. read word-by-word.
   E. speed up the reading act.

Questions 45–48 refer to the following passage:

The information about the comparison of the technology (duplex versus one-way video and two-way audio) and the comparison of online classes versus face-to-face classes tends to indicate that although there was not much of an apparent difference between classes and technology, student participation and student involvement were viewed as important components in any teaching/learning setting. For the future, perhaps revisiting what learning is might be helpful so that this component of distance learning can be more adequately addressed. The question remains whether or not student participation can be equated with learning. Participation per se does not demonstrate learning. A more <u>rigorous</u> instrument which assesses and measures learning may need to be addressed with future distance learning studies.

45. Student participation and student involvement are viewed as

   A. consequential ingredients in any teaching/learning environment.

   B. inconsequential ingredients in any teaching/learning environment.

   C. only appropriate with regards to distance learning.

   D. an unrelated component of the distance learning process.

   E. not demonstrative of distance learning.

46. Which of the following is the most complete and accurate definition of the term <u>rigorous</u> as used in the passage?

   A. Harsh

   B. Austere

   C. Uncompromising

   D. Dogmatic

   E. Precise

47. The author of the passage would tend to endorse which of the following statements?

    A. Learning consists of more than student participation.

    B. Duplex technology is better than one-way video and two-way audio.

    C. Student participation and student involvement is not important to learning.

    D. An instrument that assesses and demonstrates learning is not currently available.

    E. A review of learning is not important, as the topic has been thoroughly researched.

48. The primary purpose of the passage is to

    A. delineate the issues in distance learning.

    B. note student participation in distance learning and question this role in learning.

    C. detail the comparisons of online classes versus face-to-face classes.

    D. share information about duplex technology versus one-way video and two-way audio.

    E. request an assessment instrument that includes a learning component.

Use the excerpt below from a cookbook index to answer Questions 49 and 50 below.

Cookies, 220–241
about 220–221
bars, 230–236
caramel melts, 235
coconut, 236
blondies, 230
brownies, 230 – 234
brownie bites, 232
chocolate, 222–224
chocolate chip, 222–223
chocolate–chocolate chip, 223
oatmeal–chocolate chip, 223–224
fruit, 237–240
apricot thumbprints, 239
date drops, 238
oatmeal raisin, 240
oat, 240–241
oatmeal raisin, 240
    oat and honey, 241
nut, 225–229
almond rings, 225
almond–coconut dreams, 226
cashew crunchies, 229
peanut butter, 227
peanut butter fingers, 228

49. On which pages should one look to find information on baking cookie bars?

   A.   220–221
   B.   230–236
   C.   230–238
   D.   229–230
   E.   239–240

50. Which of the following best describes the method of organization used by the book in dealing with the different types of cookies?

   A.   by baking time
   B.   by popularity
   C.   by main ingredient
   D.   by baking temperature
   E.   by baking technique

Answer Key

Section 1: Reading

1. **A**	14. **B**	27. **A**	40. **A**
2. **D**	15. **C**	28. **A**	41. **D**
3. **D**	16. **B**	29. **E**	42. **A**
4. **B**	17. **C**	30. **B**	43. **D**
5. **A**	18. **A**	31. **C**	44. **E**
6. **A**	19. **C**	32. **C**	45. **A**
7. **C**	20. **B**	33. **B**	46. **E**
8. **C**	21. **E**	34. **B**	47. **A**
9. **C**	22. **C**	35. **C**	48. **B**
10. **B**	23. **B**	36. **A**	49. **B**
11. **E**	24. **C**	37. **A**	50. **C**
12. **D**	25. **D**	38. **C**	
13. **E**	26. **E**	39. **E**	

Section 1: Reading

1. **A**

    Choices (B), (D), and (E) present minor problems in spa maintenance, whereas choice (C) cannot be prevented. As both temperature and chemicals control bacteria and viruses, it becomes a possible source of health problems if ignored.

2. **D**

    Choice (A) is above the recommended operating temperature, while (B) is the proper bromine level, (C) the proper pH level, and (E) the chlorine level.

3. **D**

    Choices (A), (B), and (C) represent an inference that goes beyond the scope of the passage and would indicate biases of the reader. Although the passage explains spa maintenance, choice (E), the information is not adequate to serve as a detailed guide.

4. **B**

    While choice (A), Sentence 3, makes an oblique reference to the necessity for adding disinfectant, only choice (B), Sentence 9, discusses the "fertile environment for the growth of bacteria and viruses."

5. **A**

    Choices (B), (C), and (D) are appropriate chemicals. Although chlorine is an alternative to bromine, this passage indicates it should be granular as indicated in choice (A); liquid and tablet chlorines are too harsh for spas, thus, no forms are acceptable, as indicated by choice (E).

6. **A**

    Choices (B) and (C) fluctuate, while (D) and (E) negate the question, leaving choice (A) as the only viable answer.

7. **C**

    Choices (A), (B), and (D) show more consistency in their figures, while choice (E) negates the primary purpose of the graph.

8. **C**

    Choices (B), (D), and (A) all show higher profits; while choice (E) is truthful, it does not directly answer the question.

9. **C**

    Choices (A), (B), (D), and (E) present erroneous information, so choice (C) is the only relevant answer.

10. **B**

    Choices (A), (C), and (D) have overall yearly profits at a lower cumulative total, while (E) does not address the question.

11. **E**

    Choices (A), (B), (C), and (D) all connote extreme or inappropriate attitudes not expressed in the passage. The author presents an informed concern—choice (E).

12. **D**

    For the other choices, (A), (B), (C), and (E), the criteria, the role, the discussion, and the assurance for communication or learning are not provided in the passage. The passage stresses the importance of authenticity in communication—choice (D).

13. **E**

    Choices (A) and (B) are possible choices while (C) and (D) are not, but the over-all passage suggests that communication needs to be clear and well-spoken so that student responses may become more significant and authentic—choice (E).

14. **B**

    Choice (B) is the only response that ensures logical conformity and continuity in all three blank lines in the passage. Any other of the offered choices would interrupt or distort the passage's sequence or logical thread.

15. **C**

    "City" schools is another way of saying "urban" schools. Since "Problems facing Urban Schools" is one of the topics listed below the heading, "Chapter One," issues of city schools would be found in this section.

16. **B**

   The title page (A) displays the author, title and sometimes other information, such as the name of the publishing company. The correct answer (B) is the preface. In this section the author explains a bit about why the book was written, additional information she would like the readers to be aware of, and or how the book was developed. The introduction (C) is the beginning of the story or work. The chapters are the body of the book (D), (E).

17. **C**

   John Dewey is considered to be the foremost philosopher of American education. His theories on child-centered learning, the scientific inquiry approach and project-based experiences have greatly affected our educational system. Information on Dewey would be found in Chapter Two's section titled "Prominent Philosophers of Education," choice (C).

18. **A**

   The passage explicitly states that computers are capable of addressing the issues of practice and the true act of reading, choice (A). The other choices represent inferences that are not supported by the passage.

19. **C**

   Although the reader might make inferences to select (A), (B), (D), and (E), ways to use a word processor to make practice resemble the true reading act are not stated in the passage, thus choice (C) is correct.

20. **B**

   Although audiences in choices (A), (C), (D), and (E) may benefit from the information provided in the passage, the passage explicitly states that a greater understanding of the information in the passage should assist teachers—choice (B).

21. **E**

   Although meaning is found in the components of each choice, the passage states that we should begin with students' meanings before moving to the commonalities of story meaning—choice (E).

22. **C**

    Choices (A), (B), (D), and (E) might suggest variants or variations, but not of culture.

23. **B**

    Romanticism is a form of stylized representation that has its own unique properties and distinctive traits. (A), (C), (D), and (E) do not address these literary properties, thus choice (B) is correct.

24. **C**

    While choices (A), (B), (D), and (E) may be truisms, the most comprehensive purpose of the passage is to establish the clear definition of terms and philosophy.

25. **D**

    Choices (A), (B), (C), and (E) pertain to colonialism in one form or another, but (D) is reiterated from the passage.

26. **E**

    Choices (A) and (C) are not supported by the passage. Choices (B) and (D) go beyond the scope of the passage. The last sentence states, "The pattern . . . resulting in teachers prone to teach as they had been taught"—choice (E).

27. **A**

    Any choice other than (A) would be too narrow (B), overblown (E), or simply out of sync with the narrative thread [(C) and (D)].

28. **A**

    Only choice (A) has the correct sequence; the other sequences are incorrect.

29. **E**

    Choices (A), (B), (C), and (D) are statements about education, teacher education, and teachers. Choice (E)'s statement that teacher education has changed very little implies that this lack of change could be a source of dissatisfaction.

30. **B**

    Choices (A), (C), (D), and (E) are not terms for a sovereign, one who rules by divine birthright. A king is a sovereign, thus, choice (B) is correct.

31. **C**

    Choices (A), (D), and (E) are not supported by the passage. Choice (B) represents a possible conclusion, but choice (C) suggests real thought about the hawk.

32. **C**

    The hawk watches with "disdain" and the only answer that fits is choice (C).

33. **B**

    Choices (A), (C), (D), and (E) are incorrect because of their definitions. "Feudal" most clearly denotes an association to the Middle Ages.

34. **B**

    The passage explicitly states that political efficacy is a feeling that one's actions can have an impact on government—choice (A). Choices (C), (D), and (E) are not supported by the passage. Choice (B) is correct.

35. **C**

    Choices (A), (B), (D), and (E) are not supported by the passage. The passage states ". . . political socialization, a process varying according to political systems but toward the end of indoctrinating the members to the respective political system"—choice (C).

36. **A**

    Although choices (B), (C), (D), and (E) are possible definitions, the passage explicitly states that "a political system is one of inputs, conversion, and outputs by which the wants of a society are transformed into binding decisions"—choice (A).

37. **A**

    Choices (B), (C), (D), and (E) contain an incorrect concept of either Easton and Dennis or Lipset. Only choice (A) has the correct concepts for both Easton / Dennis and Lipset.

38. **C**

Choices (A), (B), (D), and (E) do not encompass the flexibility of Western European historical representations that the passage suggests—thus choice (C) is correct.

39. **E**

Non-Eurocentric voice refers to someone who is not limited to interpreting and evaluating other cultures strictly based on his or her Western European descent—thus, choice (E) is correct.

40. **A**

Eradication of narrative voice is synonymous with the premeditated obliteration of traditional beliefs, oral narratives, and ethnic heritage, thereby making non-Eurocentric voices seem more foreign or undesirable, hence, choice (A) is correct.

41. **D**

The author takes an informed and involved approach to the subject without persuasion or emotional influence, thus, choice (D) is correct.

42. **A**

Choices (D) and (E) are incorrect, as the strategy is for oral reading, not silent reading. Choices (B) and (C) are not supported by the passage—thus, choice (A) is correct.

43. **D**

Choices (A), (B), (C), and (E) include syllable and paragraph elements, which are not supported by the passage. The passage states, ". . . individual language units, which can be as small as a single letter or as large as a phrase or sentence."

44. **E**

Choices (A), (B), (C), and (D) are not supported by the passage. The passage states that "speeding up reading, not slowing it down, helps the reader make sense of a passage."

45. A

     While choice (E) does reflect the notion that student participation per se does not reflect learning, the passage does tell us that learning remains a consequential ingredient in any teaching/learning environment—thus, choice (A) is correct.

46. E

     Choices (A), (B), (C), and (D) are inappropriate for defining an instrument that assesses and demonstrates learning.

47. A

     Choices (B), (C), (D), and (E) are not supported by the passage.

48. B

     While choices (A), (C), (D), and (E) are given passing mention in the passage, it focuses on student participation and learning.

49. B

     According to the index, in this book cookie bar recipes can be found on pages 230–236. Choice (B) is the correct answer.

50. C

     This section details the cookie section of a cookbook. The general information is listed about cookies, followed by subcategories, which include chocolate, fruit, oat and nuts. These may be popular choices (B), but more clearly represent the main ingredient (C) of the cookies. This makes (C) the best choice. No information regarding baking temperature (D) or baking technique (E) is given.

ANSWER SHEET – DIAGNOSTIC TEST

Section 2: Mathematics

1. Ⓐ Ⓑ Ⓒ Ⓓ Ⓔ
2. Ⓐ Ⓑ Ⓒ Ⓓ Ⓔ
3. Ⓐ Ⓑ Ⓒ Ⓓ Ⓔ
4. Ⓐ Ⓑ Ⓒ Ⓓ Ⓔ
5. Ⓐ Ⓑ Ⓒ Ⓓ Ⓔ
6. Ⓐ Ⓑ Ⓒ Ⓓ Ⓔ
7. Ⓐ Ⓑ Ⓒ Ⓓ Ⓔ
8. Ⓐ Ⓑ Ⓒ Ⓓ Ⓔ
9. Ⓐ Ⓑ Ⓒ Ⓓ Ⓔ
10. Ⓐ Ⓑ Ⓒ Ⓓ Ⓔ
11. Ⓐ Ⓑ Ⓒ Ⓓ Ⓔ
12. Ⓐ Ⓑ Ⓒ Ⓓ Ⓔ
13. Ⓐ Ⓑ Ⓒ Ⓓ Ⓔ
14. Ⓐ Ⓑ Ⓒ Ⓓ Ⓔ
15. Ⓐ Ⓑ Ⓒ Ⓓ Ⓔ
16. Ⓐ Ⓑ Ⓒ Ⓓ Ⓔ
17. Ⓐ Ⓑ Ⓒ Ⓓ Ⓔ
18. Ⓐ Ⓑ Ⓒ Ⓓ Ⓔ
19. Ⓐ Ⓑ Ⓒ Ⓓ Ⓔ
20. Ⓐ Ⓑ Ⓒ Ⓓ Ⓔ

21. Ⓐ Ⓑ Ⓒ Ⓓ Ⓔ
22. Ⓐ Ⓑ Ⓒ Ⓓ Ⓔ
23. Ⓐ Ⓑ Ⓒ Ⓓ Ⓔ
24. Ⓐ Ⓑ Ⓒ Ⓓ Ⓔ
25. Ⓐ Ⓑ Ⓒ Ⓓ Ⓔ
26. Ⓐ Ⓑ Ⓒ Ⓓ Ⓔ
27. Ⓐ Ⓑ Ⓒ Ⓓ Ⓔ
28. Ⓐ Ⓑ Ⓒ Ⓓ Ⓔ
29. Ⓐ Ⓑ Ⓒ Ⓓ Ⓔ
30. Ⓐ Ⓑ Ⓒ Ⓓ Ⓔ
31. Ⓐ Ⓑ Ⓒ Ⓓ Ⓔ
32. Ⓐ Ⓑ Ⓒ Ⓓ Ⓔ
33. Ⓐ Ⓑ Ⓒ Ⓓ Ⓔ
34. Ⓐ Ⓑ Ⓒ Ⓓ Ⓔ
35. Ⓐ Ⓑ Ⓒ Ⓓ Ⓔ
36. Ⓐ Ⓑ Ⓒ Ⓓ Ⓔ
37. Ⓐ Ⓑ Ⓒ Ⓓ Ⓔ
38. Ⓐ Ⓑ Ⓒ Ⓓ Ⓔ
39. Ⓐ Ⓑ Ⓒ Ⓓ Ⓔ
40. Ⓐ Ⓑ Ⓒ Ⓓ Ⓔ

41. Ⓐ Ⓑ Ⓒ Ⓓ Ⓔ
42. Ⓐ Ⓑ Ⓒ Ⓓ Ⓔ
43. Ⓐ Ⓑ Ⓒ Ⓓ Ⓔ
44. Ⓐ Ⓑ Ⓒ Ⓓ Ⓔ
45. Ⓐ Ⓑ Ⓒ Ⓓ Ⓔ
46. Ⓐ Ⓑ Ⓒ Ⓓ Ⓔ
47. Ⓐ Ⓑ Ⓒ Ⓓ Ⓔ
48. Ⓐ Ⓑ Ⓒ Ⓓ Ⓔ
49. Ⓐ Ⓑ Ⓒ Ⓓ Ⓔ
50. Ⓐ Ⓑ Ⓒ Ⓓ Ⓔ

Section 2: Mathematics

DIRECTIONS: Each of the 50 questions in this section is a multiple-choice question with five answer choices. Read each question carefully and choose the one best answer.

1. This year, Central High School has 1000 students. If the enrollment next year is 650, what will be the percent decrease?

   A. 35
   B. 40
   C. 50
   D. 55
   E. 60

2. The cost of gas for heating a house in Riverview, Florida, is $1.83 per cubic foot. What is the monthly gas bill if a customer uses 145 cubic feet?

   A. $79.25
   B. $145.05
   C. $183.50
   D. $200.40
   E. $265.35

3. Which of the following is the best estimate for 2980 ÷ 95?

   A. 3
   B. 10
   C. 20
   D. 30
   E. 50

4.   What number is the result of rounding off 406.725 to the nearest tenth?

   A.   406.3

   B.   406.5

   C.   406.7

   D.   406.8

   E.   407.0

5.   The mean IQ score for 1,500 students is 100, with a standard deviation of 15. Assuming a normal curve distribution, how many students have an IQ between 85 and 115? Refer to the figure below.

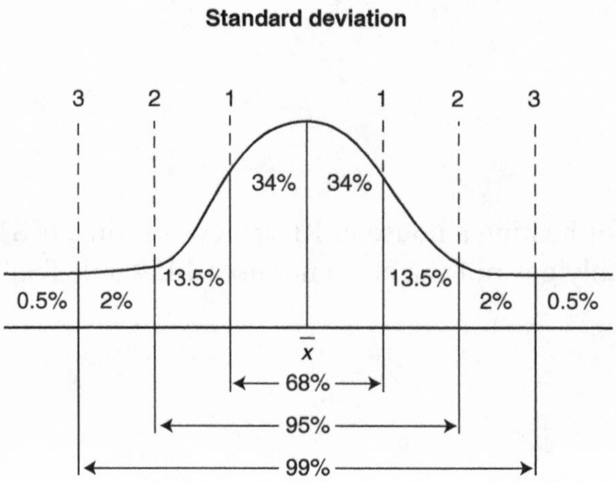

Standard deviation

   A.   510

   B.   750

   C.   1,020

   D.   1,275

   E.   1,425

6. At a special high school, each day has only four periods. Each period is the same length of time and there is a five-minute break between periods. Given the information in the table below, at what time is the last period over?

Class Period	Start Time	End Time
First	8:00 AM	9:40 AM
Second	9:45 AM	11:25
Third	11:30	1:10
Fourth	1:15	2:55

A. 2:15 PM
B. 2:40 PM
C. 2:55 PM
D. 3:10 PM
E. 3:20 PM

7. What is the sum of $1\frac{3}{5}$ and $3\frac{4}{9}$?

A. $5\frac{23}{45}$
B. $5\frac{2}{45}$
C. $4\frac{1}{2}$
D. $4\frac{2}{45}$
E. $2\frac{7}{45}$

$$1\frac{3}{5} + 3\frac{4}{9} = 1\frac{27}{45} + 3\frac{20}{45}$$
$$4\frac{47}{45} = 5\frac{2}{45}$$

8. What is the value of $-24 - (-6)$?

A. 30
B. 18
C. -4
D. -18
E. -30

$$-24 - (-6)$$
$$-24 + 6 = -18$$

9.   Suppose *P* is false and *Q* is true. Which one of the following is a true statement?

    A.   *P* and *Q*

    B.   If *Q* then *P*

    C.   *P* or *Q*

    D.   Not *Q*

    E.   *P* if and only if *Q*

10.   What is the value of *x* in the equation $8x + 20 = -12$?

    A.   −4

    B.   −1

    C.   0

    D.   1

    E.   4

Use the following pie chart for Questions 11, 12, and 13. Assume that the total U.S. population is 250 million.

U.S. Population by Region

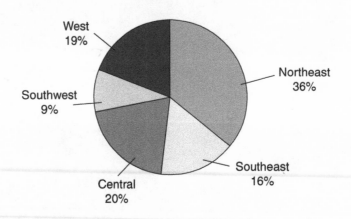

11.   In millions, how many people live in the combined regions of Northeast, Southeast, and Central?

    A.   100

    B.   120

    C.   150

    D.   180

    E.   200

12. In millions, how many more people live in the West region than in the Southwest region?

    A. 20
    B. 25
    C. 30
    D. 35
    E. 40

13. In millions, how many people would have to move from the West region to the Southeast region in order for the populations to be the same in these two regions?

    A. 12.25
    B. 10
    C. 7.5
    D. 5
    E. 3.75

14. If an ordinary die is tossed twice, what is the probability that the sum is 10?

    A. $\dfrac{1}{36}$

    B. $\dfrac{1}{20}$

    C. $\dfrac{1}{18}$

    D. $\dfrac{1}{12}$

    E. $\dfrac{1}{10}$

15. Which one of the following is equivalent to 45%?

    A. $\dfrac{9}{200}$

    B. 4.5

    C. $\dfrac{9}{20}$

    D. 0.0045

    E. 0.00045

16. In driving from Philadelphia to Pittsburgh, Linda put 10 gallons of gas in her car at a cost of $27.00. The capacity of the car's gas tank is 20 gallons. If she wants to determine the number miles per gallon of gas that her car uses, what additional information does she need?

    A. The cost to put in 20 gallons of gas

    B. The number of miles she drove

    C. The type of engine her car has

    D. The number of stops she made during her trip

    E. The number of gallons of gas she could have bought with $50

17. Ronnie is 70 inches tall. What is his height in feet?

    A. $5.08\overline{3}$

    B. 5.7

    C. 5.75

    D. $5.8\overline{3}$

    E. $5.\overline{8}$

18. A class of 25 students, including Phil, took a math test. Phil was the only student who scored 90%. If five students had a higher score than Phil, what percent of the class scored lower than Phil?

    A. 76%

    B. 80%

    C. 84%

    D. 90%

    E. 95%

19. The weight of 16 paper clips is 22.4 grams. How many grams does one paper clip weigh?

    A. 0.71

    B. 1.4

    C. 2.4

    D. 4.4

    E. 14

20. Which of the following numbers, when added to 0.175, yields a result between 0.26 and 0.273?

    A. 0.077

    B. 0.08

    C. 0.082

    D. 0.096

    E. 0.099

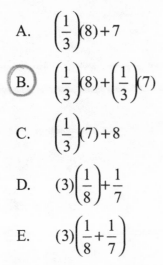

21. Which of the following is an equivalent way to compute $\left(\frac{1}{3}\right)(8+7)$?

    A. $\left(\frac{1}{3}\right)(8)+7$

    B. $\left(\frac{1}{3}\right)(8)+\left(\frac{1}{3}\right)(7)$

    C. $\left(\frac{1}{3}\right)(7)+8$

    D. $(3)\left(\frac{1}{8}\right)+\frac{1}{7}$

    E. $(3)\left(\frac{1}{8}+\frac{1}{7}\right)$

22. What is the perimeter of this triangle?

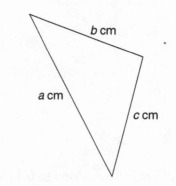

A. abc cm

B. abc cm^2

C. $(a + b + c)$ cm

D. $(a + b + c)$ cm^2

E. abc cm^3

23. In order for Susan to receive a final grade of C, she must have an average of at least 70%, but less than 80%. Her grades on the first four tests were 65%, 85%, 60%, and 90%. What range of grades on the fifth test would give her a C grade for the course?

A. At least 40% but less than 95%

B. At least 45% but less than 95%

C. At least 47% but less than 90%

D. At least 49% but less than 98%

E. At least 50% but less than 100%

24. Two college roommates spent $2,000 for their monthly expenses. The circle graph below indicates a record of their monthly expenses.

Monthly Expenses for Two Roommates

Based on the information in this graph, which of the following statements is correct?

A. They spent $700 on food.

B. They spent $550 on rent.

C. They spent $450 on entertainment and clothing combined.

D. They spent $800 on food and books combined.

E. They spent more than $1,000 on rent, clothing, and books combined.

25. Which of the following inequalities is correct?

A. $\dfrac{2}{3} < \dfrac{5}{6} < \dfrac{7}{9}$

B. $\dfrac{5}{6} < \dfrac{2}{3} < \dfrac{7}{9}$

C. $\dfrac{5}{6} < \dfrac{7}{9} < \dfrac{2}{3}$

D. $\dfrac{7}{9} < \dfrac{2}{3} < \dfrac{5}{6}$

E. $\dfrac{2}{3} < \dfrac{7}{9} < \dfrac{5}{6}$

26. Which of the following division problems results in a quotient with no remainder?

    A. 458 ÷ 12
    B. 406 ÷ 15
    C. 544 ÷ 17
    D. 898 ÷ 22
    E. 810 ÷ 26

27. One commonly used standard score is a *z*-score. A *z*-score gives the number of standard deviations by which a particular score differs from the mean, as shown in the following graph.

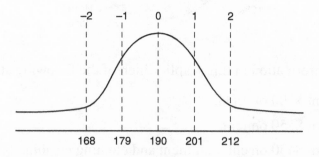

In this graph, the mean ($\bar{x}$) is 190 and the standard deviation (*s*) is 11. The score of 201 has a *z*-score of 1 and the score of 168 has a *z*-score of –2. Suppose that the mean height of a group of people is 190 cm, with a standard deviation of 11 cm. Glenn's height has a *z*-score of 1.6. What is his actual height?

Note: $z = \dfrac{x - \bar{x}}{s}$.

    A. 212 cm
    B. 207.6 cm
    C. 201 cm
    D. 190.8 cm
    E. 179.4 cm

28. The following table shows the number of hours that Jennifer worked on each of four days—Monday, Tuesday, Wednesday, and Friday. Her total hours are also displayed.

Day	Monday	Tuesday	Wednesday	Thursday	Friday	Total
# of Hours	6.8	7.0	8.4		5.5	35

How many hours did she work on Thursday?

A. 6.7
B. 6.9
C. 7.1
D. 7.3
E. 7.5

29. The statement "*P* if and only if *Q*" is true. Which of the following statements <u>must</u> be true?

A. *P* or *Q*
B. *P* and *Q*
C. If *P* then *Q*
D. *P*
E. Not *Q*

30. For which one of the following equations does $x = -1$?

A. $-6x + 9 = 3$
B. $5x + 8 = 8$
C. $-4x - 4 = 4$
D. $3x + 11 = 8$
E. $-2x + 7 = 6$

31. Jill's cat weighs 9 pounds 5 ounces. What is the cat's weight in ounces only?

A. 95
B. 109
C. 123
D. 137
E. 149

32. In a math class, there are 18 boys and 12 girls. On a particular exam, 50% of the boys and 75% of the girls earned passing grades. What percent of the entire class earned passing grades?

    A. 50

    B. 55

    C. 60

    D. 65

    E. 70

33. The cost of a bus trip to San Diego will be shared equally among 40 people. If the total cost is \$145, what is the best estimate for the cost per person?

    A. \$3.40

    B. \$3.50

    C. \$3.60

    D. \$3.70

    E. \$3.80

34. What is the value of $\frac{1}{2} \times \frac{3}{4} \div \frac{5}{3}$?

    A. $\frac{9}{40}$

    B. $\frac{3}{8}$

    C. $\frac{2}{5}$

    D. $\frac{5}{8}$

    E. $\frac{10}{9}$

35. If a fair coin is tossed three times, what is the probability of getting three tails?

     A. $\frac{1}{2}$

     B. $\frac{1}{3}$

     C. $\frac{1}{4}$

     D. $\frac{1}{6}$

     E. $\frac{1}{8}$

$$\frac{1}{2} \quad \frac{1}{2} \quad \frac{1}{2}$$

36. Jeff is an avid bowler. The scores of his last six games were 283, 215, 237, 276, 186, and 249. What was his median score?

     A. 241

     B. 243

     C. 248

     D. 252

     E. 256

186, 215, 237, 249, 276, 283

37. A certain computer normally sells for $3,200 at a store. However, the local university bookstore sells this computer at a discount of 20%. What is the price of this computer at the university bookstore?

     A. $2,370

     B. $2,560

     C. $2,750

     D. $2,930

     E. $3,120

38. Mr. Smith died and left an estate to be divided among his wife, daughter, and a charitable organization in the ratio of 6:2:1. The estate was valued at $180,000. How much money will his daughter receive?

    A. $120,000

    B. $100,000

    C. $60,000

    D. $40,000

    E. $20,000

39. Romeo is driving from his house to Juliet's house, a distance of 300 miles. His average speed is 50 miles per hour, but he plans to take two rest stops of 20 minutes each. If he leaves his house at 9:15 AM, at what time will he arrive at Juliet's house?

    A. 3:15 PM

    B. 3:35 PM

    C. 3:55 PM

    D. 4:15 PM

    E. 4:35 PM

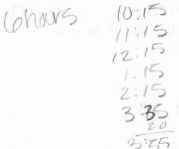

40. While Eileen was shopping, she bought three pounds of apples and five pounds of pears. The total cost for these two fruits was $8.60. Which of the following additional information would be sufficient to determine the cost per pound of the pears?

    A. The number of apples

    B. The number of pears

    C. The total cost for all the items she bought

    D. The cost per pound of the apples

    E. The total number of all the items she bought

41. Which of the following has the same value as $6 + 16 - 8 \div \frac{1}{2} \times 5$?

    A. $6 + 16 - 80$

    B. $6 + 16 - 20$

    C. $6 + 16 - \frac{16}{5}$

    D. $14 \div \frac{1}{2} \times 5$

    E. $(22 - 4) \times 5$

42. Ed has six new shirts and four new pairs of pants. How many combinations of new shirts and pants does he have?

    A. 10

    B. 14

    C. 18

    D. 20

    E. 24

43. A radio was originally listed at the price of $100. Last week, the price was discounted by 10%. This week, the price was increased by 10% over last week's price. What is the price of the radio this week?

    A. $92

    B. $95

    C. $99

    D. $100

    E. $110

44. What is the value of $1\frac{1}{2} - 3\frac{2}{5}$?

    A. $-4\frac{9}{10}$

    B. $-2\frac{1}{10}$

    C. $-1\frac{9}{10}$

    D. $1\frac{9}{10}$

    E. $2\frac{1}{10}$

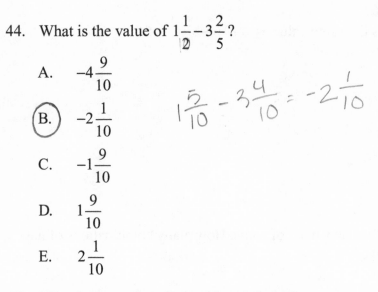

$1\frac{5}{10} - 3\frac{4}{10} = -2\frac{1}{10}$

45. What is the value of $-6 + 12 \div (-8 - 4)$?

    A. -7

    B. -6

    C. -3

    D. -2

    E. $-\frac{1}{2}$

$-6 + 12 \div (-8-4)$

$-6 + 12 \div (-12)$

$6 \div (-12)$

-2

46. The following table shows the items and the cost per item that Wendy bought for a party at her house.

Item	Bag of Chips	Bottle of Soda	Cake	Rolls
Number	4	3	1	20
Cost per Item	$2.40	$1.60		$0.50

If the total cost of these items was $46.20, what was the cost of the cake?

    A. $22.40

    B. $21.80

    C. $21.20

    D. $20.60

    E. $20.00

$\begin{array}{r} 240 \\ \times\quad 4 \\ \hline 9.60 \end{array}$ $\begin{array}{r} 160 \\ \times\quad 3 \\ \hline 4.80 \end{array}$ $\begin{array}{r} 20 \\ \times .50 \\ \hline 00 \\ 100 \\ \hline 10.00 \end{array}$

$\begin{array}{r} 9.60 \\ +\ 4.80 \\ \hline 24.40 \end{array}$ $\begin{array}{r} 46.20 \\ -24.40 \\ \hline 21.80 \end{array}$

47. Mary had been selling printed shirts in her neighborhood. She created the following pictograph to show how much money she made each week.

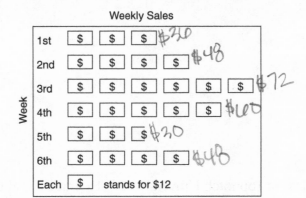

How many weeks were sales more than $55?

A. 1

B. 2

C. 3

D. 4

E. 5

48. A jar contains 20 marbles, of which 3 are red, 4 are black, and the rest are yellow. One marble will be randomly selected. What is the probability of selecting a yellow one?

A. 0.25

B. 0.35

C. 0.45

D. 0.55

E. 0.65

49. What is the value of x in the equation $\frac{2}{3}x + 15 = 9$?

    A. -9

    B. $-6\frac{2}{3}$

    C. $-5\frac{1}{3}$

    D. -4

    E. -3

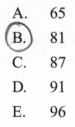

50. In a biology class at Topnotch University, the 16 grades on the final exam were as follows:

91	81	65	87
65	91	81	93
91	80	43	87
96	81	75	81

What is the mode?

    A. 65

    B. 81

    C. 87

    D. 91

    E. 96

Answer Key

Section 2: Mathematics

1.	A	14.	D	27.	B	40.	D
2.	E	15.	C	28.	D	41.	A
3.	D	16.	B	29.	C	42.	E
4.	C	17.	D	30.	D	43.	C
5.	C	18.	A	31.	E	44.	C
6.	C	19.	B	32.	C	45.	A
7.	B	20.	D	33.	C	46.	B
8.	D	21.	B	34.	A	47.	B
9.	C	22.	C	35.	E	48.	E
10.	A	23.	E	36.	B	49.	A
11.	D	24.	A	37.	B	50.	B
12.	B	25.	E	38.	D		
13.	E	26.	C	39.	C		

DIAGNOSTIC TEST – Detailed Explanations of Answers

Section 2: Mathematics

1. **A**

    Next year's enrollment will be $1000 - 650 = 350$. Then the percent decrease is $\dfrac{350}{1000} = 35\%$.

2. **E**

    The monthly gas bill is determined by multiplying $1.83 by 145.

3. **D**

    2980 is approximately 3000 and 95 is approximately 100. Thus, the answer is closest to 3000 divided by 100.

4. **C**

    The number 7 is in the tenth's place. Since the digit in the hundredths place (2) is less than 5, drop this digit and the digit in the thousandths place (5), and retain the 7. Thus, the answer is 406.7.

5. **C**

    The number 85 represents one standard deviation below the mean of 100 and the number 115 represents one standard deviation above 100. Based on the given figure, $34\% + 34\% = 68\%$ of the students have an IQ between 85 and 115. This percent represents $(1,500)(0.68) = 1,020$ students.

6. **C**

    The length of the first period is 1 hour 40 minutes. Since there is a 5-minute break between periods, the end time for each period can be found by adding 1 hour 40 minutes + 5 minutes = 1 hour 45 minutes to the end time of the previous period. Then the end time for the second period is 11:25 AM; for the third period, it is 1:10 PM; for the fourth (last) period, it is 2:55 PM.

7. **B**

The common denominator is 45. Then $1\frac{3}{5} = 1\frac{27}{45}$ and $3\frac{4}{9} = 3\frac{20}{45}$. Thus, $1\frac{27}{45} + 3\frac{20}{45} = 4\frac{47}{45} = 5\frac{2}{45}$.

8. **D**

Change $-24 - (-6)$ to its equivalent addition form $-24 + (+6)$. The sum of a negative 24 and a positive 6 becomes the negative of the difference of 24 and 6, which is -18.

9. **C**

With the connective "or," if either part is true, then the entire statement is true. Choice (A) is wrong because with the connective "and," both parts must be true. Choice (B) is wrong because "true implies false" is always false. Choice (D) is wrong because "not true" means "false." Choice (E) is wrong because "P if and only Q" is true only when P and Q are both true or both false.

10. **A**

Add -20 to each side of the equation to get $8x + 20 - 20 = -12 - 20$, which simplifies to $8x = -32$. Thus, $x = \frac{-32}{8} = -4$.

11. **D**

$36\% + 16\% + 20\% = 72\%$. Then $(0.72)(250 \text{ million}) = 180 \text{ million}$.

12. **B**

$19\% - 9\% = 10\%$. Then $(0.10)(250 \text{ million}) = 25 \text{ million}$.

13. **E**

The difference between these two regions is $19\% - 16\% = 3\%$. If 1.5% of the people from the West moved to the Southeast, then each of these two regions would comprise 17.5% of the total U.S. population. Then $(0.015)(250 \text{ million}) = 3.75 \text{ million}$.

14. **D**

In tossing an ordinary die twice, there are $(6)(6) = 36$ different outcomes.
Of these, the three outcomes whose sum is 10 are 46, 55, and 64. Thus, the required probability is $\frac{3}{36} = \frac{1}{12}$.

15. **C**

As a decimal, 45% = 0.45. As a percent, $45\% = \dfrac{45}{100}$, which reduces to $\dfrac{9}{20}$.

16. **B**

The only additional information needed is the number of miles that she traveled. Then the number of miles per gallon equals the number of miles traveled divided by the 10 gallons of gas that her car used.

17. **D**

Since 60 inches is equivalent to 5 feet, Ronnie's height is 5 feet 10 inches. Then 10 inches represents $\dfrac{10}{12} = .8\overline{3}$ of a foot. Therefore, his height in feet is $5.8\overline{3}$.

18. **A**

Phil was the only student to score 90%, so there were 24 students who scored either higher or lower than Phil. Since five students scored higher than Phil, $24 - 5 = 19$ students scored lower than Phil. Finally, $\dfrac{19}{25} = 76\%$.

19. **B**

The weight of one paper clip is found by dividing 22.4 by 16, which is 1.4 grams.

20. **D**

$0.26 - 0.175 = 0.085$ and $0.273 - 0.175 = 0.098$. Then the number we are seeking must lie between 0.085 and 0.098. Of the given selections, the only correct number is 0.096.

21. **B**

$\left(\dfrac{1}{3}\right)(8+7) = \left(\dfrac{1}{3}\right)(15) = 5$. We can calculate $\left(\dfrac{1}{3}\right)(8) + \left(\dfrac{1}{3}\right)(7)$ as $\dfrac{8}{3} + \dfrac{7}{3} = \dfrac{15}{3} = 5$.

The values of answer choices (A), (C), (D), and (E) are $9\dfrac{2}{3}$, $10\dfrac{1}{3}$, $\dfrac{29}{56}$, and $\dfrac{45}{56}$, respectively.

22. **C**

The perimeter of a triangle is the sum of all three sides, which is $a + b + c$. The units for the perimeter are identical to the units for the three sides.

23. E

An average of 70% on five tests means that Susan must have a total of $(5)(70) = 350$ points. Similarly, an average of 80% on five tests implies that she has a total of $(5)(80) = 400$ points. For the four tests she has taken, her point total is $65 + 85 + 60 + 90 = 300$. Note that $350 - 300 = 50$ and $400 - 300 = 100$. Thus, Susan needs at least 50% but less than 100%.

24. A

The amount the roommates spent on food was $(0.35)(\$2,000) = \$700$. For answer choices (B), (C), (D), and (E), the amounts spent were $500, $400, $900, and $900, respectively.

25. E

Change each fraction into a denominator of 18, which represents the least common multiple of 3, 6, and 9. Then $\frac{2}{3} = \frac{12}{18}$, $\frac{7}{9} = \frac{14}{18}$, and $\frac{5}{6} = \frac{15}{18}$. When fractions have the same denominator, their relative size is indicated by their corresponding numerators. Since $12 < 14 < 15$, we can conclude that $\frac{2}{3} < \frac{7}{9} < \frac{5}{6}$.

26. C

544 divided by 17 equals 32 with no remainder. For answer choice (A), the quotient is 38 with a remainder of 2. For answer choice (B), the quotient is 27 with a remainder of 1. For answer choice (D), the quotient is 40 with a remainder of 18. For answer choice (E), the quotient is 31 with a remainder of 4.

27. B

Use the formula $z = \frac{x - \bar{x}}{s}$. We are given $z = 1.6$, $\bar{x} = 190$, and $s = 11$. By substitution, $1.6 = \frac{x - 190}{11}$. Multiply both sides by 11 to get $17.6 = x - 190$. Thus, $x = 17.6 + 190 = 207.6$ cm.

28. D

The sum of the number of hours Jennifer worked on Monday, Tuesday, Wednesday, and Friday was 27.7. Thus, the number of hours she worked on Thursday was $35 - 27.7 = 7.3$.

29. **C**

> In order for the statement "*P* if and only if *Q*" to be true, either both *P* and *Q* are true or both *P* and *Q* are false. In either case, "If *P* then *Q*" must be true. Answer choices (A) and (B) are wrong because *P* and *Q* could both be false. Answer choice (D) is wrong because *P* could be false. Answer choice (E) is wrong because *Q* could be true.

30. **D**

> Substitute $x = -1$ into answer choice (D). Then the left side of the equation becomes $(3)(-1) + 11 = -3 + 11 = 8$, which matches the right side of the equation. The values of x in answer choices (A), (B), (C), and (E) are 1, 0, –2, and $\frac{1}{2}$, respectively.

31. **E**

> One pound is equivalent to 16 ounces. Therefore, 9 pounds 5 ounces is equivalent to $(16)(9) + 5 = 149$ ounces.

32. **C**

> The number of boys who passed the exam was $(0.50)(18) = 9$. The number of girls who passed the exam was $(0.75)(12) = 9$. This means that out of the 30 students in the class, 18 students passed the exam. Thus, $\frac{18}{30} = 0.60 = 60\%$.

33. **C**

> The cost per person is $\$145 \div 40 = \$3.625$, which is closest to \$3.60.

34. **A**

> $\frac{1}{2} \times \frac{3}{4} = \frac{3}{8}$. Then $\frac{3}{8} \div \frac{5}{3} = \frac{3}{8} \times \frac{3}{5} = \frac{9}{40}$.

35. **E**

> Let T = Tails and let H = Heads. The eight possible outcomes can be represented as HHH, HHT, HTH, THH, HTT, THT, TTH, and TTT. Since only one of these outcomes shows three tails, the probability is $\frac{1}{8}$.

36. **B**

First arrange the scores in ascending order. Then they appear as 186, 215, 237, 249, 276, and 283. The median score is the average of the third and fourth scores. Thus, the median equals $\frac{237+249}{2} = \frac{486}{2} = 243$.

37. **B**

The discount equals (0.20)($3,200) = $640. Thus, the sale price of the computer is $3,200 – $640 = $2,560.

38. **D**

There are a total of $6 + 2 + 1 = 9$ equal shares of the $180,000 estate to be divided up. Each share is worth $\frac{\$180,000}{9} = \$20,000$. Thus, the daughter will receive 2 shares that have a total worth of $40,000.

39. **C**

Without any stops, Romeo's trip would take $\frac{300}{50} = 6$ hours. Since he plans to stop twice for 20 minutes each time, the trip will actually take 6 hours and 40 minutes. Adding 6 hours to 9:15 AM leads to 3:15 PM. Finally, we add 40 minutes to 3:15 PM in order to get his arrival time of 3:55 PM.

40. **D**

If the cost per pound of the apples were known, then the cost of the three pounds of apples could be calculated by multiplying by 3. Then this cost would be subtracted from the total cost of the apples and pears in order to find the cost of the five pounds of pears. Finally, this number would be divided by 5 to yield the cost per pound of the pears.

41. **A**

The first step in evaluating $6+16-8 \div \frac{1}{2} \times 5$ is to divide 8 by $\frac{1}{2}$, which is $8 \times \frac{2}{1} = 16$. Then multiply 16 by 5 to get 80. Finally, $6 + 16 - 80 = -58$. This answer matches the computation for answer choice (A). The answers for answer choices (B), (C), (D), and (E) are 2, $18\frac{4}{5}$, 140, and 90, respectively.

42. **E**

   The number of combinations is found by multiplying 6 by 4.

43. **C**

   The price last week was 90% of the original list price. So last week's price was (0.90)($100) = $90. The price this week represents a 10% increase over last week's price. Thus, this week's price for the radio is (1.10)($90) = $99.

44. **C**

   Convert both fractions to ones with the common denominator of 10. Then after switching the order of the fractions, we have $-3\frac{4}{10}+1\frac{5}{10}$. Since $\frac{5}{10}>\frac{4}{10}$, convert the first fraction to $-2\frac{14}{10}$. Thus, $-2\frac{14}{10}+1\frac{5}{10}=-1\frac{9}{10}$.

45. **A**

   First perform the operation in parentheses. So, $-8 - 4 = (-8) + (-4) = -12$. Second, divide 12 by -12 to get -1. Finally, $-6 - 1 = -7$.

46. **B**

   The cost of the four bags of chips was (4)($2.40) = $9.60. The cost of the three bottles of soda was (3)($1.60) = $4.80. The cost of the 20 rolls was (20)($0.50) = $10.00. This means that the cost of all items except the cake was $9.60 + $4.80 + $10.00 = $24.40. Thus, the cost of the cake was $46.20 − $24.40 = $21.80.

47. **B**

   Each box with a dollar sign represents 12 weeks. Divide 55 by 12 to get approximately 4.58. The only weeks with more than four boxes are weeks 3 and 4, which had sales of $72 and $60, respectively.

48. **E**

   There are 20 − 3 − 4 = 13 yellow marbles in the jar. Thus, the probability of selecting a yellow marble is $\frac{13}{20}=0.65$.

49. A

Subtract 15 from each side of the equation to get $\frac{2}{3}x = 9 - 15 = -6$. Then divide each side by $\frac{2}{3}$. Thus, $x = -6 \div \frac{2}{3} = \left(-\frac{6}{1}\right)\left(\frac{3}{2}\right) = -9$.

50. B

The mode is the number that occurs most frequently. The number 81 occurs four times, which is greater than the frequency of any other number.

Section 3: Writing

DIRECTIONS: Carefully read the two writing topics below. Plan and write an essay on each topic, to be read by an audience of educated adults. Be sure to support your position with logical arguments and specific examples. Remember to address all aspects of the topic. Allow approximately 30 minutes per essay.

Topic 1

There is a current trend in the United States toward smaller families. Sociologists attribute the decline in childbearing to many factors, including the dramatic rise of women in the workforce, delayed marriage, divorce, and the high cost of raising and educating children. Discuss both your view of smaller family size and how smaller families may affect the future of American society.

Topic 2

Write an essay in which you contrast your values and/or personality with the values and/or personality of a member of your family. Explain how two individuals from the same family can be different in the ways you and your relative are different.

Scoring Rubric of the CBEST Writing Exam

Although there are no "right" and "wrong" answers for your essays, it will neverthe-less be graded. The graders will read your essay and assign it a score based upon how well it communicates your ideas in a clear, logical, and grammatically correct manner. Your essay will be graded holistically, which means that your score will be determined by grading the essay as a whole, not as parts. Your essay will receive one of the following four scores: Pass (4), Marginal Pass (3), Marginal Fail (2), or Fail (1). The determination of each score is based on the following Six Primary Traits of Good Writing:

- Rhetorical Force

- Organization

- Support and Development

- Usage

- Structure and Conventions

- Appropriateness

The determination of each score is based on the following criteria.

Pass (4)

A score of "4" is assigned to a well-written essay that clearly communicates a coher-ent and compelling message to its intended audience. This score is achieved by writing an essay with the following characteristics:

1. Rhetorical Force: The essay argues a central idea and maintains its focus on this thesis.

2. Organization: The essay is presented in a logical manner; smooth transitions between ideas help the reader understand the flow of the essay.

3. Support and Development: Specific examples and compelling data support generalizations and assertions.

4. Usage: Word usage is correct and precise.

5. Structure and Conventions: The writer understands how to create sentences of complexity, and only minor flaws in mechanics deter from the essay's readability.

6. Appropriateness: The essay addresses the topic given in the essay prompt, and it does so in a manner and style appropriate for the audience.

Marginal Pass (3)

A score of "3" represents an essay that adequately communicates its message to the intended audience, although several important improvements could be made.

1. Rhetorical Force: The essay showcases a thesis and primarily focuses on this thesis.

2. Organization: The ideas of the essay are organized in an effective and logical manner.

3. Support and Development: Assertions are supported with evidence, although sometimes the evidence is not entirely convincing.

4. Usage: Word choice and usage are competent, but could be improved.

5. Structure and Conventions: Errors in the mechanical conventions of writing are neither serious nor frequent.

6. Appropriateness: The response may not fully respond to the topic given in the essay prompt, but the essay nevertheless sufficiently engages with the questions at issue to create an engaged exchange of ideas.

Marginal Fail (2)

A "2" is a fragmented essay that inadequately communicates its message to the intended audience.

1. Rhetorical Force: Although the writer may present a thesis in the essay, that idea is then lost in the ensuing paragraphs; the reasoning is simplistic and lacks sophistication.

2. Organization: The essay is poorly organized and lacks logical coherence between paragraphs; the author jumps from idea to idea rather than guiding the reader from one idea to the next.

3. Support and Development: Assertions lack supporting evidence and examples; supporting evidence and examples which are present do not effectively contribute to the thesis.

4. Usage: Improperly used words hamper the reader from comprehending the essay.

5. Structure and Conventions: Errors in paragraphing, grammar, and sentence structure impede the essay's readability.

6. Appropriateness: The writing does not engage with the essay prompts, and the essay is inappropriate for its intended audience.

Fail (1)

A score of "1" is assigned to an essay that fails to communicate a meaningful message to its audience.

1. Rhetorical Force: The writer does not provide a thesis to the essay, and the reasoning behind the essay is unconvincing.

2. Organization: The meaning of the essay is difficult to decipher because the organization of ideas appears haphazard rather than logically determined.

3. Support and Development: The writer fails to support generalizations and assertions with adequate evidence.

4. Usage: Errors in word choice and usage make the essay difficult to understand.

5. Structure and Conventions: Frequent mistakes in paragraphing, sentence structure, and grammar impair readability.

6. Appropriateness: The essay fails to engage with the essay prompt, and its tone and language are inappropriate for its audience.

Try to see which of these categories your essay falls into by comparing its characteristics to the ones listed above. You may want to ask a teacher or a trusted friend to read your essay and grade it for you. Also, many colleges have writing labs which offer free tutoring; check to see if your school offers such a service.

DIAGNOSTIC TEST – Detailed Explanations of Answers

Section 3: Writing

SAMPLE SCORED ESSAYS WITH EXPLANATIONS

Topic 1 Sample Answers

Essay #1—Pass (Score = 4)

Although today people commonly complain about overcrowding and overpopulation, figures show that the average-sized family has dropped below the number needed for replacement of the population. I favor the trend toward smaller families. We need to move toward creating a world where children are guaranteed the simple things like food and shelter instead of giving birth to generations of starving and homeless people.

There are various reasons for such a steady decline in childbearing that are well worth taking note of. The high cost of raising and educating children, availability of birth control, the desire for greater freedom, and the realization that parenthood may well be a learned behavior rather than an instinct are a few examples.

The first of those points is the most obvious and rational explanation for not having children. The costs of pregnancy, and the first few years of the child's life alone can be staggering, assuming that it's a healthy child. Once you make it past that stage, parents are soon hit with the high cost of education, not to mention getting their child into the "right" school. Another factor to consider is birth control. In the past forty years we have gone from a period where sex was rarely discussed, to one where contraceptives are openly discussed, and distributed. The desire for greater freedom is another important consideration. People who grew up in large families, or whose jobs involve children, often desire the freedom of a marriage without kids. Having a family is quite obviously a lifetime commitment, and often by the time a parent may be ready to make it, it's too late. Last, but possibly the most important, is the growing belief that being a parent may be a learned behavior rather than an instinct. As I grew up I always figured that being a good parent was something that would "come to me" when the time is right. Judging by the high number of cases of abuse and abandonment, this is obviously not the case. It is true that being a good father or mother requires good instinct, but there is a bit more to it than that.

These are all issues worth considering, however they are concerned mostly with individuals, and not the "world family" in general. As I have said, I think we need to concentrate more on the kind of generations we are giving birth to, and the society they will live their lives in. It is ignorant to overlook the fact that we are giving birth to more children than we can possibly provide for. Even more importantly, it is a cruel trick to play on something so young and innocent as a baby.

Scoring Explanation for Essay #1—Pass

Essay #1 is a clear pass because it offers lucid, well-reasoned arguments about smaller family size. The writer's position is clearly stated in the introduction, and several reasons for the steady decline in childbearing are then systematically explored. Although the idea that parenthood is a learned rather than an instinctual behavior is somewhat off the initial thesis about family size, the vast majority of this writer's supporting evidence helps to build a solid foundation for the essay. In addition, the writer coherently links the ideas of the essay together with smooth transitions and logical development.

The author's syntax and grammar are well under control. The text is nearly error-free, and complex sentences are handled with ease. For example, embedded sentences, such as "People who grew up in large families, or whose jobs involve children, often desire the freedom of a marriage without kids" occur often. In addition, the author goes beyond the obvious reactions to the issue of smaller families and draws more thoughtful conclusions, such as the implications of these issues to the "world family." Finally, the essay addresses both crucial aspects the question requires, namely, to express a view on smaller family size and to speculate about how it may affect future society. It accomplishes these goals in a manner and style appropriate to its audience of CBEST graders.

Essay #2—Marginal Pass (Score = 3)

According to sociologists, Americans are having fewer children. Possible reasons to account for this trend may be the increase of women in the work force and the strain of the many problems of adolescents as well as other factors. I feel the trend toward smaller families and childlessness is a definite result of these factors and predict that in the future less importance may be placed on raising a family as part of the "American dream."

To begin with, the norms of society used to reflect that the "woman's place is in the home." Yet, women today are taking charge of their lives and realizing their own ambitions above what society dictates. Most of all they are seeing that children do not automatically have to be a part of their future. More and more women are placing their own ambitions above what society dictates and do not include children, and each generation is producing less offspring. I, for example, intend to become a nurse and will probably postpone marriage and children. Secondly, people are realizing that there truly is a great deal involved in raising a family. Commitment to the responsibility of having children sometimes slacks when a family experiences difficulty during the child's adolescent years. It is hard enough to deal with the physical, emotional, and psychological changes of young adulthood yet a teenager must also face the pressures of society which may cause personal problems. This factor is one that many couples would rather avoid and, therefore, must refrain from having children altogether in order to do so.

Thirdly, this trend toward smaller family size will most likely continue in the future, affecting society in such a way that the term "family" may not necessarily include children. It seems that many people are living for today and are not concerned about carrying on the family name. Rather, they wish to live a life that is self-fulfilling. This attitude may affect future society in that it would project selfishness as a value onto future generations.

In essence, there is a definite trend toward smaller families and childlessness due to a greater concern for recognizing one's own personal ambitions and transforming them into a successful, fulfilling life. This is particularly true for women who are becoming increasingly active in the work force. Also, raising children is not easy and some couples would rather deal with the difficulties. These and other factors will most likely result in a decrease in the importance of having children as a part of the "American dream."

Scoring Explanation for Essay #2—Marginal Pass

This essay shows adequate reasoning and organization. The introduction sets up a three-part discussion, and the ensuing paragraphs fulfill that commitment in the promised sequence. We read about (1) changing roles for women, (2) the problems involved in raising children (particularly adolescents), and (3) the resulting change in how we understand the concept of family; however, it is not clear why the author addresses the first two of these ideas in one paragraph. The ideas are not sufficiently interrelated to necessitate that they be considered in the same paragraph.

Both general ("More and more women are placing their own ambitions above what society dictates") and specific information ("I, for example, intend to become a nurse") are offered in the discussion. General assertions, however, predominate over specific ones; the author would have done better to include more specific and direct information to support the argument.

The diction and syntax are generally adequate, although some errors in punctuation and a few awkward sentences ("Commitment to the responsibility of having children sometimes slacks when a family experiences difficulty during the child's adolescent years") detract from the essay's readability. Greater attention should have been paid to word choice and sentence structure.

The writer does address the question of how smaller family size will affect future American society, predicting that smaller family size will change the "American Dream," resulting in "living for today," a lack of concern for "carrying on the family name," and selfishness. Unfortunately, the writer appears to confuse the terms "self-fulfillment" and "selfishness," resulting in a hasty generalization about the effect of smaller family size. Despite these problems in the essay's supporting assertions, the very typical strategy of restating the conclusion, and occasional errors in syntax and grammar, the essay deals with the questions and is relatively easy to follow. It is a marginal pass.

Essay #3—Marginal Fail (Score = 2)

The trend toward smaller families and childlessness definitely makes our future society better. In the future, smaller family size will allow the people to live a more carefree and enjoyable lifestyle.

In the passage sociologists point out some good reasons for the decline in childbearing. In today's society the desire of the people to live affluently, the high divorce rates, and the high costs of raising and educating children makes the people to want fewer children or not at all. It may seem selfish but to enjoy oneself one needs to have a choice not to have babies or to have a few just to suit one's lifestyle. Some notices that having a large family give financial problem, the family cannot afford to send all the children to colleges. Also, since divorce rates are high few want to consider having children; they are afraid that it will give them troubles of settling child custody problem.

Because of this major reasons stated in the passage the future society seems to be moving toward a more pleasurable lifestyle. The people tend to look forward to delaying marriage and fulfilling one's desires. Then, of course, what is a bigger problem than childbearing? There is no surprise that an average sized family is greatly reduced . . . it is necessary.

Scoring Explanation for Essay #3—Marginal Fail

The essay's introduction promises a discussion of smaller families resulting in a better society, more "carefree and enjoyable." The bulk of the essay, however, seeks to explain the reasons for the decline in childbearing. The writer has lost sight of his/her original focus or thesis, returning to it only briefly at the end of the essay.

Furthermore, the treatment of the topic is simplistic; the writer primarily explains what is evident from the question and offers little new material. Insufficient information supports the thesis, intriguing as it might be. The writer would have done better to describe in detail how smaller families would, indeed, improve society.

Grammatical errors and several instances of awkward syntax ("the high costs of raising and educating children makes the people to want fewer children or not at all") make the essay difficult to comprehend. Punctuation problems distract as well. Still, the writer did attempt to address the question, although the essay lacks the necessary development to formulate a compelling response to the essay prompt. For these reasons, the essay is a marginal fail.

Essay #4—Fail (Score = 1)

Society in the United States has changed drastic in the ideas of family life. One can contribute this change through a various amount of reasons. One of the pertanent ideas revolve around society becoming more career oriented in their jobs they have been involved with. Another idea is the cost of raising a child and finally the knowledge that has developed over the centuries has played a factor in postponing child birth until last in life.

In the past, having a big family was the desired. Although a family struggled with the demands of raising a large family, they were able to prevale because as the children grow up they could also work with the father or mother, which resulted in an extra source of income. A college education was not a common option. That one could decide to do when they reached the age of 18. At many times a son or daughter would learn it an take over the business.

Today, that idea, has been altered. Couples or even individuals have become more career oriented in their jobs. This idea also stems with stress a greater freedom wanted, and less of a interest to family. The high cost of raising a family is also a factor in less child births. A family or couple can now wait until their late thirties to have a child. Medical advancement has helped in this area of having a family later in life. Through the use of medical procedures, a couple can conceive a child even when they are older in age. Statistics in conceiving a child in the forties age group has risen substantially because of medicine.

With less child births, cities such as Los Angeles won't be as crowded as it was before. Children can get a better education because teachers will be able to devote their attention to a smaller group of students, then a larger-sized group. Lower amounts of poverty stricken families will exist. Because of the idea of couples waiting until they are financially stable before raising children. More jobs will also be available due to the decrease in child births. One can also say that the freeway system that people use every day will in time get better, and more efficient. People today are now thinking twice about bringing up a family. Becoming financially secure first, is a good idea before deciding to have a child.

Scoring Explanation for Essay #4—Fail

Essay #4 fails on a number of counts. The writer introduces an interesting idea by relating medical advancement to childbearing later in life, but this idea is not explored; rather, it is presented repetitively. The writer presents a list of benefits resulting from "less child births" that similarly go uninvestigated; also, this list ranks serious issues ("poverty stricken families") alongside trivial ones ("the freeway system will get more efficient"), resulting in an essay that does not appear to realize the seriousness of its topic. This intellectual confusion derails the beginnings of a promising idea.

The writer's sentence structure shows a serious lack of focus and knowledge of proper syntax. Some sentences are simply awkward (e.g., "Society in the United States has changed drastic in the ideas of family life"), while others are confused and exhibit missing elements or faulty logic (such as "This idea also stems with stress a greater freedom wanted, and less of an interest to family"). The writer simply does not have sufficient control over written English to merit a passing score.

Topic 2 Sample Answers

Essay #1—Pass (Score = 4)

Some people see a glass half-filled with water and say that it is half empty, while other people see the same glass of water and describe it as half-full. The former are pessimists, and the latter are optimists. This crucial distinction applies equally well to my grandmother and me. For her, the world is constantly spiraling downward into oblivion and god-awfulness, while I have a more optimistic and hopeful outlook on life. We have very different perspectives and personalities, yet we come from the same family. Strong families, however, can overcome differences in personalities if they share enough common ground in their values.

I think that my grandmother's viewpoints are generally more pessimistic than my own because her life has been much harder than mine. Her mother died when she was very young, and she also suffered through the years of the Great Depression as a young child. Money was not plentiful in her home, and her father often could not afford to give her the things she desired. I, on the other hand, had a much more secure childhood. Both of my parents are still alive today, and, although we were not extremely well off, my family lived in relative comfort and security. My grandmother often had to fear what tomorrow might bring, while I have lived comfortably as my parents have supported me through childhood and continue to help me in my college years. These differences in our childhood, I think, explain the differences between my grandmother's and my personalities.

Despite the fact that our personalities are so different, my grandmother and I share certain core values. We are both hard workers who strive to do our best, and we support our friends and family members in all their endeavors. We are loyal and loving, and we both believe that a strong family will help its members to succeed. In fact, I think that one of the reasons I am so optimistic is that my grandmother, despite her pessimism in many areas, has shown me that hard work can pay off. Although she may be grumpy and predict doom and gloom far too often, she is a survivor, and she has shown me how to work hard to achieve my goals. Even with our stark differences in personality, we share values which allow us to appreciate and love each other for the people we are, not who we would like each other to be. For my family and me, a strong loving family is one which respects differences in personality while working together to form a community founded upon core values of loyalty, love, and determination.

Scoring Explanation for Essay #1—Pass

Despite the cliché which opens this essay, it is a coherent and compelling response to the essay prompt. The author begins by describing a chief difference in personality between his/her grandmother and him/herself. The essay then considers a possible cause of this difference, noting the differences in each of their backgrounds. The essay concludes by addressing how these two people have different personalities, yet share similar values. Responding to all issues that the essay prompt suggests, the writer investigates the concepts of personalities, values, the causes behind them, and how these factors interrelate with real people to form a family.

The writing in this essay is strong throughout. The writer adeptly handles complex sentences, and the grammar and punctuation assist the passage's readability. The tone is appropriate to the given audience, and the organization of the essay moves smoothly from paragraph to paragraph. With its many strengths, the essay warrants a "4."

Essay #2—Marginal Pass (Score = 3)

People tell me quite often that my brother and I look like twins. We both have brown hair, brown eyes, a fair complexion, and the same features. Though we look like each other, our personalities clash.

Alex is only sixteen years old, and he is very advanced for his age in school. He's intelligent, determined, confident, and always does what he says he's going to do. On my part, I can say that my intelligence is at the average level, and rather than being determined and confident about the things I do, I tend to be somewhat insecure about myself.

I've always wanted to be just like Alex. Throughout my life I've always looked up to him. He's outgoing and open, and I am the shy, quiet type. He's the one who always completes his work on time and never depends on anyone else but himself. I always procrastinate, and I'm lazy.

Also, Alex is the "outgoing" type who plays sports like tennis, football and baseball. Though I was on the tennis team in 1998, I never continued to play on a regular basis. Alex likes to play sports, and I like to watch them on t.v.

My parents can similarly be compared to my brother and I. I share the same personality traits as my father, and Alex shares my mom's personality. My father is the introvert and we are both hesitant to get things done before the last minute. My mother is an open, confident woman and always trusts herself—which can similarly be compared to my brother. My father and I prefer to stay inside while my mom and brother are always on the go. When my mother was our age she was on a running team. She was involved in a lot of sports, and my father was always the one who liked to be alone.

As shown here, my brother and I are different in many ways, and so are my parents.

Scoring Explanation for Essay #2—Marginal Pass

The bulk of this marginally passing essay is spent providing the audience with a series of comparisons (ranging from physical differences to sports preferences) between the writer and his/her brother. These comparisons are offered in sentences that are readable and competent, although not very complex or sophisticated. Very few grammatical errors and only minor punctuation problems deter from easy comprehension of the writer's ideas. Despite the fact that the essay is relatively well written, it fails to show much evidence of critical thinking; rather, it mainly serves as a laundry list of differences between the two siblings.

The last major paragraph of this essay attempts to explain the differences between the siblings by offering corresponding differences between the parents. The author implies, but never clearly states, that the parental characteristics account for those of the children. Thus, the writer attempts to address the question in its entirety but fails to explain these critical ideas explicitly. The conclusion is brief and perfunctory, merely restating the general thrust of the previous paragraph. Because the essay only vaguely addresses the assignment in its entirety, though it is satisfactorily written, the essay is a marginal pass.

Essay #3—Marginal Fail (Score = 2)

Have you ever wondered if someone in your family could possibly be from the same family, do to the fact that you are so opposite? My sister Kate and I have to be one of the most opposite sisters in the world. Our likes, values, and personalities contrast terribly. At times I often ask myself: "How could we possibly be related?"

To begin with my sister has red hair, is two inches taller than me and two years younger than me. This is far different from me who is blonde, petite and older. Our looks are the outside appearance of how different we are in the inside.

When it comes to dating, Katie likes to date as many as possible, whereas I like to stick to just one. I am extremely competitive and hate to lose, especially in volleyball. Katie is more carefree and if her team loses it is not that big of a deal. Our bedrooms show a great deal of differences. Katie's room is piled with clothes and many unimportant things. She like to save everything. On the other hand I am very metuculus, and I am annoyed if there is junk laying around. Even when it comes down to the "nitty gritty" of things such as music, clothes, or jewelry Katie and I have opposite taste.

Two individuals from the same family could be different in the ways my sister and me are different, possibly because of different genes in the family. Generations of a family consist of many genes from various relatives, and those genes are passed on contributing to the different personalities of a number of relatives. Every individual is his or her own person and just because people are from the same family, it does not mean that people cannot have their own distinct values and personalities different than anyone else in the family.

Scoring Explanation for Essay #3—Marginal Fail

This essay provides a series of contrasts between the writer and her sister, beginning with physical characteristics and ending with tastes in clothing. None of the differences mentioned addresses a contrasting value system, although some minor personality differences are offered. Thus, the question is only partially answered in this essay.

The author does have a lively and unique voice in her essay, but several errors in grammar, syntax, spelling, and word choice inhibit this voice from speaking clearly. One example of an awkward construction appears in the first paragraph: "My sister Kate and I have to be one of the most opposite sisters in the world." Spelling (e.g., "do" for "due," "metuculus" for "meticulous") and punctuation are similarly irregular.

The final paragraph of the essay offers genetic differences as an explanation for the contrasts between the sisters. The author relies on this biological explanation exclusively, although she does not appear to be well-versed with genetics. The author concludes with a wordy restatement of her belief that despite blood ties, family members can differ. The writer is confused, therefore, about how genetics actually do or do not contribute to differences between siblings, and she thus fails to do justice to a promising idea. This problem with reasoning contributes to the essay's marginally failing score.

Essay #4—Fail (Score = 1)

My uncle Gary and I are completely different peoples. First of all, my Uncle Gary is an atheist. I on the other hand am a religious person. I do not go to church every Sunday but I do believe in God. Secondly, my Uncle does not speak to anyone in the family. He has totally sheltered himself from everyone. I love to be with my family at family gatherings. I will admit they get on my nerves sometimes. But I would never want to lose contact with them. Last, but not least, my Uncle is a democrat. I am a Republican. This would be a good discussion topic. If my uncle would ever go to family gatherings. So there you have two completely different people. From the same family.

Scoring Explanation for Essay #4—Fail

This essay suffers from a serious lack of development. Its simplistic listing of differences between the author and his/her uncle only minimally addresses the question. No discussion of these differences is advanced, and the writer concludes without even attempting any explanation beyond: "So there you have two completely different people. From the same family."

Despite the essay's extreme brevity, the author also makes many errors in syntax and grammar. Sentence fragments appear regularly, and the author does not know when to capitalize letters. A lack of attention to the demands of the question, incomplete development, and errors in writing make this essay a clear fail.

CHAPTER

Reading Skills Review 3

Overview

The reading section of the California Basic Educational Skills Test (CBEST) is designed to measure your ability to understand information presented in the form of literary and nonfiction passages, graphs, directions, and tables. Reading selections vary in style, length, and difficulty. Some include charts that you will be asked to interpret, while others take the form of indexes, tables of contents, and instructions. Each selection is followed by a series of questions (typically 2 to 5). The questions are aimed at assessing your reading skills, not your knowledge of the content discussed. All necessary information can be obtained solely from the reading selections. The questions emphasize Critical Analysis, Evaluation, Comprehension, and Research Skills. You will be able to determine the correct answers by using these four essential reading skills.

Each of the main skill areas—Critical Analysis, Evaluation, Comprehension, and Research/Reference—represent a percentage of questions included on the reading portion of the CBEST. In this section, approximately 60 percent, or 30 questions, will involve Comprehension and Research Skills and approximately 40 percent, or 20 questions, will be based on the use of Critical Analysis and Evaluation.

Quick Tips for Any Reading Selection

- Read all of the questions carefully first to focus your attention while reading.

- Quickly review the answer choices.

- Read critically, keeping the questions in mind.

- Reread what you do not initially understand.

- Determine the tone, main idea, and audience.

- Do not spend too long on any one reading selection.

A Closer Look at the Two Main Skill Areas

Skill Factor 1: Critical Analysis and Evaluation

Critical Analysis

What does it mean to use critical analysis while reading? Let's take a closer look at these words and how you will use this skill while taking the CBEST. In this context, the word "critical" means sensible or well thought-out. Analysis is the act of analyzing, which means to separate the parts of something in order to determine their relationship to the whole. In this case, you will not only read a passage, you will study it from a critical standpoint. When you analyze a reading selection, you will be investigating various aspects of the writing, such as the vocabulary, the tone, the details or information, the author's intention, and audience. Studying or noticing the different components of a passage will be crucial in understanding the big picture as well as in identifying smaller parts that will be referred to in the questions. As a reader, careful examination of details will allow you to identify key factors presented in each reading selection.

Evaluation

What does it mean to use evaluation while reading? Evaluation means to evaluate or determine the value, significance, or quality of something. When you evaluate you make an assessment of worth or importance. Let's consider how evaluation relates to reading as well as the types of questions that utilize this skill. Many of the evaluation questions focus on the author of the reading passage. While no explicit information on the author will be provided directly, you will be able to determine the author's purpose, audience, style, opinions, and point of view by reading thoughtfully. You may be asked to determine if the author presents an effective argument or expresses a clear point of view. You may also be asked to identify the target audience of the piece. The tone of the passage reflects the author's feelings regarding the specific topic, the wording and content reveal the author's point of view as well as the intended audience, and the main idea presents the author's purpose and beliefs.

Skill Factor 2: Comprehension and Research

Comprehension

What does it mean to comprehend what you are reading? Let's answer that question and look at how you will use this skill while taking the CBEST. Comprehension is a perception or understanding of concepts or ideas—the ability to know. In this case, to comprehend is to take in or grasp the meaning of a reading passage. When you employ strong comprehension skills, you will be able to construct meaning from a text. It is said that no piece of writing is complete until somebody engages in the task of reading what has been written. Reading at the deepest level of comprehension involves using your experiences, knowledge, and beliefs to construct an understanding of the text in addition to simply decoding the words. There will be several different types of questions that will require you to rely on your comprehension skills. You may be asked to identify specific concepts or points of view expressed in the reading selection. You may be asked to recognize the main idea, draw conclusions, and make predictions regarding outcomes or to make generalizations based on the information provided. Questions may center on the meanings of specific words, phrases, and sentences, the sequence of events depicted, or directions. You will be expected to comprehend a variety of reading materials, such as texts, memos, resource materials, articles, and graphs.

Research and Reference

What do research and reference refer to in relation to the readings section of the test? Research means to conduct a methodical and organized investigation into a subject area. The purpose of research is to discover facts, theories, and concepts in a thorough manner. Reference refers to the types of resources that assist a reader in conducting research.

They may take the form of indexes, tables of contents, appendixes, and other similar sections of a text. You may be asked to locate the place in a book, chapter, or article where a specific kind of information can be found, or you might be asked to explain how a reading selection is organized. Some questions will require you to draw logical conclusions, make comparisons, and identify relationships that are presented in the form of a table or graph. Questions may ask you to determine the function of specific parts of a text. You will need to use your knowledge of glossaries, indexes, prefaces, tables of content, and appendixes to answer correctly research and reference-based questions.

Quick Tips for Any Skill-Based Question

- Determine the focus of the question.

- Examine the answers for the best choice.

- Find details that support that choice in the reading selection.

- Read the answer choices one last time to make your final decision.

- Answer the questions using only the information provided.

- Trust your instincts! Your initial choice is often the correct one.

A Closer Look at the Questions

Let's take a look at the ways you may need to analyze or evaluate a passage while completing the CBEST Reading section. You will be faced with a variety of questions that will require you to use specific strategies and techniques to answer. This review will assist you in developing those necessary skills to be successful. We will use the reading selections and corresponding questions from the diagnostic test you just completed to explore the essential reading proficiencies that fall under the four main skill areas.

Concept or Information Questions

Some questions will be based directly on the information that is explicitly included in a reading passage, while others require you to use the details provided to make assumptions that go beyond the passage. In these instances you may be asked to *identify facts and details presented and to draw conclusions or generalizations from material pre-*

sented. Other questions will be based on information that is implicit or implied by the author. These will call for you to *make inferences and recognize implications based on information from a reading selection.* You will need to use the details that are included and logic to determine the correct answers. We will take a closer look at one of the reading selections and questions you completed while taking the diagnostic test that focuses on these skills.

> In view of the current emphasis on literature-based reading instruction, a greater understanding by teachers of variance in cultural, language, and story components should assist in narrowing the gap between reader and text and improve reading comprehension. Classroom teachers should begin with students' meanings and intentions about stories before moving students to the commonalities of story meaning based on common background and culture. With teacher guidance, students should develop a fuller understanding of how complex narratives are when they are generating stories as well as when they are reading stories.

Where does the passage suggest that meaning begins?

    A.   In culture, language, and story components

    B.   In comprehension

    C.   In students' stories

    D.   In the teacher's mind

    E.   In students and narratives

The correct answer is (E). This question requires you to draw conclusions and to make inferences. The answer is not clearly or directly stated within the passage, as it may be in other instances. You may have noticed a clue to this in the question itself. The word *suggest* lets you know that the concept is implied in the passage and that you will need to make a connection between the details in the piece and the answer choice that comes closest to representing them. The passage does state that teachers should start with *students' meanings and intentions about stories.* Choices (A), (B), and (D) do not mention students at all and can be eliminated. When you compare the remaining choices, you will notice that (C) refers only to students, while choice (E) mentions both students and stories, making it the best match.

Some questions may require you to *compare and contrast ideas or information presented* in different portions of a reading selection. In order to do this, you will need to read each selection once through to develop an overall sense of the piece. Then you will need to reread sections mentioned in the questions in order to determine specific elements that are referenced. It is important to look at the information that is addressed in the passage objectively when comparing and contrasting ideas. You may agree or disagree with the ideas presented. This should not interfere with your ability to analyze the reading selection. You may be asked to *identify the relationships between general and specific ideas and to recognize implied relationships between people, ideas, or events.*

Example

Reduced to its simplest form, a political system is really no more than a device enabling groups of people to live together in a more or less orderly society. As they have developed, political systems generally have fallen into the broad categories of those which do not offer direct subject participation in the decision-making process and those which allow citizen participation in form, if not in actual effectiveness.

Let us consider, however, the type of political system that is classified as the modern democracy in a complex society. Such a democracy is defined by Lipset (1963) as "a political system which supplies regular constitutional opportunities for changing the governing officials and a social mechanism which permits the largest possible part of the population to influence major decisions by choosing among alternative contenders for political office."

Proceeding from another concept (that of Easton and Dennis), a political system is one of inputs, conversion, and outputs by which the wants of a society are transformed into binding decisions. Easton and Dennis (1967) observed: "To sustain a <u>conversion</u> process of this sort, a society must provide a relatively stable context of political interaction, as a set of general rules of participating in all parts of the political process." As a rule, this interaction evolves around the settling of differences (satisfying wants or demands) involving the elements of a "political regime," which consists of minimal general goal constraints, norms governing behavior, and structures of authority for the input-output function. In order to persist, a political system would seem to need minimal support for the political regime. To insure the maintenance of such a support is the function of political socialization, a process varying according to political systems but toward the end of indoctrinating the members to the respective political system. "To the extent that the maturing members absorb and become attached to the overarching goals of the system and its basic norms and come to approve its structure of authority as legitimate, we can say that they are learning to contribute support to the regime." The desired political norm (an expectation about the way people will behave) is that referred to as a political efficacy—a feeling that one's action can have an impact on government.

Adapted from Easton, B. and J. Dennis, "The Child's Acquisition of Regime Norms: Political Efficacy," American Political Science Review, March 1967.

The major distinction between the concepts of Easton and Dennis as opposed to the concepts of Lipset is

A. that the concepts of Easton and Dennis are based on the wants of a society, whereas Lipset's concepts are based on change of governing officials.

B. that Easton and Dennis's concepts are based on arbitrary decisions, whereas Lipset's concepts are based on influencing major decisions.

C. that Easton and Dennis's concepts must have a set of general rules, whereas Lipset's concepts provide for irregular constitutional opportunities.

D. that Easton and Dennis's concepts have no inputs, conversion, and outputs, whereas Lipset's concepts allow for no regular constitutional opportunities.

E. that Easton and Dennis's concepts evolve around the settling of differences, whereas Lipset's concepts permit the largest conflict possible.

To answer this question you must pay attention to the details. The answer choices are lengthy, but do not let this throw you off track. It is basically asking you to determine what Easton and Dennis believe, as opposed to what Lipset believes. Read the passage with this in mind and single out the concepts presented by each side. In this case, they are expressed in quotations. Choices (B), (C), (D), and (E) contain an incorrect concept of either Easton and Dennis or of Lipset. The only choice that contains all accurate information for both sides is (A).

In response to a reading selection, you may be asked to *determine whether facts or ideas are relevant to an argument*. Sometimes extraneous information will be included within a passage. These statements may stand out to you as being clearly off the topic; alternatively, they may be related to the topic but not completely relevant to the main idea or argument. You will need to decide which facts or thoughts are essential to the passage. In addition to evaluating the relevance of statements, you may be asked to *distinguish between facts and opinions* in a reading selection. A fact is a piece of information that has been proven to be true. It is an objective and verifiable statement. Alternately, an opinion reflects the thoughts, beliefs, and attitudes of the person expressing the statement. While you may agree with the statement, you will need to ask yourself if others might disagree. Opinions often contain subjective words such as *beautiful, horrible, best, worst, easy,* and *difficult*. If you examine statements to determine facts from opinions while reading, you will be prepared to respond to the corresponding questions. Let's take another look at the brief reading selection about reading instruction.

> A major problem with reading/language arts instruction is that practice assignments from workbooks often provide short, segmented activities that do not really resemble the true act of reading. Perhaps more than any computer application, word processing is capable of addressing these issues.

Would you consider the two statements to be based on fact or opinion? Could it perhaps be a mix of both? As a reader you will need to pick apart the author's statements to analyze both their relevance and accuracy. Whether or not the use of workbooks is a problem would depend on one's perspective. It would be difficult to test this statement. However, one could prove or disprove that *segmented activities*, such as the ones found in workbooks, do not accurately resemble what most experts would consider to be reading in the true sense of the word. The second sentence in the passage can also be broken into fact and opinion. While one could verify that *word processing is capable of addressing these issues,* proving that it would *more than any computer application* would pose some difficulties.

It is likely that questions will require you to *recognize the main idea or purpose of a reading selection.* This task may be less obvious than you would expect. Read the selection once through to obtain a sense of what it is about. Then read the answer choices to see if one of them stands out to you as being correct. If you are attempting to choose between two or more main idea answer choices, you will need to reread the piece with them in mind. To establish the main idea in a longer passage, you can count the number of sentences that mention a specific concept. However, in a shorter passage each sentence may seem to stand on its own. You will need to look at the reading selection as a whole to identify the one that reflects most of the statements. Let's take a look at an example from your diagnostic test.

To define Jonathan Edwards as a representative of the Colonial period in American Literature (1607–1765) requires a brief definition of that era's key ideologies. In the midst of a continuing conflict between advancing scientific frontiers and diversifying religious exegetical interpretations came advances in technology, industrialization, and colonial expansion. Reason and enlightenment were the maxims of the day. For the sake of this argument, the term Colonialism will refer to a direct conquest and control of another's land, culture, heritage, government, and so on. Imperialism will denote the ideology of globalization of capitalist productions. Romanticism, with reference to both these issues, will suggest a form of diluted or tranquilized representation, which thereby makes the horrific realities of these colonial practices gentler to endure, both for the oppressor as well as the oppressed.

The main idea of the passage is

    A.   to introduce Jonathan Edwards.

    B.   to present the turmoil of the Colonial period.

    C.   to define terminology and philosophy.

    D.   to comment on the evils of colonial practices.

    E.   to endorse colonial expansion.

The main purpose of this selection is to define terminology and philosophy, which means (C) is the correct answer to this question. Through careful reading and analysis you can determine that most of the statements are in fact definitions of important terms.

While the other choices may refer to or are mentioned in the passage, they do not represent the central message of the reading selection.

Determining the main idea of a passage should allow you to *identify accurate paraphrases or summaries of ideas* as well. We will take a look at another example from your diagnostic test.

_____. This theme has been traced through the following significant occurrences in education: Benjamin Franklin's advocacy in 1749 for a more useful type of education; Horace Mann's zealous proposals in the 1830s espousing the tax-supported public school; John Dewey's early twentieth-century attack on traditional schools for not developing the child effectively for his or her role in society; the post-Sputnik pressure for academic rigor; the prolific criticism and accountability pressures of the 1970s; and the ensuing disillusionment and continued criticism of schools through the turn of the millennium. Indeed, the waves of criticism about American education have reflected currents of social dissatisfaction for any given period of this country's history.

As dynamics for change in the social order result in demands for change in the American educational system, so, in turn, insistence has developed for revision of teacher education (witness the more recent Holmes report [1986]). Historically, the education of American teachers has reflected evolving attitudes about public education. With slight modification, the teacher education pattern established following the demise of the normal school during the early 1900s has persisted in most teacher preparation programs. The pattern has been one requiring certain academic and professional (educational) courses, often resulting in teachers prone to teach as they had been taught.

Which sentence, when inserted into the blank line, would best present the main idea of the passage?

A.   Seldom has the American school system not been the target of demands for change to meet the social priorities of our times.

B.   Times have been tough lately for the nation's schools.

C.   Teachers' unions have expressed growing concern over the wide-spread use of so-called high-stakes testing.

D.   Teaching is not the easiest profession.

E.   America's public schools are under siege.

The correct answer is (A). As a reader you are asked to focus on the theme of this reading selection from the first lines. If you did not initially determine the main idea or theme while you read, scan through the passage and see what stands out. You will notice that the timeframe referenced spans from 1749 to the 1970s. You will also notice the use of words such as *historically, persisted,* and *pattern,* which imply that the reading refers to an ongoing issue. Choice A is the only answer that is comprehensive enough to represent the ideas expressed in the writing. Choice (B) is too general, and choices (C) and (D) are not discussed in the passage. Choice (E) can be ruled out because it does not reflect the tone and purpose of the reading selection. When determining the main idea, it is important to analyze these aspects.

Author-Centered Questions

Some questions may require you to *recognize the attitude, opinion, or viewpoint expressed by the author toward his or her subject.* You will need to pay close attention to clues that reveal the author's attitude and/or beliefs about the topic. The choice of words used by the author will provide insight. Examine the passage for negative and positive words. How are they used in relation to the subject? Does the author support the issue under discussion? Remember to read carefully to ensure that you recognize authorial point of view. When you evaluate aspects of the author's argument, you will also be able to *recognize the various persuasive techniques used.* Evaluate how the author makes the point or conveys the main idea of the reading selection. Are two sides of an argument presented equally? Does the author site specific examples or make sweeping generalizations? Are opinions or facts presented? You may be asked to *identify logical assumptions upon which the author bases the argument* of a reading selection. Quite a bit of information about the author can be discovered within a short reading passage. People often read without considering the author's standpoint or techniques. You will need to practice evaluating an author's perspective while reading. We will use an example from your diagnostic test.

A major problem with reading/language arts instruction is that practice assignments from workbooks often provide short, segmented activities that do not really resemble the true act of reading. Perhaps more than any computer application, word processing is capable of addressing these issues.

The author would tend to agree that a major benefit of computers in reading/language arts instruction is that

    A.   the reading act may be more closely resembled.

    B.   short, segmented assignments will be eliminated.

    C.   the issues in reading/language arts instruction will be addressed.

    D.   computer application will be limited to word processing functions.

    E.   reading practice will be eliminated.

The correct answer is (A). By looking at the author's reasons, examples, details, or facts in the above reading selection, you can make interpretations concerning that information. The passage explicitly states facts about computers and their ability to address the issues of practice and the "true act of reading." Choice (A) supports that same information and reflects the author's beliefs. The other choices represent inferences that are not reinforced by the details in the passage; therefore we cannot assume the author supports those statements.

You may be asked to *identify the reasons, examples, details, and facts that support the author's main idea*. In order to do this, you will need to determine the most important concept, feeling, or goal of the writing presented. It is likely that each reading selection touches on more than one important point; however, there is only one main idea that most of the sentences revolve around. Analyze each sentence and ask yourself what it is referring to. Most of the details and information included will support one central subject or thought. That will be the main idea or topic.

There may be several types of questions that require you to evaluate the author's beliefs, attitude, tone, and persuasive writing techniques. You will need to examine the overall attitude conveyed in the writing and consider the purpose of the piece and how the author feels about the topic under discussion. Once you have recognized the author's beliefs, you may be asked to *challenge the statements and opinions presented* and to *identify those statements that strengthen or weaken arguments*. When you read critically or with an investigative stance, you should question the author's standpoint. You will need to consider the statements of opinion and evaluate their credibility or worth. Do you agree or disagree with the author's viewpoint? Do you think the author's opinions are well-supported with statements that back them up? Does the author weaken the argument through contradictions or ineffective testimony? Can you detect *inconsistencies or differences in points of view* within one reading selection? For the following reading selection from your diagnostic test, three out of the four questions focused on analyzing the statements made by the author. Let's take a closer look at one of those questions to determine what the author means.

Because Western European historicism constructs a worldview in its own imaginary image, marginal authors such as María Amparo Ruiz de Burton must reclaim or redefine a non-Eurocentric voice in order not only to be heard but to reenter mainstream society by reestablishing an ethnic identity. One of the ways of recognizing the influence of Western imperialism is by "acknowledging how effectively it naturalizes its own [imperially constructed] history, how it claims precedence for its own culture by identifying culture with nature," and how it thus assimilates or eradicates indigenous narrative voice (Deane, 357). One such example would be the attempted eradication of the Native American Indian from the social consciousness by speaking of their culture in the past tense, thus implying an extinction process of natural selection. The continuity of this same narrative ideology proposed by Deane (1995) is reflected and reconstituted in Homi Bhabha's DissemiNation (1990) assertion that, "turning Territory into Tradition provides marginal voices [or minority discourse] a place from which to speak" (Bhabha, 300).

What does the author mean by a ***non-Eurocentric voice***?

    A.   Someone from Europe who cannot speak English

    B.   Someone who is born in Europe and moves to America

    C.   Someone from America who moves to Europe

    D.   Someone from America who cannot speak European

    E.   Someone whose worldview is not filtered through the lens of Western European cultural touchstones

The correct answer is (E). "Voice "refers to being heard or having one's point of view recognized on a societal level. This author characterizes a person having a Eurocentric voice as somebody whose perspective is based on a Western European "imaginary image." Therefore, a person who expresses a non-Eurocentric voice would be someone whose view is not based on Western European culture and values. This is a controversial line of reasoning that can either weaken or strengthen the author's arguments, depending on the reader's own beliefs. In this case you are not asked to challenge the author's logic but to identify what is meant by a specific statement. Process of elimination is a beneficial strategy to use, as the other choices are fairly weak. There is no direct mention of people moving (B), (C) or being able to speak a language (A), (D).

Audience-Centered Questions

The audience is another crucial component of any piece of writing. Some questions may require you to *recognize the audience that a reading selection addresses.* The tone of the passage will give you the necessary information to determine who the selection is aimed at. You may be asked to *identify the language that creates an inappropriate or inconsistent tone, given the intended audience and purpose.*

Examine the word choice as well as the sentence structure. Is the language formal or informal? For instance, are contractions or colloquialisms used? Does the tone seem conversational or more professional? Who is the author trying to reach? Since the passage will not explicitly state the audience, for these questions you should read the answer choices and cancel the ones that are least likely in order to choose the best one. Once again we will refer to the reading selection about reading instruction for our example.

> In view of the current emphasis on literature-based reading instruction, a greater understanding by teachers of variance in cultural, language, and story components should assist in narrowing the gap between reader and text and improve reading comprehension. Classroom teachers should begin with students' meanings and intentions about stories before moving students to the commonalities of story meaning based on common background and culture. With teacher guidance, students should develop a fuller understanding of how complex narratives are when they are generating stories as well as when they are reading stories.

Who is the intended audience for the passage?

    A.   Parents with young children just entering school

    B.   English teachers using literature-based curriculum

    C.   Administrators who develop school curriculum

    D.   Teachers with multicultural classroom populations

    E.   Students of language and literature

The correct answer is (B), *English teachers using literature-based curriculum*. In this example none of the answer choices stands out as being clearly wrong. The choices in (A), (C), (D), and (E) could certainly all benefit from the information provided in the passage. Process of elimination alone is not likely to be helpful in this situation; rather you will need to refer to the passage for help. You will see that *teachers* are referred to three times in the selection. They are clearly the target audience. Choices (B) and (D) both refer to teachers; however, (D) can be eliminated because there is no reference to multiculturalism in the passage. The focus is on literature-based instruction, which makes (B) the best choice.

Sequence and Outcome Questions

The questions may ask you to *identify the sequence of events or steps in a process* and to perhaps *arrange the ideas into an outline or another form of graphic organization*. These types of questions can be based on written directions or on an explanatory passage. It may be helpful for you to number the sentences or steps (if it is not already marked) in order to maintain a clear notion of the sequence. For example in this passage from your diagnostic test:

[1]Spa water quality is maintained by a filter to ensure cleanliness and clarity. [2]Wastes such as perspiration, hairspray, and lotions that cannot be removed by the spa filter can be controlled by shock treatment or super chlorination every other week. [3]Although the filter traps most of the solid material to control bacteria and algae and to oxidize any organic material, the addition of disinfectants such as bromine or chlorine is necessary.

[4]As all water solutions have a pH which controls corrosion, proper pH balance is also necessary. [5]Based on a 14-point scale, the pH measurement

determines if the water is acid or alkaline. [6]High pH (above 7.6) reduces sanitizer efficiency, clouds water, promotes scale formation on surfaces and equipment, and interferes with filter operation. [7]Low pH (below 7.2) is equally damaging, causing equipment corrosion, water which is irritating, and rapid sanitizer dissipation. [8](When pH is high, add a pH decreaser such as sodium bisulphate [e.g., Spa Down]; when pH is low, add a pH increaser such as sodium bicarbonate [e.g., Spa Up].)

[9]The recommended operating temperature of a spa (98°–104°) is a fertile environment for the growth of bacteria and viruses. [10]This growth is prevented when appropriate sanitizer levels are continuously monitored. [11]Maintaining a proper bromine level of 3.0 to 5.0 parts per million (ppm) or a chlorine level of 1.0–2.0 ppm can also control bacteria. [12]As bromine tablets should not be added directly to the water, a bromine floater will properly dispense the tablets. [13]Should chlorine be the chosen sanitizer, a granular form is recommended, as liquid chlorine or tablets are too harsh for the spa.

The primary purpose of the passage is to

    A.   relate how spa maintenance can negate the enjoyment of the spa experience.

    B.   provide evidence that spas are not as practical as swimming pools.

    C.   suggest that spa maintenance is expensive and time consuming.

    D.   explain the importance of proper spa maintenance.

    E.   instruct you on how to care for your spa.

The primary purpose of the passage is to explain the importance of proper spa maintenance, which is choice (D). While you may assume the information provided in answer choices (A), (B), and (C), these points are not included in the reading selection itself and may be eliminated. The reading selection focuses on why a spa needs to be maintained; however, it does not provide the detailed instructions on how to care for your spa (E). You many have some difficulty deciding between choices (D) and (E). They are both correct to some degree, so you may need to reread the passage to determine what portion is dedicated to actual instructions on how to maintain a spa, versus what portion focuses on the necessity of maintenance. You will find that the passage centers on *why* rather than *how*.

In the reading section of the test, you may be asked to *make predictions about the outcome of an event* based on information provided in the passage. As mentioned earlier, all information needed to answer a given question will be provided in the accompanying reading selection. However, when you are required to make a prediction after reading, you will need to make a sensible judgment on your own. While the outcome will not be explicitly offered, the reading selection will include sufficient details to enable you to make a prediction based on the given facts. Like a detective, you will need to identify clues that will point you in the right direction. Use this information along with the answer choices to determine the most likely outcome. Once again consider the passage on spa maintenance that is cited above.

> Which of these numbered sentences directly states why the use of disinfectant is necessary in the spa?
>
> A.   Sentence 3
>
> B.   Sentence 9
>
> C.   Sentence 7
>
> D.   Sentence 11
>
> E.   Sentence 1

The correct answer is (B), Sentence 9, which discusses the *fertile environment for the growth of bacteria and viruses*. As a reader, you need to make a judgment regarding the result of adding disinfectant to the spa. It would lead to the removal of bacteria and viruses, as well as prohibiting further growth. Although choice (A), Sentence 3, makes some reference to the necessity for adding disinfectant, it is an indirect reference. The question asks you specifically to identify the sentence that *directly* mentions why disinfectant is important for spa maintenance.

There will be questions that involve your knowledge of grammar and sentence structure. You may be asked to *use context clues, syntax, and structural analysis (e.g., affixes, prefixes, roots) to determine the meanings of unknown words and figurative or colloquial language.* Other questions will involve vocabulary skills, such as analysis of words, sentences, and paragraphs. These questions may ask you to *recognize and identify differ-*

ent interpretations that can be made of a word, sentence, or paragraph and to recognize how the meaning is affected by the context in which it appears. You may also be asked to demonstrate your understanding of *the function of key transition indicators.* This includes words such as *however, by contrast, in conclusion, nevertheless,* and *still.* We will look at the following example from your diagnostic test.

Learning to communicate well is very important. _____ communicate articulately, one must understand the meaning embedded in the language. _____ , one must understand a word's connotations (implied meanings) and denotations (literal meanings) in order to communicate clearly. Obviously, articulate communication in the classroom is essential. By being positive role models, teachers can help students develop the skills necessary to put their thoughts and feelings into words. Without <u>articulate</u> communication skills, an individual's thoughts, words, and feelings appear random, confused, and, ultimately, insignificant.

Learning theorists emphasize specific components of learning: behaviorists stress behavior in learning; humanists stress the affective in learning; cognitivists stress cognition in learning. All three of these components occur simultaneously and cannot be separated from each other in the learning process. In 1957, Festinger referred to dissonance as the lack of harmony between what one does (behavior) and what one believes (attitude). Attempts to separate the components of learning either knowingly or unknowingly create dissonances wherein language, thought, feeling, and behavior become diminished of their authenticity. _____ , ideas and concepts lose their content and vitality, and the manipulation and politics of communication assume prominence.

Which of the grouped words or phrases, if inserted in order into the passage's blank lines, would address the logical sequencing of the narrative?

    A.   For example, to; Consequently; Nonetheless

    B.   In order to; That is; As a result

    C.   Thus, to; Moreover; Consequently

    D.   Surprisingly; Thus; Initially

    E.   Ironically; That is; Finally

The correct answer is (B). When answering questions in which words are omitted, it is important that you try each of the answer choices in the blanks. Reading the passage with the range of possibilities will allow you to determine which word choice makes sense in the sentence as well as in the greater piece. In this case, only choice (B) includes words or phrases that make sense in the three blank areas.

Reference and Graph Questions

Let's consider how research and reference relates to the reading portion of the CBEST, as well as the types of questions that involve this area. Some questions may ask you to u*se the table of contents, section heading, and index to locate information.* These questions will follow reading selections that are comprised of these sections of a book. A *table of contents* is found in the beginning of a book. It details the parts of the book, such as the preface, introduction, sections, chapters, glossary, and bibliography as well as their corresponding page numbers. Not all books contain all of the parts mentioned above; however, questions will likely refer to these parts. The preface is usually a brief note from the author that includes a bit of information he or she would like the reader to be aware of before starting the book. The introduction is often one to several pages in the front of a text that is either written by the author of the book or another individual. The purpose is to set the context, introduce the author, or explain the topic or the research and writing process. Glossaries are brief dictionaries that provide definitions of key words from the book. They are located toward the end of the book. Some books have bibliographies or reference pages, which provide details regarding any published books, articles, or reports that are cited in the text. The *index* is found in the back of a book and provides a quick reference to the page numbers of the subjects, people, dates, and more that are included in the book.

You may encounter questions that require you to review an index or table of contents in order to *locate the place where a specific kind of information can be found.* You will need to determine where a topic would be found according to the given reference. This involves studying the book sections and chapters or other parts to decide what category the topic falls under.

You will also be asked to identify page numbers and to demonstrate that you *understand how a reading selection is organized.* For example: Use the excerpt below from a cookbook index to answer the two questions that follow.

Figure 3.1
Index

Cookies, 220-241

      about 220-221

      bars, 230-236

      caramel melts, 235

      coconut, 236

      blondies, 230

Which of the following best describes the method of organization used by the book in dealing with the different types of cookies?

    A.   by baking time

    B.   by popularity

    C.   by main ingredient

    D.   by baking temperature

    E.   by baking technique

The general information is listed about cookies, followed by subcategories, which include chocolate, fruit, oat, and nuts. Those subcategories represent main ingredients of the different types of cookies. The correct answer is (C). If the correct answer is not immediately obvious to you, the best approach is to use process of elimination. No information regarding baking temperature (D) or baking technique (E) is given, so these answer choices can be eliminated immediately. Chocolate, fruit, oats, and nuts may all be popular choices (B), but they more clearly represent the main ingredient (C) of the cookies. This makes (C) the best choice.

In addition to the passage-based and reference-based reading selection, this portion of the CBEST includes charts and graphs. The types included vary and can include bar graphs, line graphs, pie charts, and tables. These will require you to read the information presented and to answer the associated questions. You will be asked to *formulate logical conclusions, generalizations, or implied relationships that are supported by information.* Reading charts and graphs correctly calls for you to carefully examine the labels, portions, keys, and attributes provided. For example:

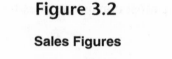

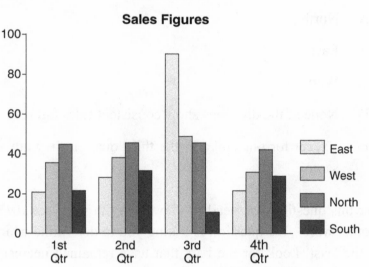

The four divisions of Company X (North, West, South, and East) are represented in the graph by region. The numbers along the left-hand side represent profits from sales in thousands of dollars, while the numbers along the bottom represent the company's fiscal year divided into quarters.

To understand the graph, first you must note the key on the right of the bars. The four categories, in this case sales areas (East, West, North, South) are differentiated by the color or markings of the bars. For instance, East is a solid shaded box and South is marked by dark dots. Next you will need to examine the attributes marked on the x (horizontal) and y (vertical) axes. The horizontal axis presents four bars representing each of the four sales areas in each of the four sales quarters. The vertical axis presents numbers and no further information. You must read the small passage under the graph, which provides an explanation of the numbers. In this case the numbers along the left-hand side represent profits from sales in thousands of dollars. In order to fully interpret the graph, you must examine all the information that is provided—title, labels, keys, and explanatory statements. Let's take a look at the first question:

Which region shows the most consistent sales figures for the fiscal year?

- A. North

- B. East

- C. West

- D. None of the divisions show consistent sales figures.

- E. Except for one spike in the third quarter, they are all about the same.

To answer this question you need to know that the word *consistent* means steady or constant. In other words, the question is asking you to determine which of the sales areas has changed the least. Look for the bars that have remained nearest to the same height over the four quarters. The bars with the light dots throughout are all about the same, which means North is the region with the least change—or the most consistent.

Extended List of Quick Tips for the Reading Section

- Read all of the questions carefully first to focus your attention while reading.

- Quickly review the answer choices.

- Read critically, keeping the questions in mind.

- Re-read what you do not initially understand.

- Determine the tone, main idea, and audience.

- Determine the focus of the question.

- Examine the answers for the best choice.

- Find details that support that choice in the reading selection.

- Read the answer choices one last time to make your final decision.

- Answer the questions using only the information provided.

- Do not spend too long on any one reading selection.

- Trust your instincts! Your initial choice is often the correct one.

Mathematics Review

Overview

The following is intended as a review of the basic mathematical skills assessed on the mathematics section of the CBEST. It is not intended as a substitute for a comprehensive mathematics curriculum. If you are planning to take the CBEST, this section should be an efficient means of reviewing a wide range of mathematics topics you have studied before.

The mathematics portion of the CBEST assesses cumulative knowledge of mathematics traditionally taught in elementary and secondary school. All teachers need to know mathematics whether they teach the subject or not.

Knowledge of three categories of mathematics is assessed:

1. **Identifying Processes Used in Problem Solving**
   Questions in this category assess your ability to set up problems and to determine what is required to solve problems. Questions in this category may not ask you to actually solve the problem. Examples of tasks you may be required to perform are identifying appropriate units of measure, recognizing that sufficient information is or is not given to solve the problem, recognizing different methods of solving a problem, or translating expressions into mathematical statements. The problems in this section may require identify-

ing the arithmetic, algebraic, geometric, logical, or graphical processes used in solving word problems.

2. **Solution of Word Problems**

   Questions in this category assess your ability to solve word problems. Mathematical topics included in this category are arithmetic, algebra, geometry, probability, and statistics.

3. **Demonstrating an Understanding of Mathematical Concepts and Relationships**

   Questions in this category assess your ability to understand basic mathematical concepts. Examples include terminology (e.g., measures of central tendency, order (greater than, less than, equal to), relationships demonstrated by charts and graphs, statistics, and elementary probability.

The mathematics section of the CBEST consists of 50 multiple-choice questions with five possible answer choices. The questions in the mathematics section are divided into the three areas as follows: approximately 15 questions are focused on *Estimation, Measurement, and Statistic Principles,* about 18 questions are on the areas of *Computation and Problem Solving,* which leaves approximately 17 questions on *Numerical and Graphical Relationships.*

This mathematical review covers all the content that will appear on the mathematics section of the CBEST. The review is divided into five sections:

- **Basic Mathematical Concepts**. Topics included in this section are: sets of numbers, our numeration system, whole numbers, integers, fractions, decimals, operations on numbers, percents, ratio and proportion, and comparison of numbers.

- **Elementary Statistics and Probability.** Topics included in this section are: measures of central tendency, statistical terminology, and elementary probability including addition, multiplication, and complement rules.

- **Algebra.** Topics included in this section are: algebraic expressions, solving linear equations and inequalities, and word problems.

- **Measurement and Estimation.** Topics included in this section are: systems of measurement, estimation, and rounding.

- **Reading Charts and Graphs.** Topics included in this section are: analyzing bar charts, pie charts, histograms and pictograms.

Basic Mathematical Concepts

Sets of Numbers

- The set of *natural* or *counting numbers* is {1,2,3,...}.

- The set of *whole numbers* is {0,1,2,3,...}.

- The set of *integers* is {...,–3,–2,–1,0,1,2,3,...}.

- The set of *positive integers* is {1,2,3,...}. and the set of *negative integers* is {–1,–2,–3,...}. Note that 0 is neither a positive nor a negative integer. Keeping this in mind, the set of *non-negative integers* is {0,1,2,3,...} and the set of *non-positive* integers is {0,–1,–2,–3,...}.

- The set of *even numbers*, or *even* integers, is {...,–4,–2,0,2,4,...}. All even numbers are divisible by 2.

- The set of *odd numbers*, or *odd integers*, is {...,–3, –1,1,3,5,...}. Each odd number is one more than an even number. There are no numbers which are both even and odd.

- The set of *rational numbers* is the collection of all numbers which can be written in the form $\dfrac{m}{n}$ where m and n are both integers and $n \neq 0$. For example, $\dfrac{2}{3}, \dfrac{-25}{7}$, and $2\dfrac{1}{5}$ are rational numbers. All rational numbers can also be written either as a terminating *decimal,* such as $\dfrac{3}{4} = 0.75$, or as a *repeating decimal* such as $\dfrac{2}{7} = 0.285714285714...$ which is usually written as $0.\overline{285714}$ to indicate that the six digits repeat indefinitely.

- The set of *prime numbers* is the collection of all positive integers greater than 1 each which has only itself and one as its positive integer divisors. The first 10 prime numbers are 2, 3, 5, 7, 11, 13, 17, 19, 23, 29.. It is interesting to note that 2 is the only even prime number; this is because an even number greater than 2 is divisible by 1, 2, and itself. Integers greater than 1 which are not prime are called *composite numbers*. The first 10 composite numbers are 4, 6, 8, 9, 10, 12, 14, 15, 16, and 18.

Our Numeration System

- Our numeration system uses the *Hindu-Arabic numerals* 0, 1, 2, 3, 4, 5, 6, 7, 8, 9 to represent numbers.

- This system has a *base-ten place value* design in which each place value in a number is ten times the place value to the right; this also means that each place value in a number is one-tenth the place value of that on the left. For example, the place values in the number 2,065,381 are:

2	0	6	5	3	8	1
millions	hundred thousands	ten thousands	thousands	hundreds	tens	ones or units

- The *expanded form* of 5,381 is 5 thousands + 3 hundreds + 8 tens + 1 ones.

- In the expression 4^5, the 4 is called the *base* and the 5 is called the *exponent*. Its meaning is $4^5 = 4 \times 4 \times 4 \times 4 \times 4$.

- Using exponents, the expanded form of the number 5,381 can be written $5000 + 300 + 80 + 1 = (5 \times 10^3) + (3 \times 10^2) + (8 \times 10^1) + 1$

Integers and Operations

The Absolute Value Operation

- The *absolute value* of a number x is defined to be the distance between x and 0 on the number line. Thus, the absolute value of x, which is indicated by $|x|$, is never a negative number. So, if x is non-negative then $|x| = x$, but if x is a negative number then $|x| = -x$ ($-x$ is the opposite of x and so is a positive number if $x < 0$.). For example, $|-18.3| = -(-18.3) = 18.3$.

The Operations of Addition and Subtraction

- Addition of whole numbers represents the combination of two sets of objects into a larger collection of objects. For example $2 + 5 = 7$ represents combining one set of 2 objects with another set of 5 objects to get a set of 7 objects. In the addition operation, $a + b = c$, the numbers a and b are called *addends* while c is called the *sum*.

- Subtraction of whole numbers is defined using addition. $a - b = c$ is true for whole numbers a, b, and c when $c + b = a$. In the subtraction operation, $a - b = c$, a is called the *minuend*, b is called the *subtrahend*, and c is the *remainder*.

- When adding two integers, m and n, there are two possibilities: the two integers have (i) the same sign (that is, m and n are both positive or both negative) or (ii) different signs (one is positive and the other is negative).

- If the addends have the same sign then the addition operation is completed by adding the absolute values of the addends and then giving the sum the same sign as the addends. For example, $8 + 15 = 23$ and $-8 + -15 = -23$

- If the addends have different signs then the addition operation is completed by subtracting the absolute values of the addends, lesser from greater, and then giving this result the sign of the original addend with the greater absolute value. For example, $-16 + 11 = -(16 - 11) = -5$.

- Subtraction of integers is defined using addition: For integers a and b, $a - b = a + (-b)$. For example, $-6 + (-11) = -(6 + 11) = -17$.

The Operations of Multiplication and Division

- Multiplication of two whole numbers is defined as repeated addition. This means for whole numbers a and b, $a \times b = \underbrace{b + \ldots + b}_{a \text{ terms of } b}$. For example, $3 \times 5 = 5 + 5 + 5 = 15$. In the operation $3 \times 5 = 15$, 3 and 5 are called the *factors* and 15 is called the *product*. Notice that $0 \times b = 0$ for any number b.

- Division of whole numbers is defined using the operation of multiplication. If a, b, and c are whole numbers with $b \neq 0$, then $a \div b = c$ provided $c \times b = a$. For example, $24 \div 6 = 4$ because $4 \times 6 = 24$. In the operation $a \div b = c$, a is called the *dividend*, b is called the *divisor*, and c is called the *quotient*.

- When multiplying two integers, multiply the absolute values of the factors. If the factors have the same sign (are both positive or both negative), then assign the product to be a positive number. If the factors have different signs (one is positive and the other is negative), then assign the product to be a negative number. For example, $7 \times (-4) = -28$ and $-9 \times (-3) = 27$.

- Division of integers is defined using the operation of multiplication. If a, b, and c are integers with $b \neq 0$, then $a \div b = c$ if $c \times b = a$. For example, $27 \div (-3) = -9$ because $(-3) \times (-9) = 27$.

- The *least common multiple* of two positive integers m and n, LCM (m, n), is exactly what it sounds like! It is the least positive integer that is a multiple of both m and n. For example, given the integers 12 and 15, note that the multiples of 12 are 12, 24, 36, 48, 60, 72... and the multiples of 15 are 15, 30, 45, 60, 75, 90,... While $12 \times 15 = 180$ is a common multiple of 12 and 15, 60 is the least common multiple of 12 and 15.

Fractions and Operations

- A *fraction* is a number that can be written in the form $\frac{m}{n}$ where m and n are both integers and $n \neq 0$. In the expression $\frac{m}{n}$, the m is called the *numerator* and n is called the *denominator*.

- A fraction is in *lowest terms* or *reduced form* if the numerator and denominator have no common (positive integer) factors other than 1. For example, $\frac{21}{27}$ is not in lowest terms because 21 and 27 have 3 as a common factor. If both the numerator and denominator of $\frac{21}{27}$ are divided by 3, the result is $\frac{7}{9}$ which is in lowest terms since 7 and 9 have no common factors other than 1.

- When writing an answer for a problem which involves a fraction, always reduce the fraction to lowest terms.

- *Equivalent fractions* are fractions that represent the same rational number. $\frac{12}{24}=\frac{6}{12}=\frac{3}{6}=\frac{1}{2}$ so $\frac{12}{24}$, $\frac{6}{12}$, $\frac{3}{6}$, and $\frac{1}{2}$ are equivalent fractions.

- A *mixed number* is a number that consists of an integer and a fraction. For example, $3\frac{1}{2}$ is a mixed number.

- The fraction $\frac{m}{n}$ is called a *proper fraction* if the numerator is less than the denominator ($m < n$), and is called an *improper fraction* if the numerator is greater than or equal to the denominator ($m > n$ or $m = n$). For example, $\frac{10}{13}$ is a proper fraction while $\frac{40}{13}$ is an improper fraction.

- An improper fraction may be written as a mixed number by dividing the denominator into the numerator to obtain the integer part of the mixed number and then using the remainder as the numerator of the proper fraction part. For example, $\frac{40}{13}$ can be changed into a mixed number: divide 13 into 40 to obtain 3 as the integer part; $3 \times 13 = 39$ so there is a remainder of 1. Thus the mixed number equivalent to $\frac{40}{13}$ is $3\frac{1}{13}$.

- A mixed number can be expressed as an improper fraction. Multiply the denominator of the fraction by the integer part and adding this product to the numerator of the fraction to obtain the numerator of the improper fraction. Keep the denominator of the fraction part of the mixed number as the denominator of the improper fraction. For example, the mixed number $2\frac{3}{7}$ can be written as $\frac{(2\times7)+3}{7}=\frac{17}{7}$.

- *Addition of fractions* can only be completed when the fractions have the same denominator. When this happens it is said that the fractions have a *common denominator*. To add fractions with a common denominator, add the numerators and keep the common denominator as the resulting fraction's denominator: $\frac{a}{c}+\frac{b}{c}=\frac{a+b}{c}$. An example is: $\frac{6}{8}+\frac{1}{8}=\frac{7}{8}$.

- When two fractions, $\frac{a}{b}$ and $\frac{c}{d}$, do not have a common denominator, one must be determined so that the sum can be computed. Usually the *least common denominator* is used to add $\frac{a}{b}$ and $\frac{c}{d}$ when b is not equal to d. Once the LCM(b, d) is determined, $\frac{a}{b}$ and $\frac{c}{d}$ are rewritten as fractions with the common denominator and then added. For example, to compute $\frac{1}{20}+\frac{7}{15}$, the first step is to find LCM(20, 15) which is 60. Then, rewrite each fraction with denominator 60: $\frac{1}{20}=\frac{3\cdot1}{3\cdot20}=\frac{3}{60}$ and $\frac{7}{15}=\frac{4\cdot7}{4\cdot15}=\frac{28}{60}$. Hence, $\frac{1}{20}+\frac{7}{15}=\frac{3}{60}+\frac{28}{60}=\frac{31}{60}$ which is in reduced form.

- *Subtraction of fractions* is defined using addition: $\frac{a}{b}-\frac{c}{d}=\frac{a}{b}+\frac{(-c)}{d}$ and then using the rules for *adding signed numbers* and *fractions*. For example, $\frac{1}{2}-\frac{11}{15}=\frac{1}{2}+\frac{-11}{15}=\frac{1\cdot15}{2\cdot15}+\frac{-11\cdot2}{15\cdot2}=\frac{15+-22}{30}=\frac{-(22-15)}{30}=\frac{-7}{30}$.

- *To multiply two fractions*, first multiply the two numerators and then multiply the two denominators; i.e., $\frac{a}{b}\times\frac{c}{d}=\frac{a\times c}{b\times d}$. Then reduce the resultant fraction to lowest terms. For example, $\frac{2}{3}\times\frac{9}{14}=\frac{18}{42}=\frac{3}{7}$.

- Given a fraction, $\frac{a}{b}$, its *reciprocal* is computed by interchanging the numerator and denominator to obtain $\frac{b}{a}$. For example, the reciprocal of $\frac{-5}{9}$ is $\frac{9}{-5}$.

- To divide two fractions, multiply the first fraction (the dividend) by the reciprocal of the second fraction (the divisor): $\frac{a}{b}\div\frac{c}{d}=\frac{a}{b}\times\frac{d}{c}$. For example, $\frac{5}{28}\div\frac{10}{7}=\frac{5}{28}\times\frac{7}{10}=\frac{35}{280}=\frac{1}{8}$.

Decimals and Operations

- We can expand our place value system to include *negative integer powers of ten* as follows:

$$\frac{1}{10} = 10^{-1} = 0.1 \text{ which is read as "one-tenth."}$$

$$\frac{1}{100} = 10^{-2} = 0.01 \text{ which is read as "one-hundredth."}$$

$$\frac{1}{1000} = 10^{-3} = 0.001 \text{ which is read as "one-thousandth."}$$

For example, 5.274 is "five and two hundred, seventy-four thousandths."

- To add or subtract decimal numbers, line up the decimal points of each fraction and use the same procedure as in adding whole numbers. For example,

$$
\begin{array}{r}
27.03 \\
+ \ 8.295 \\
\hline
35.325
\end{array}
\qquad
\begin{array}{r}
276.500 \\
- \ 19.832 \\
\hline
256.668
\end{array}
$$

- When *multiplying two decimal numbers*, follow the same procedures as for multiplying integers, and then place the decimal point so that the total number of digits to the right of the decimal point in the product is equal to the sum of the number of decimal places in the two factors. For example, $2.43 \times 0.05 = 0.1215$.

- To *divide a decimal number by a whole number*, divide as if there was no decimal point, then place the decimal point in the quotient directly over the decimal point in the dividend. For example, to compute $35.4 \div 8$, we write $8\overline{)35.400}$ with quotient 4.425.

- To *divide a decimal number by a decimal number*, first move the decimal point of the divisor to the right so that no digits remain to its right. Then move the decimal point of the dividend the same number of places to the right. Next complete the division as when dividing by a whole number. For example, to divide 708.2 by 0.16 we first change the problem into a new one: $708.0 \div 0.16 \rightarrow 70820 \div 16 = 4426.25$.

- To *convert a decimal into a fraction*, write a fraction with the numerator equal to the given decimal but without the decimal point, and with the denominator as 10^p where p is the number of digits the given decimal has to the right of the decimal point; then reduce to simplest terms. For example, $7.064 = \dfrac{7064}{10^3} = \dfrac{7064}{1000} = \dfrac{883}{125}$.

- To convert a fraction to a decimal, divide the denominator of the fraction into the numerator until the division terminates or repeats. For example, $\dfrac{1}{4} = 0.25$ and $\dfrac{5}{12} = 0.41666... = 0.41\overline{6}$.

Percents

- "*Cent*" in the word "*percent*" means 100. and "*percent*" means per 100. For example, 23 percent, which is written 23%, means $\dfrac{23}{100}$.

- To *convert a decimal to a percent*, move the decimal point two places to the right and insert the percent symbol. For example, $0.246 = 24.6\%$.

- To *convert a percent to a decimal*, move the decimal point two places to the left and remove the percent symbol. For example, $35.6\% = 0.356$.

- To *convert a fraction to a percent*, first convert the fraction to a decimal. Then convert the decimal to a percent. For example, $\dfrac{3}{5} = 0.60 = 60\%$.

- To *find the percentage of a given number*, change the percent to a decimal and then multiply this decimal by the given number. For example, to calculate 30% of \$252, $30\% \times \$252 = 0.3 \times \$252 = \$75.60$.

Ratio and Proportion

- A *ratio* of two numbers, a and b, is the comparison of a and b (b cannot be equal to zero) as a quotient. It is written $\dfrac{a}{b}$ or $a:b$. For example, *the ratio of girls to boys in Mr. Fini's class is 3:2*, means that if you are told there are 10 boys then there are $\dfrac{3}{2} x\, 10 = 15$ girls in the class. Or if you are given that there are 25 students in the class, then having the ratio of girls to boys as 3:2 means that there are $3x$ girls and $2x$ boys; therefore: $3x + 2x = 25 \Rightarrow 5x = 25 \Rightarrow x = 5$ from which it follows that there are girls $3x = 15$ and $2x = 10$ boys in the class.

- A *proportion* is an equation that sets two ratios equal. For example, $\dfrac{4}{5} = \dfrac{24}{30}$. In this example, the first and last terms (4 and 30) are called the *extremes* while the middle two terms (5 and 24) are called the *means*.

- A property of proportions (Cross Product rule) is that *in a proportion the product of the extremes is equal to the product of the means;* that is, $\dfrac{a}{b} = \dfrac{c}{d}$ is equivalent to $ad = bc$. An example of a problem that would use this rule is: If a lamppost is represented in a drawing as 2.2 inches tall and each inch in the drawing represents 6.2 feet then we can let x be the actual height in feet of the lamppost and write a proportion to represent the problem: $\dfrac{x \text{ feet}}{2.2 \text{ inches}} = \dfrac{6.2 \text{ feet}}{1 \text{ inch}}$. To solve the problem use the Cross Product rule: $x = (2.2)(6.2) = 13.64$ feet.

Comparison of Numbers

Figure 4.1
Comparison Symbols

Symbol	Meaning	Example in Symbols	Example in Words
>	greater than	$7 > 4$	7 is greater than 4
<	less than	$4 < 7$	4 is less than 7
=	equal to	$7 = 7$	7 is equal to 7
≥	greater than or equal to	$7 \geq 4$	7 is greater than or equal to 4
≤	less than or equal to	$4 \leq 7$	4 is less than or equal to 7

- To *compare two whole numbers*, if the two whole numbers do not have the same number of digits, then the one with more digits is greater. For example $27,018 > 8,103$. But if the numbers have the same number of digits we compare them starting with the left most or greatest place value; find the first place value where the digits are unequal and compare those digits. For example, comparing 7935 and 7512, we see that the thousands place digit is the same but they differ in the hundreds place with $9 > 5$ so that $7935 > 7512$.

- To *compare two rational numbers in decimal form*, if the two numbers do not have the same number of digits to the left of the decimal point, then the one with more digits is greater. For example 27,018.3 > 8,103.97. But if the two numbers have the same number of digits to the left of the decimal point, we compare them starting with the left most or greatest place value; find the first place value where the digits are unequal and compare those digits. For example, comparing 79.435 and 79.9512, we see that the tenths place digit is the first digit, comparing from left to right, which is not the same with 9 > 4 so that 79.9512 > 79.435.

- To compare two proper fractions, if the fractions have a common denominator then the fraction with the greater numerator is greater. For example, $\frac{17}{23} > \frac{15}{23}$. If the fractions do not have a common denominator then one must be found. For example, to compare $\frac{5}{6}$ and $\frac{7}{9}$ we can use the least common denominator which is 18 and find equivalent fractions, then compare. $\frac{5}{6} = \frac{15}{18}$ and $\frac{7}{9} = \frac{14}{18}$, so $\frac{5}{6} > \frac{7}{9}$.

Elementary Statistics and Probability

Measures of Central Tendency

- The *average* or *mean* of a set of numbers is found by finding the sum of these numbers and then dividing by the number of elements in the set. For example, to find the mean of the numbers 12, 18, 23, 15, and 20: $\frac{12+18+23+15+20}{5} = \frac{88}{5} = 17.6$.

- The *median* of a set of numbers is the middle number. So to find the median, list the numbers from greatest to least and choose the middle number. If there are two middle numbers, average them. For example, the median of the set of numbers 5, 9, 16, 8, 22, 17, 7 is found by first rearranging the numbers from greatest to least: 22, 17, 16, 9, 8, 7, 5 and then seeing that 9 is the middle number; so 9 is the median. Or another example, to find the median of the set of numbers 26, 18, 34, 12, 44, 24 first we rearrange in order to arrive at 44, 34, 26, 24, 18, 12. The two middle numbers are 26 and 24. The median is the average of 26 and 24 which is 25.

- The *mode* of a set of numbers is the number that appears most frequently in the collection. There may be no mode or more than one mode. For example, the mode of the collection 4, 17, 18, 22, 16, 18 is 18 since there are two 18's and only one of each of the other numbers. However, there are two modes for the collection 6, 3, 6, 6, 5, 2, 5, 4, 5, 9, 11, 10 because the numbers 5 and 6 both occur three times while the other numbers occur once. But in the case where no number appears more than another, such as in the collection 26, 38, 72, 37, 27, we say that there is no mode.

Other Statistical Terminology

- The *range* of set of numbers is the difference between the greatest number of the set and the least. For example, the range of the collection 94, 67, 81, 30 is $94 - 30 = 64$.

- When a score on an exam is referred to being in the *p*th *percentile,* this means that the score is greater than or equal to $p\%$ of all the scores on the exam.

- The *deviation* of a score x from the mean is $x - \bar{x}$ where $\bar{x}$ is the notation of the mean of the set.

- The *standard deviation* measures how far a score tends to be from the mean. It is calculated by finding the deviations of each score, then squaring the deviations, after which the mean of these squares is calculated. The standard deviation is the square root of this mean. For example, consider the scores 68, 92, 86, and 84. To compute the standard deviation of this set, first find the mean: $\bar{x} = \dfrac{68+92+86+84}{4} = \dfrac{330}{4} = 82.5$. Then we can use a table to compute the standard deviation as follows:

x	$x - \bar{x}$	$(x - \bar{x})^2$
68	−14.5	210.25
92	9.5	90.25
86	3.5	12.25
84	1.5	2.25

The mean of the right column is $\dfrac{315}{4} = 78.75$ so the standard deviation is $\sqrt{78.75} \approx 8.87$ ($\approx$ means approximately.) The larger the standard deviation means the greater the spread of the data.

- In standardized testing, the terminology *stanine* is often used. The word "stanine" means STAndard NINE and is a method of scaling test scores so that the mean is five and standard deviation is two. The scale ranks scores from 1 to 9 with 1 being the lowest score and 9 the highest. The lowest 4% of scores are assigned the stanine 1, the next 7% are assigned the stanine 2, the next 12% are assigned the stanine score 3, the next 17% are assigned a 4, the middle 20% are assigned a 5, and so on as shown in this table:

grouped ranking	4%	7%	12%	17%	20%	17%	12%	7%	4%
stanine score	1	2	3	4	5	6	7	8	9

- For example, a stanine score of 7 in a standardized reading test indicates that the test taker scored in the third highest stanine group.

Elementary Probability

- An *experiment* is an occurrence which produces *outcomes*. The set of all possible outcomes is called the *sample space*. For example if the experiment is rolling a die the sample space would be {1, 2, 3, 4, 5, 6}.

- An *event* is a subset of the sample space. For example if a single die is rolled an event might be that an even number is rolled. So the event is {2, 4, 6} which is a subset of {1, 2, 3, 4, 5, 6}.

- The likelihood or chance that an event will take place is called the *probability* of the event.

- *Empirical probability* is the probability determined by an actual physical experiment. *Theoretical probability,* which we discuss here, assumes that each outcome in the *sample space* of the event has an equally likely chance of occurring. For example when flipping a coin it is assumed that 50% of the time the outcome "heads" will occur and 50% of the time "tails" will occur. So when we write "probability" we mean theoretical probability.

- Let $n(E)$ represent the number of elements in an event and let $n(S)$ be the number of elements in the sample space. Then the *probability that event E will happen* is $P(E) = \dfrac{n(E)}{n(S)}$. So the probability that when a die is rolled the number is even is $P(even) = \dfrac{3}{6} = \dfrac{1}{2}$.

- Note that the probability of an *impossible event* is 0 and the probability of a *certain event* (must happen) is 1. For example, when randomly choosing a marble out of a box with 6 blue and 8 black marbles, the probability of choosing a red marble is 0 and the probability of choosing a marble is 1.

- Probabilities are always a number between 0 and 1, inclusive.

- The *Addition Rule of Probability* is that the probability either of the events E and F happening is $P(E \text{ or } F) = P(E) + P(F) - P(E \text{ and } F)$. For example, the probability, when randomly choosing a card from a standard deck of cards, of choosing a ten or a heart is $P(10 \text{ or heart})$
$= P(10) + P(\text{heart}) - P(10 \text{ of hearts}) = \dfrac{4}{52} + \dfrac{13}{52} - \dfrac{1}{52} = \dfrac{16}{52} = \dfrac{4}{13}$.

- The *Complementary Rule* is that if E is an event then *the probability of E not happening is* $P(\text{not } E) = 1 - P(E)$. For example, if the probability of *rain tomorrow* is 30% then the probability of *no rain tomorrow* is $1 - 0.30 = 0.70 = 70\%$.

- The *Multiplication Rule of Counting* (or *Fundamental Counting Principle*) is that if an event E can occur in m ways and, another event F that occurs after E can occur in n ways then the number of ways that event E followed by event F can occur is $m \cdot n$ (m times n). For example, when tossing a pair of dice (we assume one die stops after the other), the number of possible outcomes is $6 \cdot 6 = 36$ since there are 6 different numbers on each die.

- The *Multiplication Rule* of *Probability* is that the probability that event E happens followed by event F happening is $P(E) \cdot P(F)$. For example, what is the probability that, given a box with 8 black socks and 6 brown socks, if two socks are randomly chosen from the box, one after the other, that a pair of black socks will have been chosen? The probability that the first sock chosen is black is $P(\text{black}) = \dfrac{8}{14}$ and the probability that the second sock is black is $P(\text{black}) = \dfrac{7}{13}$, so the probability that both are black is
$P(2 \text{ black}) = \dfrac{8}{14} \cdot \dfrac{7}{13} = \dfrac{8}{2 \cdot 13} = \dfrac{4}{13}$.

Algebra

Algebraic Expressions

- An *algebraic expression* is an expression using letters, numbers, symbols, and arithmetic operations to represent a number or relationship among numbers. For example, $2x + 6xy^2$.

- A *variable*, or unknown, is a letter that represents a number in an algebraic expression. A *coefficient* is a number that precedes a variable. For example, in the term $-8m^3$ the letter m is the variable while the number -8 is the coefficient.

- A *monomial* is the product of a number and variables raised to non-negative integer powers. A *binomial* is the sum of two monomials. A *trinomial* is the sum of three monomials. A *polynomial* is the generic expression for sums of monomials. For example, $6x$ is a monomial, $9y - 5$ is a binomial, $2a^2 - 5a + 1$ is a trinomial, and all three of the examples are polynomials.

- In polynomials, *like terms* are those monomials with the same variables raised to the same power. For example, in the expression $2x^2 + x - 6 + 2x$, x and $2x$ are like terms.

- To *simplify* an algebraic expression, always work with parentheses first and then all exponents, always working from left to right. Next do all multiplication and division from left to right. Lastly carry out all addition and subtraction from left to right. For example, $6 - 8(2x + 4) - x = 6 - 16x - 24 - x = (6 - 24) - (16x + x) = -26 - 17x$.

Solving Linear Equations and Inequalities

- A *linear equation (or inequality)* is an equation (or inequality) which involves the sum of constant terms and terms with single variables raised to the first power. For example, $6x - 2 = 5$ is a linear equation and $8 + x < 3 - 2x$ is a linear inequality.

- To *solve a linear equation*, use the following steps:

  (1) Eliminate parentheses by distributing using the Distributive Property: $a(b + c) = ab + ac$.

  (2) Isolate the variable by grouping all terms with variables on one side of the equation and constant terms on the other side.

(3) Combine terms on each side of the equation.

(4) Divide both sides of the equation by the coefficient of the variable.

(5) Check your answer by substituting your answer into each side of the original equation.

- For example, consider the equation $24 - 2x = 5(x + 2)$. The steps to solving the problem are:

(1) $24 - 2x = 5(x + 2) \Rightarrow 24 - 2x = 5x + 10$

(2) $24 - 2x = 5x + 10 \Rightarrow 24 - 2x + -5x + -24 = 5x + 10 + -5x + -24$

(3) $24 - 2x + -5x + -24 = 5x + 10 + -5x + -24 \Rightarrow -7x = -14$

(4) $-7x = -14 \Rightarrow \dfrac{-7x}{-7} = \dfrac{-14}{-7} \Rightarrow x = 2$

(5) Check: Left side: $24 - 2(2) = 24 - 4 = 20$

   Right side: $5(2 + 2) = 5(4) = 20$

- To *solve a linear inequality*, use the same procedure as for solving linear equalities except step (4) which becomes

(4)* Divide both sides of the inequality by the coefficient of the variable using the following rule: If dividing by a negative number the sense of the inequality changes; that is, if the inequality is "less than" it will change to "greater than" and vice versa.

For example, $-2x \le 8 \Rightarrow \dfrac{-2x}{-2} \ge \dfrac{8}{-2} \Rightarrow x \ge -4$. Note that numbers less than -4 produce a false statement; e.g., substituting $x = -5$ into the original inequality gives us $-2(-5) \le 8 \Leftrightarrow 10 \le 8$ which is clearly false.

Solving Word Problems

- A general procedure for solving word problems begins with reading the problem carefully and identifying what is known and what is to be found. Label the unknown(s). Next a method (or several) for solution must be chosen and attempted. Then a solution of the problem must be determined. The last step is to check that the answer is correct.

- Some problem solving strategies are:

  (a) Using inductive or deductive reasoning.

  (b) Drawing a diagram.

  (c) Guessing and checking.

  (d) Working backwards.

  (e) Writing an equation or inequality.

  (f) Making a list or table.

  (g) Using a graph.

  (h) Estimating.

- When solving *algebraic word problems*, read the problem carefully several times and identify the unknown(s); choose variable(s) to represent the unknowns. Next translate the problem into an equation or inequality. Look for words such as "is, are, were" which translate into the mathematical symbol "=". Use inequalities for "greater than" (>) and" less than" (<). Other symbols to look for are shown in the table below:

Operation	Key Words	Examples	In Mathematics
addition	more, increased by, sum, total	six more than x x increased by 6 the sum of x and 6 the total of x and 6	$x + 6$
subtraction	less, fewer, difference	4 less than y 4 fewer than y the difference of y and 4	$y - 4$
multiplication	of, product, times	15% of m 8 times z the product of 8 and z	$0.15m$ $8z$
division	out of, per, ratio, quotient	10 out of 17 10 per 17 the ratio of 10 and 17 the quotient of 10 and 17	$\dfrac{10}{17}$

Some Examples of Word Problems:

(a) **Problem:** What percent of 125 is 30?

Solution: Let m be the percent you are seeking. Translate the question into an equation: $m \times 125 = 30$ or $125m = 30$. Then solve: $125m = 30 \Rightarrow m = \dfrac{30}{125} = 0.24 = 24\%$.

(b) **Problem:** Jenny has 10 less dollars than twice what Ben has in his pocket. The sum of their money is $200. How much money does Jenny have?

Solution: Let x be the amount of money that Ben has. Then Jenny has *10 less than twice Ben* which can be written as "$2x - 10$." The word "sum" indicates to add these two amounts.

So the mathematical translation is $x + (2x - 10) = 200$. Solving: $x + (2x - 10) = 200 \Rightarrow 3x - 10 = 200 \Rightarrow 3x = 210 \Rightarrow x = 70$.

Thus, since Ben has $70, Jenny has $[2(70) - 10] = 140 - 10 = \$130$.

(c) **Problem:** Tim's dog weighs 42 pounds and his cat weighs 11 pounds. What is the difference between Tim's pets' weights?

Solution: $42 - 11 = 31$ pounds.

Measurement and Estimation

Systems of Measurement

- The *English* system of measurement historically grew out of using body parts for measurements such as a foot or arm.

- Units of Measurement in the English system are:

	English System	**Equivalents**
Length	inch (in), foot (ft), yard (yd), mile (mi)	12 inches = 1 foot 3 feet = 1 yard 5280 feet = 1 mile
Weight/Mass	ounce (oz), pound (lb), ton	16 ounces = 1 pound 2000 pounds = 1 ton
Capacity/ Volume	teaspoon (tsp), tablespoon (tbsp), cup (c), pint (pt), quart (qt), gallon (gal)	3 teaspoons = 1 tablespoon 16 tablespoons = 1 cup 2 cups = 1 pint 2 pints = 1 quart 4 quarts = 1 gallon

- The *Metric* system of measurement is related to the base ten place value system.

	Metric System	**Equivalents**
Length	millimeter (mm), centimeter (cm), meter (m), kilometer (km)	1000 millimeters = 1 meter 100 centimeters = 1 meter 1000 meters = 1 kilometer
Weight/Mass	milligram (mg), centigram (cg), gram (g), kilogram (kg)	1000 milligram = 1 gram 100 centigram = 1 gram 1000 gram = 1 kilogram
Capacity/Volume	milliliter (ml), centiliter (cl), liter (l), kiloliter (kl)	1000 milliliter = 1 liter 100 centiliter = 1 liter 1000 liter = 1 kiloliter

- Conversion between systems is not usually necessary but a general sense of comparison in the measurements is good to know. So this chart is for that purpose.

Metric to English	**English to Metric**
Length: 1 mm = 0.04 in 1 cm = 0.39 in 1 m = 39.37 in = 3.28 ft 1 m = 1.09 yd 1 km = 0.62 mi	Length: 1 in = 2.54 cm 1 ft = 30.48 cm = 0.305 m 1 yd = 0.914 m 1 mi = 1.609 km
Weight: 1 g = 0.035 oz 1 kg = 2.2 lb	Weight: 1 oz = 28.350 g 1 lb = 0.453 kg
Capacity: 1 ml = .2 tsp 1 l = 1.057 qt	Capacity: 1 tsp = 5 ml 1 c = 236 ml 1 qt = 0.946 l 1 gal = 3.785 l

- *Temperature* is measured in degrees using either the *Celsius* system or the *Fahrenheit* system. In the Celsius system, 0° C is the freezing point of water while 100° C is the boiling point of water. In the Fahrenheit system water freezes at 32°F and the boiling point of water is 212° F. The relationship between the systems can be expressed by $F = \frac{9}{5}C + 32$.

- Time is measured in seconds, minutes, hours, days, weeks, and years. where 60 sec. = 1 min., 60 min. = 1 hour, 24 hrs. = 1 day, 7 days = 1 week, 52 weeks = 1 year.

Estimation

- *Estimation* is used before computation to arrive at an approximate answer to a more difficult problem.

- *Rounding off* is an important estimation technique. To round off a decimal number:

  (a) First identify the place value you want to round off at (the "rounding digit") and look at the digit immediately to the right of it.

  (b) If that digit is less than 5, do not change the rounding digit. If that digit is instead greater than or equal to five, add one to the rounding digit.

  (c) Next if the rounding number's place value is greater than 1, change all digits to the right of the rounding digit to 0 and drop all digits to the right of the decimal point. If the rounding number's place value is less than or equal to 1, drop all digits to the right of it. For example, if you are asked to round 6731.24 to the hundreds place (which has digit 3 on its right), change the tens and ones digit to zero and drop off the .24 on the end to get 6700. If you need to round 6731.24 to the tenths place (which has the digit 4 on its right), just drop off the last digit to get 6731.2 as your estimate. As another example, consider the number 7593.648. To round off to the thousands place (which has digit 5 to its right) add 1 to the rounding digit, change the hundreds, tens, and ones digits to zero and drop off the .648 to get 8000.

Graphs, Charts, and Tables

Pie Charts

- A *pie chart* is a circle which has been divided into sectors which represent categories. The pie chart itself represents the whole collection of categories. The size of each sector is proportional in size to the percentage that the corresponding category represents of the whole.

- The parts of the pie chart that you should note are the *title, categories,* and *the sizes of the* categories.

For example, consider the pie chart below:

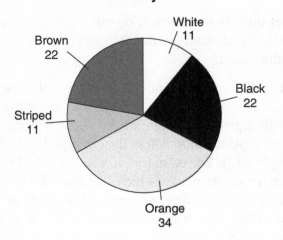

Sara's Toy Cats

This pie chart represents the cat toy collection owned by someone named Sara. The five categories indicated on the pie chart are clearly marked along with the percentage of the collection that each category contains.

A possible question might involve which category is the greatest in size. (orange) Or how much larger Sara's collection of black and brown cats is than her collection of striped cats? ($22 + 22 - 11 = 33\%$)

Bar Graphs

- A *bar graph* has two axes and rectangles whose heights represent the quantity or frequency of occurrences of specific categories. Bar graphs are used to compare categories.

- The important parts of the bar graph are the *title, axes labels, units,* and *scales,* and the *height of the bars.*

- One axis of the bar graph is *the frequency axis* which is used to indicate the frequency of the category, and the other is the *grouped data axis* which identifies how the data has been grouped.

For example, observe the bar graph here:

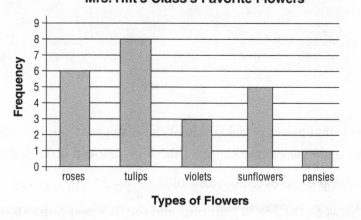

Mrs. Hilt's Class's Favorite Flowers

Some questions that might be asked about the information given by the bar graph are (a) What is the favorite type of flower of the students in Mrs. Hilt's class? (tulips), (b) How many more students like tulips versus pansies? ($8 - 1 = 7$), or (c) How many students are in Mrs. Hilt's class? ($6 + 8 + 3 + 5 + 1 = 23$).

Histograms

- A *histogram* is a type of bar graph in which the bars (rectangles) are adjacent (no space between them) and each bar's width represents an interval. The bars are always vertical in a histogram.

- The important parts of histogram are the *title, axes labels, units,* and *scales,* the *intervals of the categories,* and the *height of the bars.*

For example, a histogram is shown here which groups people into categories according to their ages.

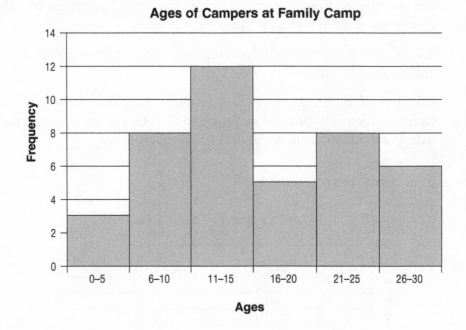

Ages of Campers at Family Camp

Some questions that might be asked about the histogram are: (a) Which group of people was least represented at Family Camp? (the 0–5-year-old group), (b) What percentage of people at the camp were over 20 years old? ($\frac{14}{42} = 33.3\%$), or (c) What is the difference in number between the 25–30 year olds and the 0–5 year olds? (6 − 3 = 3).

Line Graphs

- A *line graph* is a way to represent the relationship between two variables. In statistics the frequency could be one of the variables.

- The important parts of a line graph are the *title, axes labels,* and *value points.*

Consider the line graph shown below which illustrates the average temperature in a town in California for the first six months in 2010. Some questions that might be asked about this graph are: (a) Between which two months was the increase in average temperature the greatest? (between March and April) or (b) Between which two months is the percentage increase the least? (January to February =

$$\frac{\text{change}}{\text{original amount}} \approx \frac{48-42}{42} = \frac{6}{42} \approx 14.3\%, \text{ February to March} = \frac{52-48}{48} = \frac{4}{48} \approx 8.3\%,$$

$$\text{March to April} = \frac{72-52}{52} = \frac{20}{52} \approx 38.7\%, \text{ April to May} = \frac{74-72}{72} = \frac{2}{72} \approx 2.7\%, \text{ May to}$$

$$\text{June} = \frac{80-74}{74} = \frac{6}{74} \approx 8.1\%, \text{ so the least percentage increase occurred between April to}$$

May.)

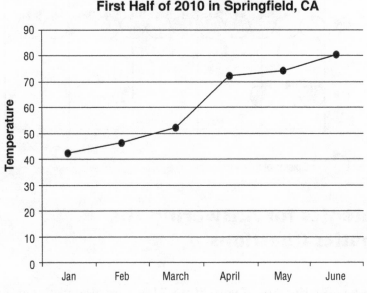

**Average Temperatures in the
First Half of 2010 in Springfield, CA**

Pictograph

- A *pictograph* is a variation of a bar graph in which a figure or picture of an object is used to represent a quantity of the object.

- The important parts of a pictogram are the *title, categories*, and the *key* which indicates the quantity each picture represents.

In the example below the apple symbol represents 2 pieces of fruit eaten. Some questions that might be asked about the pictograph might be (a) How many pieces of fruit did David eat in May? ($7.5 \times 2 = 15$) (b) How many more pieces of fruit did Mary eat than Ben in May? ($24 - 6 = 18$).

Number of Apples Eaten in May

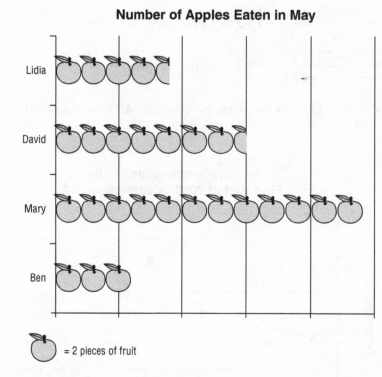

= 2 pieces of fruit

Key Strategies for Answering the Mathematics Questions

1. **Make effective use of your time.** There are 50 questions on the mathematics section of the CBEST. If you find yourself taking more than 2 minutes on a problem, mark the answer you think is most likely to be correct, circle the number of the item in the test booklet, and come back to the problem later if time allows.

2. **Answer all questions in this section of the test.** There is no penalty for incorrect answers on this portion of the test so do not leave any questions unanswered. If you are not sure of the correct answer to a particular problem, narrow the choices to two or three most likely, and choose one. Eliminate answers that could not possibly be correct before you choose.

3. **Read each problem carefully.** Identify what the problem is asking for, identify relevant information, and eliminate irrelevant information.

4. **Devise a plan for answering the question.** Draw a diagram, table, or chart to organize the information; label unknowns, write an equation, guess and check, think of a simpler but similar problem.

5. **Check your answers.** If there is time, substitute answers back into equations, ask yourself if your answer is logical and meets all the conditions in the original problem.

6. **Write in the test booklet.** Write in all space available, label or mark diagrams, or write relative information to help you strategize. Also, writing in the booklet your ideas will save time if you return to the problem later.

Practice Problems

Basic Mathematical Concepts

1. $16 - 6 \times (2 + 5) - 3^2 =$

   A. 4,489

   B. 61

   C. 16

   D. −35

   E. −841

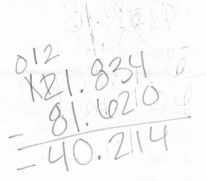

2. $81.62 - 121.834 =$

   A. −114.672

   B. −40.214

   C. −0.40214

   D. 40.772

   E. 11.36720

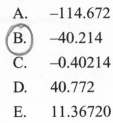

3. $\dfrac{7}{12} + \dfrac{11}{42} =$ $\dfrac{49}{84} + \dfrac{22}{84} = \dfrac{71}{84}$

49
+22
71

A. $\dfrac{1}{28}$

B. $\dfrac{1}{3}$

C. $\dfrac{3}{7}$

D. $\dfrac{16}{21}$

(E.) $\dfrac{71}{84}$

4. $|10 - 13| - |12 + 2| =$ $|-3| - |14| = 3 - 14 = -11$

A. -17

(B.) -11

C. 9

D. 11

E. 17

5. $2.1 \times 3.05 =$

(A.) 6.405

B. 6.4005

C. 0.645

D. 0.6405

E. 0.06405

$$2.10 \times 3.05$$
1050
0000
+103000
640 50

6. Solve for x; round your answer to the nearest hundredths place: $\dfrac{1500}{x} = \dfrac{35}{20}$

A. 900

B. 800

C. 857.15

D. 857.142

E. 857.14

$35x = 1500 \times 20$

$\dfrac{35x}{35} = \dfrac{30,000}{35}$

857.14
35)38,000

7. Which of the following mathematical statements is correct?

   A. $7.435 < 7.443 < 7.449$

   B. $7.435 > 7.443 > 7.449$

   C. $7.449 > 7.435 > 7.443$

   D. $7.449 < 7.435 < 7.443$

   E. $7.443 > 7.435 > 7.449$

8. $\dfrac{3}{10} \div \dfrac{6}{25} =$

   A. $\dfrac{9}{125}$

   B. $\dfrac{4}{5}$

   C. $\dfrac{5}{4}$

   D. $\dfrac{9}{5}$

   E. $\dfrac{125}{9}$

9. Consider the inequality:

$$\frac{2}{3} < p < \frac{7}{8}$$

For which of the following values of p will the given inequality be true?

   A. $p = \dfrac{9}{10}$

   B. $p = \dfrac{7}{6}$

   C. $p = \dfrac{1}{2}$

   D. $p = \dfrac{6}{11}$

   E. $p = \dfrac{8}{11}$

10. What is 22% of 140?

    A. 5.6
    B. 30.8
    C. 308
    D. 560
    E. 3080

$$\begin{array}{r} 140 \\ \times .22 \\ \hline 280 \\ 2800 \\ \hline 3080 \end{array}$$

Basic Statistics and Probability

11. What is the mode of the following collection of data?

    14, 12, 22, 14, 8, 23, 25, 21

    A. 8
    B. 14
    C. 17
    D. 17.375
    E. 17.5

12. There are 14 black, 6 blue, and 10 brown socks in a box. A sock is randomly chosen from this box. What is the probability that the chosen sock is brown?

    A. 10

    B. $\dfrac{2}{3}$

    C. $\dfrac{1}{2}$

    D. $\dfrac{1}{3}$

    E. $\dfrac{1}{5}$

$$\frac{10}{30} = \frac{2}{6} = \frac{1}{3}$$

13. Jim has three dogs. The dogs weigh 15, 24, and 12 pounds respectively. What is the average weight of Jim's dogs?

    A.   14

    B.   15

    C.   17

    D.   18

    E.   20

14. Bryan's stanine score on this year's standardized reading test is a 6. This indicates that:

    A.   Bryan scored better than 60% of all test takers.

    B.   Bryan scored in the fourth highest stanine group.

    C.   Bryan scored about 60% on the test.

    D.   Bryan scored 94% on the test.

    E.   Bryan's reading level is 6th grade.

15. When randomly choosing one card from a standard deck of 52 cards what is the probability of choosing a red ace?

    A. $\dfrac{1}{13}$

    B. $\dfrac{2}{13}$

    C. $\dfrac{1}{26}$

    D. $\dfrac{1}{52}$

    E. $\dfrac{1}{104}$

16. What is the median of the following collection of data?

33, 55, 22, 12, 28, 22

A. 25
B. 55
C. 12
D. 28
E. 22

17. Sherri roles a die twice. What the probability that the first roll produces an even number and the second roll produces the number 6?

A. $\dfrac{2}{3}$

B. $\dfrac{1}{6}$

C. $\dfrac{1}{2}$

D. $\dfrac{1}{4}$

E. $\dfrac{1}{12}$

18. In Dr. Jones's history class of 100 students, 65% like to eat hamburgers, 44% like to eat chicken, and 8% do not like to eat either hamburgers or chicken. If one student is randomly chosen from Dr. Jones's history class, what is the probability that this student likes to eat both chicken and hamburgers?

A. 17%
B. 23%
C. 27%
D. 29%
E. 31%

19. Approximately, what is the standard deviation for the following collection of data?

    8, 14, 10, 20

    A. 3
    B. 1.5
    C. 4.5
    D. 2
    E. 5.5

20. What is the range of the following collection of data?

    41, 18, 14, 30, 25, 53

    A. 53
    B. 27
    C. 39
    D. 35
    E. 24

Algebra

21. Solve the following equation for x: $3x - 8 = 4$

    A. $-\dfrac{4}{3}$
    B. -1
    C. $\dfrac{4}{3}$
    D. 4
    E. 6

22. Solve the following inequality: $2x - 5 > 4 - 6x$

A. $x > -\dfrac{9}{4}$

B. $x < -\dfrac{9}{4}$

C. $x > \dfrac{9}{8}$

D. $x < \dfrac{9}{8}$

E. $x > \dfrac{1}{4}$

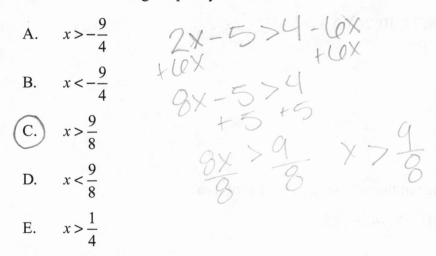

23. There are two integers whose sum is 134 and one integer is 10 less than twice the other. What is the larger integer?

A. 77

B. 80

C. 86

D. 90

E. 92

24. What percent of 235 is 85? Find your answer to the nearest tenth of a percent.

A. 13.5%

B. 13.6%

C. 36.1%

D. 36.2%

E. 30.3%

25. If *m* represents the number of students in Mr. Pall's Geometry class and Ms. Inca has sixteen more than half as many students in her English class, which of the following represents the number of students in Ms. Inca's class?

   A. $\frac{1}{2}m+16$

   B. $\frac{1}{2}m-16$

   C. $2m - 16$

   D. $2m + 16$

   E. $16 - 2m$

26. This table represents a linear function with input value *x* and output value *y*.

x	y
0	3
1	4.6
2	6.2
3	7.8
4	
5	11

   What is the missing value of *y*?

   A. 8.8
   B. 9.0
   C. 9.2
   D. 9.4
   E. 9.6

27. Dwight used 5 eggs to make 48 cupcakes. At this rate, how many eggs will Dwight need to make at least 122 cupcakes?

   A. 12 eggs
   B. 13 eggs
   C. 14 eggs
   D. 15 eggs
   E. 16 eggs

28. Craig spent one-third of his money on tickets to a ball game. Next he paid $25 for hotdogs and soda at the game. After buying the food, Craig spent one-fifth of his remaining money on a souvenir. If Craig had $12 left over after all his spending, how much money did Craig have to begin with?

    A. 54
    B. 60
    C. 62
    D. 78
    E. 86

29. Cheryl drove 20 miles from work to home in 30 minutes. How much faster should Cheryl have driven to arrive home in 25 minutes?

    A. 2 mph
    B. 4 mph
    C. 5 mph
    D. 6 mph
    E. 8 mph

30. This month Jade bought fifteen less than twice the number of cups of coffee than she did last month. If the total number of cups of coffee that Jade bought this month and last month is 84, how many cups of coffee did Jade buy this month?

    A. 28 cups
    B. 33 cups
    C. 41 cups
    D. 51 cups
    E. 65 cups

Measurement and Estimation

31. Which of the following is the most appropriate unit of measure for expressing the capacity of water in a fish tank?

    A.   pounds
    B.   ounces
    C.   centimeters
    D.   liters
    E.   yards

32. Which of the following is the most appropriate unit of measure for expressing the length of a car?

    A.   yards
    B.   grams
    C.   miles
    D.   pounds
    E.   quarts

33. The scale of the diagram on the right is 1 inch equals 5.6 feet. What is the approximate height of the flagpole?

    A.   6.2 feet
    B.   9.3 feet
    C.   10.5 feet
    D.   11.9 feet
    E.   15.6 feet

 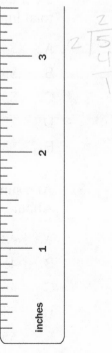

34. Round 8256.74 to the tens place.

    A. 8256.7

    B. 8256.8

    C. 8257

    D. 8250

    E. 8260

35. There are 835,831 people living in Delray Bay and 3,803,037 in West Beach. Which of the following is the best estimate of how many more people live in West Beach than in Delray Bay?

    A. 3,400,000

    B. 3,200,000

    C. 3,000,000

    D. 2,800,000

    E. 2,600,000

36. Ben spends approximately $7.42 on lunch each work day. If his daily lunch expenses are rounded to the nearest dollar, which of the following is the best estimate of his total lunch expenses for the 5 day work week?

    A. $40

    B. $39

    C. $37

    D. $36

    E. $35

37. At a summer baseball camp there were 192 children. 104 of the children were boys. About what percent of the children were girls?

    A. 42%

    B. 45%

    C. 46%

    D. 54%

    E. 55%

38. Which of the following is the best estimate for 3734 × 34?

    A.   120,000
    B.   140,000
    C.   160,000
    D.   180,000
    E.   185,000

39. If 15 of the same type and size buttons weigh 1.5 ounces, approximately how much would 217 of these same buttons weigh?

    A.   1 pound 2 ounces
    B.   1 pound 5 ounces
    C.   1 pound 8 ounces
    D.   1 pound 13 ounces
    E.   2 pounds

40. What is the best estimate for 23% of 8713?

    A.   2000
    B.   2100
    C.   2140
    D.   2200
    E.   2350

Graphs, Charts, and Tables

For problems 41–42, consider the pie graph below which shows the results of a poll of 200 women who have to travel to their place of employment. Each person was asked to name her main mode of transportation.

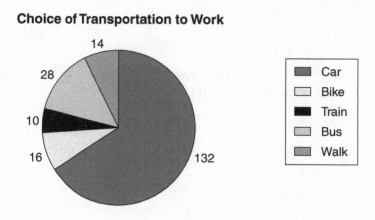

Choice of Transportation to Work

41. What percent of the polled women walk or ride a bike to work?

    A.   15%
    B.   19%
    C.   22%
    D.   30%
    E.   38%

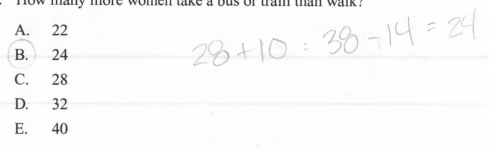

42. How many more women take a bus or train than walk?

    A.   22
    B.   24
    C.   28
    D.   32
    E.   40

Problems 43 and 44 refer to the bar graph below that shows the total number of miles Mr. Koll walked each month for seven months last year.

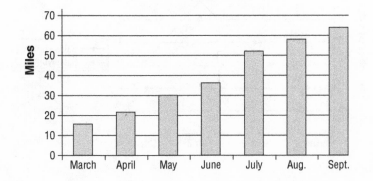

Miles Walked Per Month

43. In what period was Mr. Koll's increase in his total monthly walking distance the greatest?

    A. March to April

    B. April to May

    C. June to July

    D. July to August

    E. August to September

44. In what period did the greatest percentage increase in total miles occur?

    A. March to May

    B. April to June

    C. May to June

    D. June to July

    E. July to September

Consider the line graph below for problems 45 and 46.

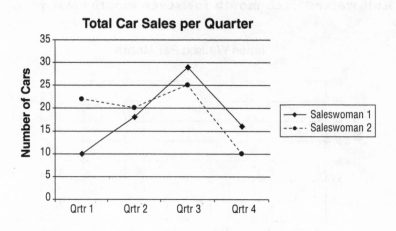

Total Car Sales per Quarter

45. In which quarter did the two saleswomen together sell the least number of cars?

    A. Quarter 1
    B. Quarter 2
    C. Quarter 3
    D. Quarter 4

46. What is the approximate difference in the number of cars saleswoman 1 and saleswoman 2 sold in the second and third quarter?

    A. 2
    B. 4
    C. 6
    D. 8
    E. 10

For problems 47 and 48 refer to the pictograph below.

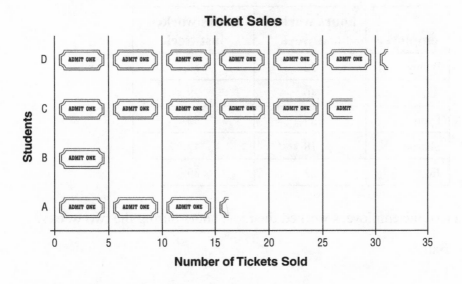

47. How many tickets did students A and D sell in total?

    A.   16

    B.   21

    C.   44

    D.   47

    E.   56

48. How many more tickets did student D sell than student B?

    A.   3

    B.   10

    C.   15

    D.   19

    E.   26

Consider the table below for problems 49 and 50.

employee	hours worked last week	hours worked last week
Bailey	32	40
Kent	40	28
Lynn	35	35
Shayna	18	47
Jin	22	39

49. Which of the employees worked the most hours during the two weeks?

    A. Bailey

    B. Kent

    C. Lynn

    D. Shayna

    E. Jin

50. Which of the employees had the greatest change in work hours from week one to week two?

    A. Bailey

    B. Kent

    C. Lynn

    D. Shayna

    E. Jin

Answers to Practice Problems

1.	D	14.	B	27.	B	40.	A
2.	B	15.	C	28.	B	41.	A
3.	E	16.	A	29.	E	42.	B
4.	B	17.	E	30.	D	43.	C
5.	A	18.	A	31.	D	44.	A
6.	E	19.	C	32.	A	45.	D
7.	A	20.	C	33.	D	46.	A
8.	C	21.	D	34.	E	47.	D
9.	E	22.	C	35.	C	48.	E
10.	B	23.	C	36.	E	49.	A
11.	B	24.	D	37.	C	50.	D
12.	D	25.	A	38.	A		
13.	C	26.	D	39.	B		

Detailed Explanations of Answers

Basic Math Concepts

1. **D**

    The first step is to add 2 and 5 to get 7. Then the expression reads $16 - 6 \times 7 - 3^2$. The second step is to square 3, which yields 9. Now the expression reads $16 - 6 \times 7 - 9$. The third step is to multiply 6 and 7 to get 42. Thus, the expression becomes $16 - 42 - 9$, which simplifies to -35.

2. **B**

    Rewrite 81.62 as 81.620. Now subtract 81.620 from 121.834 to get 40.214. Finally, since 121.834 is larger than 81.62, the answer becomes -40.214.

3. **E**

    The lowest common denominator of 12 and 42 is 84. Change each fraction so that its denominator is 84. So, $\dfrac{7}{12} = \dfrac{49}{84}$ and $\dfrac{11}{42} = \dfrac{22}{84}$. Then $\dfrac{49}{84} + \dfrac{22}{84} = \dfrac{71}{84}$.

4. **B**

    $|10 - 13| = |-3| = 3$ and $|12 + 2| = |14| = 14$. Then $3 - 14 = -11$.

5. **A**

    Multiply 21 by 305 to get 6405. The total number of decimal places for the two numbers 2.1 and 3.05 is three. Therefore, count three decimal places from the right to get the answer of 6.405.

6. **E**

    Cross-multiply to get $35x = (1500)(200) = 30,000$. Then $x = \dfrac{30,000}{35} \approx 857.14$, rounded off to the nearest hundredth.

7. **A**

    In comparing 7.435 and 7.443, they match in the tenths digit, but 7.435 has a lower hundredths digit (3) than does 7.443 (4). This means that $7.435 < 7.443$. Now compare 7.443 with 7.449. They match in both the tenths and hundredths digits but the thousandths digit of 7.443 (3) is less than the thousandths digit of 7.449 (9). Then 7.443 < 7.449. Finally, we have 7.435 < 7.443 < 7.449 .

8. **C**

 When dividing by a fraction, multiply by its reciprocal. Then the original problem becomes $\frac{3}{10} \times \frac{25}{6}$. To reduce these numbers, we can divide 3 and 6 by 3 to get 1 and 2, respectively. Also, divide 10 and 25 by 5 to get 2 and 5, respectively. Now, the multiplication becomes $\frac{1}{2} \times \frac{5}{2} = \frac{5}{4}$.

9. **E.**

 The fastest method to locating a number between the two given fractions is to convert them to their decimal equivalents. So, $\frac{2}{3} \approx 0.667$ and $\frac{7}{8} = 0.875$. The decimal equivalents for answer choices A through E are 0.9, 1.167, 0.5, 0.545, and 0.727, respectively. The only one of these five numbers between 0.667 and 0.875 is 0.727 (answer choice E).

10. **B.**

 The phrase "22% of 140" means the same as "22% times 140." Change 22% to its decimal equivalent 0.22. Then $(0.22)(140) = 30.8$.

Basic Statistics and Probability

11. **B**

 The mode is the number that occurs most frequently. In this data set, the number 14 occurs twice, whereas each of the other numbers occurs only once. Thus, 14 is the mode.

12. **D**

 There are a total of $14 + 6 + 10 = 30$ socks, of which 10 are brown. The required probability is $\frac{10}{30} = \frac{1}{3}$.

13. **C**

 The average weight of the dogs is $\frac{15 + 24 + 12}{3} = \frac{51}{3} = 17$ pounds.

14. **B**

> A stanine score, which is any of the integers 1 through 9, represents a scaled score on a normal distribution. The values of 1, 2, 3 indicate "below average"; the numbers 4, 5, 6 indicate "average"; the numbers 7, 8, 9 indicate "above average." Thus, the stanine score of 6 is in the fourth highest group.

15. **C**

> The two red aces are the ace of diamonds and the ace of hearts. Thus, the required probability is $\frac{2}{52} = \frac{1}{26}$.

16. **A**

> In order to determine the median, we must first arrange the six numbers in ascending order. The numbers will read as 12, 22, 22, 28, 33, 55. The median is the average of the third and fourth numbers, which is $\frac{22+28}{2} = \frac{50}{2} = 25$.

17. **E**

> For the first roll, there are three even numbers (2, 4, 6) out of the six numbers 1 through 6; the associated probability is $\frac{3}{6} = \frac{1}{2}$. For the second roll, there is only one 6, so the associated probability is $\frac{1}{6}$. These two rolls of the die are independent events, so the probability of both occurring is equal to the product of their individual probabilities. Thus, the required probability is $\frac{1}{2} \times \frac{1}{6} = \frac{1}{12}$.

18. **A**

> There are 65 students who like hamburgers, 44 students who like chicken, and 8 who like neither hamburgers nor chicken. The total of 100 students equals the number who like hamburgers, plus the number who like chicken, plus the number who like neither, minus the number who like both hamburgers and chicken. Let x represent the number of students who like both hamburgers and chicken. Then $65 + 44 + 8 - x = 100$. This equation simplifies to $117 - x = 100$, so $x = 17$. Finally, the required probability is $\frac{17}{100} = 17\%$.

19. **C**

First we find the mean of these numbers, which is $\frac{8+14+10+20}{4}=\frac{52}{4}=13$. The standard deviation is the square root of the average of the squared differences between each of the four given numbers and the mean. The formula for the standard deviation of these numbers is $\sqrt{\frac{(8-13)^2+(14-13)^2+(10-13)^2+(20-13)^2}{4}}=$ $\sqrt{\frac{25+1+9+49}{4}}=\sqrt{21}\approx4.58$. Answer choice C is closest to this value.

20. **C**

The range is the difference of the highest and lowest numbers. Thus, the range for this set of numbers is 53 − 14 = 39.

Algebra

21. **D**

Add 8 to both sides of the equation to get 3x = 12. Then $x=\frac{12}{3}=4$.

22. **C**

First add 6x to both sides of the inequality to get 8x − 5 > 4. Second, add 5 to both sides to get 8x > 9. Finally, divide by 8 to get $x>\frac{9}{8}$.

23. **C**

Let x and 2x − 10 represent the two integers. Since their sum is 134, we can write x + (2x − 10) = 134. Then 3x − 10 = 134. Adding 10 to both sides, we get 3x = 144. Then $x=\frac{144}{3}=48$. Thus, the larger number is (2)(48) − 10 = 86.

24. **D**

The required percent is found by $\frac{85}{235}\approx0.362=36.2\%$.

25. **A**

The term $\frac{1}{2}m$ means " half as many as m." Then "sixteen more than $\frac{1}{2}m$" means that we must add 16 to $\frac{1}{2}m$. The correct answer is $\frac{1}{2}m+16$.

26. **D**

 We notice that the differences between consecutive y values is 1.6. For instance, $4.6 - 3 = 1.6$ and $6.2 - 4.6 = 1.6$. This means that to find the missing y value, we simply add 1.6 to 7.8. Thus, the missing y value is 9.4.

27. **B**

 Let x represent the number of eggs needed for 122 cupcakes. We use the following proportion to find x: $\dfrac{5}{48} = \dfrac{x}{122}$. Cross-multiply to get $48x = (5)(122) = 610$. Then $x = \dfrac{610}{48} \approx 12.7$. Since the number of eggs must be a whole number, we round up the answer to 13.

28. **B**

 Let x represent the amount of money in dollars that Craig originally had. After spending $\dfrac{1}{3}$ of x on the tickets, he had $\dfrac{2}{3}x$ dollars left. After buying food at the ball game, he had $\left(\dfrac{2}{3}x - 25\right)$ dollars left. Since he spent one-fifth of $\left(\dfrac{2}{3}x - 25\right)$ dollars on a souvenir, this means that he had four-fifths of $\left(\dfrac{2}{3}x - 25\right)$ dollars left. This is equivalent to $\left(\dfrac{4}{5}\right)\left(\dfrac{2}{3}x - 25\right)$ dollars. We know that the amount left is \$12, so $\left(\dfrac{4}{5}\right)\left(\dfrac{2}{3}x - 25\right) = 12$. Using the Distributive law, this equation becomes $\dfrac{8}{15}x - 20 = 12$. Then $\dfrac{8}{15}x = 32$, which means $x = (32)\left(\dfrac{15}{8}\right) = \$60$.

29. **E**

 Since Cheryl drove 20 miles in 30 minutes, her rate in miles per hour (60 minutes) was $(20)(2) = 40$. Let x represent the rate in miles per hour in order for her to travel 20 miles in 25 minutes. Then we can use the proportion $\dfrac{x}{60} = \dfrac{20}{25}$. Cross-multiply to get $25x = (20)(60) = 1200$. Solving, $x = \dfrac{1200}{25} = 48$. Thus, Cheryl would have had to drive $48 - 40 = 8$ miles per hour faster.

30. **D**

 Let x represent the number of cups of coffee Jade bought last month. Then $2x - 15$ would represent the number of cups of coffee she bought this month. Since the total number of cups of coffee is 84, we can write $(2x - 15) + x = 84$. Then $3x - 15 = 84$, which simplifies to $3x = 99$. Solving, $x = 33$. Thus, The total number of cups of coffee bought this month is $(2)(33) - 15 = 51$.

Measurement and Estimation

31. D

The word "capacity" is associated with volume. The only answer choice that relates to volume is D, which is liters. Pounds and ounces are associated with weight. Centimeters and yards are associated with length.

32. A

The length of a car can be appropriately expressed as either feet or yards. Miles represents too large a unit. Grams and pounds are used as measurements of weight. Quarts are associated with capacity or volume.

33. D

The scale drawing of the flagpole corresponds to $2\frac{1}{8}$ inches. Since 1 inch corresponds to 5.6 feet in actual height, the flagpole's height is $\left(2\frac{1}{8}\right)(5.6) = (2.125)(5.6)$ $= 11.9$ feet.

34. E

In rounding off to the tens place, remove the decimal point and any digits to the right of the decimal point. The number 6 in the ones place is greater than 5, so raise the digit in the tens place to the next highest digit. Thus, the 5 becomes a 6 and the 6 in the ones place becomes zero. The answer becomes 8260.

35. C

Round off each number to the nearest hundred thousand. Then 835,831 becomes 800,000 and 3,803,037 becomes 3,800,000. Therefore, the best estimate of the difference between the original numbers is approximately 3,800,000 – 800,000 = 3,000,000.

36. E

The number $7.42, rounded off to the nearest dollar, becomes $7. Then ($7)(5) = $35.

37. C

The number of girls was 192 – 104 = 88. The percent of girls equals $\frac{88}{192} \approx 0.46 = 46\%$.

38. **A**

   $3734 \times 34 = 126,956$. Of the given answer choices, the number 120,000 is the best estimate.

39. **B**

   The weight of one button is $\dfrac{1.5}{15} = 0.1$ ounce. Then the weight of 217 buttons is $(217)(0.1) = 21.7$ ounces, which is 1 pound and 5.7 ounces. Of the given answer choices, 1 pound 5 ounces is the best estimate.

40. **A**

   23% of 8713 becomes $(0.23)(8713) = 2003.99$. Of the given answer choices, 2000 is the best estimate.

Graphs, Charts, and Tables

41. **A**

   The number of women who walk or ride a bike is $14 + 16 = 30$. Then the corresponding percent is $\dfrac{30}{200} = 15\%$.

42. **B**

   The number of women who take a bus or a train is $28 + 10 = 38$, whereas the number of women who walk is 14. Thus, the difference is $38 - 14 = 24$.

43. **C**

   In June, his walking distance was approximately 36 miles. In July, his walking distance was approximately 52 miles. This difference of 16 miles was the largest increase between any two consecutive months.

44. **A**

   The number of miles that Mr. Koll walked each month was as follows:
   March: 16   April: 22   May: 30   June: 36   July: 52
   August: 58   September: 64.
   The percentage increase from March to May was $\dfrac{30-16}{16} = 0.875 = 87.5\%$. This percentage increase was greater than that for any other answer choice's time period.

45. **D**

   In Quarter 4, the two saleswomen sold a total of 10 + 16 = 26 cars. This was lower than their total for any other quarter.

46. **A**

   For the second and third quarters, saleswoman 1 sold 18 + 29 = 47 cars. During those same quarters, saleswoman 2 sold 20 + 25 = 45 cars. Thus, saleswoman 1 sold two more cars than saleswoman 2.

47. **D**

   Student A sold 16 tickets and student D sold 31 tickets. Their total was 47 tickets.

48. **E**

   Student D sold 31 tickets and student B sold 5 tickets. The difference is 26 tickets.

49. **A**

   Bailey worked a total of 32 + 40 = 72 hours, which exceeded the total hours worked by any of the other employees.

50. **D**

   The change in the work hours for Shayna was 47 − 18 = 29 hours. This change was larger than the change for any of the other employees.

Writing Skills Review

Overview

The writing section of the California Basic Educational Skills Test is designed to measure your ability to compose two different types of essay. In one composition you must analyze a given situation or a particular statement; in the other, you will write about a personal experience. These essays test your ability to compose effective prose and to communicate your ideas to your intended audience. In order to communicate through the written word skillfully, you must first be aware of the mechanics involved in the writing process. Once you are comfortable with the many technical aspects of writing, such as grammar, vocabulary, spelling, and organization, you will be able to concentrate on the expressive aspects. This involves being able to convey your ideas, thoughts, arguments, and experiences to the audience through a strong, clear authorial voice.

You will need to demonstrate understanding of both the technical and telling sides of writing in the essays you compose for the CBEST readers. Let's take a look at each of the skill areas in order to prepare you for your writing tasks. First you will spend some time reviewing general information regarding the mechanics of writing. Later in the chapter you will read about specific strategies related to the writing and scoring of CBEST essays.

A Closer Look at the Two Main Skill Areas

Skill Factor 1: Writing Skills and Knowledge

Grammar (Syntax)

Grammar is the study and the formulation of how words relate to one another in a sentence. Remarkably, by the time children are three years old they have "learned" the grammar of their native languages. However, unless we study our language, we may be unaware that the connections we make are not natural, nor are they given. Rather, we have absorbed a human-made system.

We speak and write our language following rules about how the words and phrases can be strung together. Grammar, or syntax, is the collection of rules that describes how to connect words –what goes next to whatand in which order. To communicate what is inside our heads or hearts to another, we need to know what words and phrases can and can't go together.

Functions: In addition to rules of relationship, grammar also identifies what the different parts do, or their function. Let's examine the following sentence:

> *Jack looked at Jill lovingly.*

Jack is the subject. That is, the function of the word *Jack* is as doer of an action. *Looked* is the action that *Jack* did. We call such action words *verbs*. *Jill*, unlike Jack, is "the done to." Jill's function is as *object*, not *subject*. Then, take the word *lovingly*. This word functions to describe the verb/action (how did *Jack* look?). *Lovingly* is functioning as an adverb, a part of speech we will soon discuss.

The words and groups of words in any sentence are identified, then, by their function, the way the players in a baseball game are identified. Alex Rodriguez Williams may be the batter at one time, and at another, a third-base player. It depends on what function he is performing. So, too, a word can play various functions depending upon how it relates to other words in a sentence. In the example above, *look* is an action verb, what *Jack* did. However, consider the difference: *The look of love is in your eyes*. In this case, *look* is a noun and subject of the sentence.

Eight Parts of Speech: Describing Their Functions

English grammar is built upon the interrelationships of eight functions, or parts of speech: *nouns, pronouns, verbs, adjectives, adverbs, voice, prepositions,* and *conjunctions.*

These are described and studied in this section. We will also identify the grammar and punctuation problems that often occur with parts of speech. Some of these problems are discussed again in other sections.

Nouns

Nouns name people, things, places, and animals—items that have shape and form and that we can touch. Things, however, can also be less tangible and refer to abstractions such as ideas of freedom and independence, concepts such as number and shape, or disciplines such as the sciences and the arts. Some nouns name groups of persons or things.

Number: Nouns change in number—they can be one (singular) or more than one (plural). Most nouns show this change in number by adding an *s*. One boat becomes two boats. However, some nouns show number change differently. One woman doesn't become two womans; rather, she becomes two women.

Collective nouns often cause difficulties because of number. They can be confusing because they refer to something made up of more than one.

jury (of citizens)	flock (of geese)	team (of players)
band (of musicians)	collection (of coins)	committee (of members)

But grammatically they are treated as singulars, as *its* rather than *theys*. For instance,

> *"the team played their last game"* is grammatically incorrect and should be *"the team played its last game."*

Table 5.1 Types of Nouns

Common Nouns		Proper Nouns	
book, bicycle, cat, ice cream, cars, house, skyscraper		Tom Cruise, Macy's, General Lee, Madonna	
Concrete	**Abstract**		**Collective**
stone, hand, skunk, picture	democracy, free speech, freedom, independence		club, army, squadron, team, committee, group

Noun Case: What do nouns do? First, the subject of a sentence is always a noun, as was *Jack*. But nouns can also be objects, as was *Jill* (the receiver of the verb's action). Or, in their Possessive Case form, nouns are expressing belonging to, or a quality of. Case, then, means the function a noun plays in relationship to other words. There are three cases, and we will see the same when we examine pronouns.

Table 5.2 Types of Noun Case

Subjective Case a noun that is the subject	**Objective Case** a noun that is an object	**Possessive Case** a noun that owns or belongs to something
The cat chased the mouse. *Cat* is a noun in subjective case.	*The cat chased the mouse.* *Mouse* is a noun in objective case.	*I lost Jack's ticket.* *Jack's* is a noun in possessive case.

Pronouns

Pronouns stand in for a noun and give us ways to substitute for nouns, and thus we can speak with fewer and shorter words and phrases and with greater variety! Consider what we would face without pronouns:

> *Jimi Hendrix is well-established in the history of music. Hendrix is the King of Rock, and Hendrix's guitar playing is legendary. Jimi Hendrix's death by an overdose made Hendrix an icon of the 1960s. Like Janis Joplin, Jimi Hendrix is the image of overindulgent youth.*

Now, with pronouns:

> *Jimi Hendrix is well-established in the history of music. He is the King of Rock, and his guitar playing is legendary. Jimi Hendrix's death by an overdose made him an icon of the 1960s. Like Janis Joplin, he is the image of overindulgent youth.*

Antecedents: Because a pronoun substitutes for a noun, when one is used, the noun for which it is substituting has to be clear. For example, the pronoun *he* only communicates if we know the noun for which *he* is substituting. An example would be: *He died by assassination*. This sentence, without a reference to which the pronoun is referring, makes little sense. However, the following sentence clears up any confusion:

> *Abraham Lincoln is a symbol as much as he is a former President. He died by assassination.*

Now, the pronoun *he* is comprehensible because we have the antecedent noun for which it is substituting: Abraham Lincoln is *he*.

Pronoun Types and Cases: In the examples above, we have used different forms of pronouns (he, him, I, and me), so let's give these differences a name and description. Glance at the left column in the table below to view the eight various types of pronouns.

Table 5.3 Pronouns: Their Number and Function

Pronoun Types	Singular/Plural	Plural	Function
Personal	I, me	we, us	Refer to specific persons or things, always to a noun: *The ship is lost. It was last in contact two days ago.*
	you, you	you, you	
	he, it, she, him, her	they, them	
Possessive	my, mine	our, ours	Indicate possession: *my dog; your cat; his car; our home; their luggage*
	your, yours	your, yours	
	his, her, hers, its	their, theirs	
Reflexive (intensive)	myself	ourselves	Emphasize a noun or pronoun: *I, myself, was shocked.* *You can get your candy yourselves.*
	yourself	yourselves	
	him, her, itself	themselves	
Relative	that, which, who, whom, whose		Introduce a relative clause that describes/modifies a subject: *the book that caused great controversy*

(continued on next page)

Table 5.3 Pronouns: Their Number and Function
(continued from previous page)

Pronoun Types	Singular/ Plural	Plural	Function
Interrogative	that, which, who, whom, whose		Introduce a question: *Who said that?*
Demonstrative	this, that, these, those		Point to a specific noun, and may also serve as the subject. *That book is controversial.* *That solves the problem.*
Indefinite	every, each, everyone, nothing, something, everything no one, nobody, neither, everything, anybody, one		Refer to nonspecific things; mostly function as nouns. But also can work as adjectives. *Something must be done.* *Each day is better than the last.*
	few, both, many, several		Number agreement *Many are called but few are chosen.*
	all, any, more, most, some (can be singular or plural)		*Some of the mail has arrived.* *Some of the letters have arrived.*
Reciprocal	Same as reflexive above.		*I gave myself a haircut.*

In addition to the eight types, **pronouns,** like nouns, have three cases. Recall, case refers to function in relations with other words. For instance, the personal pronoun *I* is the **Subjective Case** since its meaning (the doer, the subject) also puts it in a specific relation to another word, a verb:

I gave my ticket away.

I, however, has different meanings and relations with verbs, and these differences are expressed by case. Thus, when *I* is not the doer/subject of the verb, it may be the *done to* and object of the verb. When this occurs, the pronoun *I* changes its case to the **Objective Case** and becomes *me.*

John gave me his ticket.

Table 5.4 Personal and Relative Pronouns

Pronoun Type	Subjective (Nominative) Case		Objective Case		Possessive Case	
	Singular	Plural	Singular	Plural	Singular	Plural
Personal Pronoun	I	we	me	us	my, mine	our, ours
	you	you	you	you	your	yours
	he, she,	they	him, her	them	his, hers	their, theirs
	it		it		its	
Relative Pronouns	who	whoever	whom	whomever	whose	whosever

Notice, too, *his,* which expresses belonging, is in the **Possessive Case**. Only two of the eight pronoun types have the case form or aspect. Unlike nouns that show possession by adding an apostrophe *s* or by changing their ending (e.g., *woman* to *women*), pronouns in the possessive case remain unchanged. The **relative pronouns** bring up an important topic. That is, how we speak is sometimes different from how we write. In speech, we are allowed to be ungrammatical. For instance, many, perhaps most of us, would ask: *Who did you go to the movies with*? But this is not correct. *Who* is not the subject, *you* is the subject. It is the object of the preposition *with*; hence, the question needs the objective case: *Whom did you go to the movies with*? Again, like nouns, pronouns are either singular or plural.

Verbs

Verbs are where the action is! *The cannibals ate their victims.* The **action verb** is *eating*. Another kind of verb doesn't so much describe an action, but rather it connects, and is called a **linking verb**. For example: *Jack seems excited to have gotten that telephone call. Seems* is a linking verb; it doesn't describe an action such as eating, travelling, or snoring. It does connect *Jack* to *excited*, and in making this link, it tells us something about *Jack.*

A third kind of verb is called a **helping verb**. These help another verb—which is the major one—to express a nuance, often a time aspect of the main verb. For instance: *I am going to the movies. Going* is the real action, the main verb; *am* is helping by giving *going* the sense of in process. Or, consider this sentence: *I had seen her before she saw me. Seen* is the main verb (act of seeing); *had* is its helping verb. It expresses that the seeing was done earlier, *before she saw me*. In fact, *to be* and *to have* are the most common helping verbs, and they are used primarily to indicate verb tense, as you will see below. However, there are other, less common helping verbs, and there are a few more things to be said about active verbs, so let's examine this table below before moving on to verb tenses.

Table 5.5 Types of Verbs

Action Verbs Two forms	Linking Verbs Connect the subject to a complement, usually an adjective or a subject complement (see below)	Helping or Auxiliary Verbs Two forms
Transitive Verb is one that can have an object: *Lincoln gave his famous speech.*	Major linking verbs: *be, feel, become, seem, smell, remain, look, taste, keep, appear, stay, grow, act*	*Auxiliary*: *to be, to have; to do.* The verbs *to be* and *to have* are so frequently used that you should be familiar with their various forms.

Intransitive Verb does not have an object and is usually followed by an adverb:
  The DOW fell sharply today.
	I feel good. Good is an adjective. *Dr. Jekyll became Mr. Hyde.* Mr. Hyde is the subject complement.
	  The speaker of the house is Nancy Pelosi.
	Nancy Pelosi is the subject complement.
		Modal Auxiliaries express special meanings, such as *obligation, doubt, possibility, can, must, may, should, could,* and *ought to.*
		  He should see a doctor.
		  You can travel now.
		  She must be on time.

Verbs have various forms. Identifying these helps us to understand the various ways a verb is used. Right from the start, we need to know how to distinguish between the two forms. Regular verbs that follow the same general pattern add *–s* on to the verb base to form the third person, singular in present tense. Past tense adds *–ed* to the base verb. Irregular verbs are stubborn individuals who follow their own patterns. Consequentially, since the irregulars are individuals who dance to their own tune, we cannot apply rules to them and have to learn them as individuals. Irregular verbs change either the third person singular or the past tense, or both, and some verbs like to make unique changes in other persons and tenses (see *lie, lay, rise* below).

Look at the tables above where both *to be* and *to have*, irregular verbs, can be studied and contrasted with regular verbs. All regular verbs follow the same pattern in third person singular and in past tense.

Table 5.6 Verb Tense

Present Tense		Past Tense		Past Perfect		Verb Tense
Singular	**Plural**	**Singular**	**Plural**	**Singular**	**Plural**	**Verb Number**
I am you are he/she/ it is	you are we are they are	I was you were he/she/it was	we were you were they were	I have been you have been he, she, it has been	we have been you have been they have been	The underlined verbs identify where agreement problems occur. Note that the verb *to be* uses the verb *to have* as its helping verb to express a past tense.
I have, you have he/she it has	we have you have they have	I had you had he, she, it had	we had you had they had	I have ha d you have had he, she, it has had	we have had you have had they have had	Note that *to have* uses itself as a helping verb to express the past perfect time.

Verb Tenses: Verbs also change according to the time of their action or linking. These time changes are called **tenses**. Consider how tense adds to our ability to communicate with one another. Imagine, for instance, arriving at someone's house who, being a generous host, offers you lunch. We take for granted that it's a simple matter to decline without offense by explaining: *No, thank you, I ate lunch an hour ago*. If we had no past tense, we would be forced to act out and hope to be understood, perhaps by "I eat . . ." and then indicating past by gesturing behind our shoulder with our hand.

In writing, we dramatically alter the meaning of what we say by our use of tense:

I was studying when the lights went out and threw the dorm into darkness for the rest of the evening.

I had already studied when the lights went out and threw the dorm into darkness for the rest of the evening.

Present Tense: actions occurring now, actions occurring regularly, or general truths:

I see you sitting there, every day.

I speak to the homeless man.

Love is stronger than hate.

Past Tense: actions that happened before now and are over and done with:

I ate dinner an hour ago.

Future Tense: actions that will happen in the future:

I will eat dinner within the hour.

Subject Verb Agreement: Speaking directs native speakers to follow this rule quite "naturally"; however, there are some grammatical structures that give many writers problems. First, let's look at the typical sentence and how the law of agreement works:

Yesterday the children ate their lunches at their desks.

The verb must agree with the subject's person and number. The subject is *children*; its number is plural, and its person is the third (see chart above). Now it's true that the writer also had to know the correct past form of the verb *eat,* which is *ate* and not *eated*, and also the correct tense.

Most agreement problems have to do with number, which means determining if the subject is singular or plural. Indeed, verb agreement with subject is very similar to pronoun agreement with antecedents, and the chart below will help this.

Table 5.7 Verb Agreement

Problem or Issue	Verb must agree with number of subject	Pronoun must agree with number of antecedent
Compound subject: two subjects connected by *and* (N5P)	Susan B. Anthony and Elizabeth Cady Stanton <u>were</u> extraordinary women; they <u>were</u> geniuses.	Susan B. Anthony and Elizabeth Cady Stanton were extraordinary women; <u>they</u> were geniuses.
Compound Subject: one entity despite appearing to be two subjects (N5S)	Ben & Jerry's <u>makes</u> the best ice cream.	Do you like Ben & Jerry's? <u>It's</u> my favorite!
Subject separated from verb can confuse	The winner amongst all the contestants goes to the Caribbean. Or, The winners of the race go to the Caribbean.	The winner amongst all the contestants goes to the Caribbean. He or she will be happy. The winners of the race go to the Caribbean. They will be happy.
Indefinite Pronoun	<u>Each</u> of the contestants <u>gets</u> a new car. Generally Singular	Each of the contestants gets a new car. <u>He or she</u> will select a model.
Correlative Conjunctions: Neither . . . nor Either . . . or	Verb agrees with number of the subject closest to it (or the 2nd subject) Neither the stockholders nor the <u>CEO seems</u> concerned about the sudden dip in profits.	Pronoun agrees with the antecedent closest to it. Neither the stockholders nor the <u>CEO seems</u> concerned about the sudden dip in the profits of <u>his</u> company.
Collective Nouns (N5S) Generally Singular	The committee <u>announces</u> the much awaited decision today. Economics is a tough subject as is statistics. Measles/mumps <u>keeps</u> you in bed.	The committee announces <u>its</u> much awaited decision today. Economics gets <u>its</u> bad reputation from its many false predictions.
Postponed subject: subject follows the verb Verb agrees with subject (not complement)	At the end of the corridor is a <u>small door.</u> The <u>real power</u> is the men behind the scenes.	At the end of the corridor is a small door, <u>it's</u> black and tan. The real <u>power</u> is the men behind the scenes, hidden though it is, it's what really makes things happen
Who, which, that can confuse	Lucinda is the <u>one</u> who rescued the bird. The boys want to be on the <u>team</u> that <u>scores</u> highest.	
Gerund phrase: a gerund with object Gerund phrases take singular form	<u>Following speeding cars</u> is a dangerous thing to do.	Following speeding cars is dangerous. Doing <u>it</u> is a foolish thing to do.

Voice: Active and Passive

English strongly prefers that the subject come first, followed by the verb, then by the object or recipient of the actions, or, if a linking verb, by a subject complement or an adjective.

> *The batter hit →→ the ball hard.*

> *The Academy of Film Arts gave →→ Julia Roberts an award.*

This pattern with the subject going toward (with the verb) the object (formula, S+V+O) is the *Active Voice*.

However, writers sometimes (correctly, often incorrectly) use the *Passive Voice*. This reverses the formula, O+V+S, making a sentence with the object of the verb first, then the verb, and finally, the subject.

> *The ball was hit hard by the ← batter.*

The action is turned around; the subject, *batter*, fades, and the focus is on the object, the *ball*. In short, the passive voice puts the object in the limelight, and it weakens both the act (the verb action) and the subject (the doer). By contrast, then, the active voice highlights the subject and emphasizes that she/he is the doer. So, when is it correct to use the passive voice? Answer: when the object is more important than the subject. Consider:

> *Julia Roberts was awarded an Oscar for her performance in* Erin Brockovich.

Or in the active voice:

> *The committee awarded Julia Roberts an Oscar.*

The first sentence is preferred because the fact that Roberts won the Oscar is more important than the committee that did the awarding. Now let's examine the structure of that passive voice: *Julia Roberts* is the object, *was rewarded*, the verb, and the subject has so faded from importance that it isn't even in the sentence! *Was rewarded* also shows us the formula for a passive voice verb = to be + past participle.

Adjectives and Adverbs

Adjectives are words that describe nouns or pronouns. We use adjectives a lot in speech and writing; many common ones pepper our conversations. For example: *a good day*; *a soft sound*; *a yellow car*.

Adverbs have more possible roles than adjectives. Adverbs can describe verbs (*he spoke slowly*); they can describe adjectives (*His face had a sickly yellow look. She is very sad.*); they can describe adverbs like *themselves*; and they can describe infinitives (*he was urged to go quickly.*)

> *Adverbs often answer the question how? How did he go? Quickly.*
>
> *Adverbs often end in –ly: quickly, smoothly, sleepily, coldly*

Those adverbs that don't end in *–ly* are often those that refer to time and frequency:

> *today, yesterday, often tomorrow, soon, never, always, never, sometimes*

Prepositions

"Never end a sentence with a preposition!" But what's a preposition? We use them very frequently (look at the list below), but defining them clearly is difficult. Prepositions, for instance, are words that connect a noun to other parts of its sentence. Or, prepositions are words that express space (on the table), time (at the appointed hour), and direction (towards the North Pole). There are two kinds of prepositions: simple, one-word prepositions and group prepositions.

It's easier to get a handle on the simple, one-word prepositions by identifying them in the prepositional phrase (where they most often are to be found, except when they end a sentence by themselves). You will find the preposition before a noun or a pronoun, and it will almost always be working as an adjective or an adverb, modifying a part of the sentence of which it is itself a part. The most common:

> *behind, except, off, toward*
>
> *above, below, for, on, under*
>
> *across, beneath, from, onto, underneath*
>
> *after, beside, in, out, until*

against, between, inside, outside, up

along, beyond, into, over, upon

among, by, like, through, with

around, despite, near, throughout, within

at, during, of, to, without

Group prepositions are made up of more than one word:

in addition to	*in place of*
next to	*in front of*
as well as	*along with*
according to	*due to*
in conjunction with	*because of*

Conjunctions

Conjunctions come in four basic varieties. They work to join parts of a sentence, to join together words, or phrases, or clauses, or even to join sentences. *And* is probably the most used conjunction—observe how frequently we use it to join words: *apples and oranges*; *work and play*; *sing and dance*; *toys and hobbies*; *Bill and Sally*.

And is also one of a group of **coordinating conjunctions**: *for, and, nor, but, or, yet, so*. These words help create compound sentences, and when they serve this role, a comma comes before their use.

Correlative conjunctives: Remember these by their "relatives." These are twins such as *neither/nor, either/or, not/only, but/also, both/and*.

Subordinating conjunctions are

after	*if so*	*that*
although	*in case*	*than*
as if	*in that*	*though*
as though	*insofar as*	*unless*
because	*no matter how*	*until*
before	*now that*	*when, whenever*
even if	*once*	*where, wherever*
even though	*provided that*	*whether*
how	*since*	*while*

Conjunctive adverbs make connections between clauses with semicolons and commas.

however, then	*She went to the film; however, I didn't go.*
therefore, hence	*It rained hard and fast; therefore, we stayed home.*
also, consequently	*The book focused on a popular topic; also, its central character was controversial.*
thus, nevertheless	*The importer pays the taxes, then sells the articles at an inflated price; thus it is the consumer who ultimately pays.*

Interjections: These are odd-balls in that they almost contradict our definition of a part of speech as defined by its function to other words. This is because they do not really function in relationship, but rather stand outside the grammatical connections. An interjection is a strong expression, a powerful emotion, a cry from the soul that sometimes is barely a word:

Oh, she cried

Yikes!

Help!

Articles: These are so common that we want to give them a special focus even though they are not one of the eight parts of speech. The articles, *a, an, the,* always come before a noun. *A* or *an* functions to identify a noun referring to something in general: *a book*; *a door*; *a cat. The* functions to identify or point to a specific noun: *the book, the cat, the door. A* is used when the noun it identifies starts with a consonant: *a book, a door, a cat. An* is used when the noun starts with a vowel: *an elf, an apple, an ice cream cone, an ox, an ulcer.*

The Sentence

The previous section reacquainted you with grammar or syntax: the laws of relationships and the function of the components of English, the eight parts of speech. This section focuses on the sentence—what it is (definition), what it does (function), what it's made of (structure and criteria), its four forms (meanings), and its four types (variations in structure)—and the punctuation that sentences use to fulfill their function: to express a thought! In this section we will also identify the major grammatical and punctuation problems related to sentence structure.

What defines a sentence? Basically it is a complete thought—that is, it's a grammatical unit that is composed of one or more clauses. Clauses are units of words that form a complete thought. The function of a sentence is to express an idea, a fact, or a desire.

Example   *I want ice cream.*

We left the restaurant at midnight.

Table 5.8 Sentence Function

Type	Example	Grammar Rules
Declaratory Sentence: States, expresses a point <u>Thesis statement</u> is a declaratory sentence.	*Logan, the adorable pit bull, licked his owner's face.*	All sentences begin with a capital; declaratory sentences end with a period.
Interrogatory Sentence Asks a question	*Did Logan lick her face?*	Begins with a capital; interrogatory sentences end with question marks.
Imperative Sentence Gives an order or a direction to another	*Lick her face and jump all over her.*	Begins with a capital; ends usually with a period, but sometimes with an exclamation point. The subject is often hidden, or "understood." The subject is whoever is being given the direction (Logan, you) *lick her face, jump all over her—right now!*
Exclamatory Sentence Expresses emotion	*What a handsome dog!*	Begins with a capital; often exclamatory sentences end with exclamation points. Writers are urged to use such sentences and punctuation only rarely. Overuse takes away their expressive power.

As we speak, the listener knows when our thought is complete by our inflection, by the tone of our voice, or by our body language. In writing, two signals "tell" the reader: "Mission accomplished!" The capital marks the start, and the ending punctuation (period, question mark, exclamation point) in effect, says, "I'm done." When we incorrectly give the signal telling the reader that we are finished, but it isn't a complete thought, we cause confusion. This signal malfunction creates a ***sentence fragment***. To qualify as a sentence and earn its punctuation marks, a group of words must meet three criteria:

1. It must have a subject.

2. It must have a verb (and often has a verb predicate, verb other words).

3. It must be a complete thought. (This is the criteria that a fragment does not meet!)

Table 5.9 Sentence Fragments

Fragment	Analysis	Corrective Sentence	Structure
Seeing you in the supermarket.	No subject (actually no verb either as you will see in the section on phrases). Seeing is a gerund.	I saw you in the supermarket.	Subject (I) verb (saw) predicate (<u>you in the supermarket</u>)
In the produce section at the back of the store.	No subject. No verb. Two prepositional phrases	I saw you in the produce section at the back of the store.	Subject (I) verb (saw) predicate (you in the produce section at the back of the store)
Since it rained last night.	Subject (it) Verb predicate (rained last night). Complete thought? No!	Since it rained last night, we cancelled our star gazing appointment.	The additional words complete the thought and meet the criteria. Subject (we) verb (cancelled) predicate (our star gazing appointment)

Types of Sentences

Simple Sentence: doesn't mean short, nor does it mean is non-complex. Rather, it refers to its structure—to what its parts are. A simple sentence can be very long, but it will have only one **independent clause**.

Independent Clause: is a synonym for sentence. Another way of saying this: A sentence is an independent clause, or it is made up of more than one independent clause. Whenever you come across the phrase *independent clause*, think—it meets the three criteria for a sentence. We'll examine clauses in the paragraphs below. Here is a short, simple sentence.

Proust and Gide are the best known French writers of the twentieth century.

Here's another, a little longer.

Both Proust and Gide wrote for a twentieth-century audience and yet retained their relevance for readers of the twenty-first century.

And longer still:

> *In the end, against our wishes, in opposition to all advice, <u>our son</u>, John,*
> *<u>and the neighbor's daughter, Janice, dropped out of school</u>, left all their*
> *friends and family, and <u>embarked</u> on a trip across country despite the poor*
> *weather and the high cost of fuel.*

Note: the underlined sections identify the skeleton of the one independent clause: compound subject and compound verb (three of them). The rest of the sentence is primarily prepositional phrases.

Compound Sentence: is one that has more than one independent clause, and no dependent clauses.

Examples   <u>The children baked three pies</u>, and <u>they took all of them to the patients</u>.

<u>Barack Obama began the presidential campaign of 2008 behind Hillary Clinton</u>, but <u>he still managed to win</u>.

Look closely at each of the <u>underlined sections</u>. Think back on the sentence pattern.

Identify how each has a subject-verb predicate and each is a complete thought. Therefore, each of them <u>could be</u> a separate sentence. As the examples above demonstrate, ***compound sentences*** connect independent clauses into one sentence rather than allowing them to stand alone. They do this in **two** ways **only**:

1. With a ***coordinating conjunction*** (*for, and, nor, but, or, yet, so*) and, as the two sentences above illustrate, a ***comma before*** the coordinating conjunction.

2. ***Compound sentences*** are also linked with semicolons, as in the examples below.

    The victor is the quickest; Jane Levin's the sure winner! Or:

    Wealth is often coarse; poverty is frequently refined.

When do you choose a connection, or the semicolon? The semicolon is often used to pull the two independent clauses closer together for dramatic effect. Consider the dramatic difference between these two sentences:

John studied hard, but he still failed.

John studied hard; he still failed.

Or imagine how much less dramatic without a connection word:

He came; he saw; he conquered.

Linking **two independent clauses** is generally the **only** correct use of a semicolon in the middle of a sentence. When you see a semicolon, check on each side for a sentence that could stand alone. Other, less frequent semicolon use is to separate items in series, when the items have internal punctuation.

The next sentence type is the ***complex sentence***. It contains one independent clause plus one or more dependent clauses (IC +DC, or IC+DC+DC). Let's look at a complex sentence with more than one dependent clause:

<u>When the ship comes in</u>, he will get a handsome paycheck <u>even though he never lifted a hand in actually delivering the goods to port.</u>

This combination of one or more dependent clauses in a sentence with an independent clause forms a ***complex sentence***. Let's examine how dependent clauses in a complex sentence function:

Linguists have discovered at least three ancient languages.

This is a **simple sentence: one independent clause**. However, we change it to a ***complex sentence*** by adding a dependent clause:

Linguists have discovered at least three ancient languages that may be the origin of all others.

Complex–compound sentences are made of at least one dependent clause (making it complex) and two or more independent clauses (making it compound):

Because Gene has always been a big eater, *<u>no one was surprised at his obesity</u>, and <u>his congestive heart diagnosis also came as no surprise</u>.*

The underlining identifies the two independent clauses. The phrase in bold is the dependent clause. It's not the length of the sentence but its structure that makes it a **compound-complex sentence**—at least two independent clauses plus at least one dependent clause (2 IC+DC).

Placement of adverbs: *only, just, merely*

Proper placement of these adverbs can determine and alter the **meaning** of a sentence.

For instance, consider the different meanings of:

I eat <u>only</u> one dessert per day.

I <u>only</u> eat one dessert per day.

Again:

<u>Only</u> I can eat the ritual meal.

I can <u>only</u> eat the ritual meal

I can eat <u>only</u> the ritual meal.

Finally:

I can see <u>merely</u> the shadows

I can <u>merely</u> see the shadows.

Punctuation, Mechanics, and Usage

Basic Rules and Conventions, Major Errors

This section focuses on the most important and most frequently occurring punctuation and mechanics errors—most important because they have negative effects on the clarity of meaning. Some are repeats and, because they are often difficult to identify, the repetition should help you learn to "see" them more readily.

Sentence Fragments: A **sentence fragment** is a group of words wrongly punctuated as if it were a sentence. The group starts with a capital and it ends with a period, question mark, or exclamation point. But it is not a sentence because it lacks one or more of the three ingredients: subject + verb + expression of a complete thought.

Fragments confuse readers who expect a complete thought but who get a partial product, causing them to try to "figure it out." Thus, fragments undermine the purpose of writing clear communication, and they frustrate readers who do not want the burden of puzzle-solving.

The most common configuration you will find is illustrated as follows (from a student paper):

> *After everyone takes their* share, I refuse to take treasure; instead, I offer*
> *it to my good friend, Gandalf. <u>Which shows how good natured I am.</u>*

The underlined fragment (dependent clause) comes after a correct sentence. The fragment expresses a point that is related to the sentence, but it is a dependent clause. Note: Dependent clauses are often the most difficult for students to identify because they meet two criteria of a sentence; they have a subject and a verb. They are not, however, complete thoughts.

*Note this student's pronoun error. *Everyone* is singular and should be paired with either *his* or *her*.

Run-on Sentences and Comma Splices

Like the fragment, these errors violate the rules of sentence structure. In this case, it's about connections and misconnections. A railroad analogy helps explain this common error. Imagine that sentences are railroad cars. Now, like them, sentences or separate cars can be linked together—or coupled; they don't have to be separate. Often to get an idea communicated most effectively, as to transport materials across the country, linking is the most effective method. But how?

To begin with, there must be a link. Just as you can't expect to connect by placing two cars next to one another without a coupling mechanism, so, too, the writer cannot simply place two sentences (independent clauses) together without a link, as in:

The evening showers were soft and <u>warm they</u> made the night enchanting.

Dublin, king of his breed, strutted as he patrolled his <u>yard his</u> posture blared his dominance through every street and alleyway.

The underlining identifies where two independent clauses have been fused, or run on, without a coupler.

Comma splice is the second type of fused sentence. Again, it's a problem of connection. You can't link two railroad cars with rubber bands; they are not strong enough. You can't link two independent clauses with a comma—it's not strong enough to do the job of communicating clearly.

The evening showers were soft and warm, they made the night enchanting.

Dublin, king of his breed, <u>strutted as</u> he patrolled <u>his yard</u>, his posture blared his dominance through every street and alleyway.

ONLY the connection words or the semicolon can do the communication job:

The evening showers were soft and warm, and they made the night enchanting.

Dublin, king of his breed, strutted as he patrolled <u>his yard</u>; his posture blared his dominance through every street and alleyway.

Semicolons are confusing to many students. Yet their correct usage is straightforward and very limited. There are three grammatical situations which require them.

Commas

I have spent most of the day putting in a comma and the rest of the day taking it out.

Oscar Wilde

Wilde's wry observation about comma choice highlights two important points: First, and this guides you in editing your and others' writing, that placing commas where they don't belong is a bigger problem with students' writing than failing to use them where they do belong; two, that while we do have rules to guide these decisions, it is often not clear-cut when a comma is necessary.

The uses and misuses of commas are probably the single most troubling punctuation question. Perhaps this is because there are so many situations that do require them and also so many situations in which they are incorrectly used. The correct use of commas is crucial to communicating meaning and also to the coherence of writing. Readers are ornery; they don't like to be confused; they do like the sensation of smooth flowing writing—that's what coherent writing produces.

One guiding principle for all comma use is your best tool. That principle simply is that commas help the reader keep the various parts of a sentence in their proper places. Consider, for instance:

After leaving his friend John made his way to his mother's apartment.

When you read the above sentence, you probably experienced a moment of confusion because your brain connected *friend* to *John*, which is not the meaning of the sentence.

Rather:

After leaving his friend, John made his way to his mother's apartment.

Here, the comma helps the reader; it "tells" the reader, "pause to meet John, who is the person who left his unnamed friend." As for writing that is incoherent, consider this:

Since Alice hadn't cooked the family decided to dine out.

To which the reader does a double-take: Did Alice cook the family? After a confusing moment, the reader may succeed in getting it right—but not without some annoyance.

The correctly placed comma avoids the confusion:

Since Alice hadn't cooked, the family decided to dine out.

Now let's look at a different comma problem. Consider: *John took a walk, and talked with Mary about their engagement.* This illustrates a frequently made error: placing a comma to separate a *compound verb*. The comma both breaks the flow of the verb action, putting a brake on the forward movement of walk and talk, and it confuses the meaning, suggesting that walking and talking are being compared or that they happened at a different time.

Pronouns: Case, Agreement, and Reference

These frequent problems involve the all-important connection between a pronoun and the word to which it refers—its antecedent. As we have previously discussed, confusion in this relationship will obstruct meaning. Pronoun agreement is a very frequent error!

Agreement: Does the pronoun match (agree) the number (singular/plural), gender (male/female), and person (first, second, third) of its antecedent?

> **Example**   *Athletes frequently suffer injuries to <u>their</u> bodies.*

Athletes, the antecedent, is **plural** in number, **neutral** in gender, and in the **third** person. *Their* is plural in number, neutral in gender, and in the third person.

> **Example**   *A reader must focus his/her attention sharply in order to see the miniscule marks in the margins.*

A reader, the antecedent, is singular in number, either male or female, and in the third person. So, too, are *his* and *her*.

To be inclusive, whenever an antecedent can be either male or female, you need to use both *his* and *her* (so as not to exclude either the male or the female). However, too many of these constructions in a piece of writing make for awkwardness. To avoid these gender constructions often requires creating different sentence formats. For instance, changing the antecedent to plural removes the awkwardness because the plural doesn't have different gender form.

> *Readers must focus their attention sharply in order to see the miniscule marks in the margins.*

Agreement Challenges: Once the basic "mirror relationship" is understood, it seems easy to follow the agreement rule. However, there are several words and grammar constructions which cause difficulties.

Collective nouns are nouns that refer to more than one person, such as *team*, *jury*, *committee*, *army*. Note these words are singular in form; they therefore require a singular pronoun, as in this example:

The committee left the boardroom and announced <u>its</u> decision to the court.

Sometimes, however, a writer does mean to describe the <u>separate</u> members of a collective, and in this case, since the reference is to more than one, the pronoun should be plural.

The committee left the boardroom and went to their offices to cast <u>their</u> votes for the proposal.

Personal pronouns are called indefinites because they don't specify gender or number and take the **singular**.

<u>*Everyone*</u> *is responsible for <u>his/her</u> belongings and must take precautions to secure them.*

<u>*Anybody*</u> *can apply by submitting <u>his/her</u> qualifications and years of experience.*

<u>*Each*</u> *student has <u>his/her</u> own computer.*

<u>*Every*</u> *book must be returned with <u>its</u> cover.*

Commonly Used Indefinite Pronouns

everything	anyone	something	nothing	each
everyone	anything	someone	nobody	every
everybody	anybody	somebody	no one	

Faulty or Unclear Pronoun Reference

Consider the pronouns in the sentence:

Jane hit the ball so hard that she sent it flying twenty feet over the fence.

We understand this because we clearly understand that the antecedent of *she* is *Jane* and that the antecedent of *it* is *ball*. This clear relationship is sometimes ambiguous or incorrect.

Claudia threw the vase at the window and broke it.

It is ambiguous; is it the window or the vase that was broken?

The Andersons told the next door neighbors that their children were chasing the chickens.

Pronoun Case

Subjective case is for pronouns functioning as subjects.

Examples   *She purchased every bottle the store had. (subjective, singular)*

We purchased every bottle the store had. (subjective, plural)

Objective case is for pronouns functioning as objects.

Examples   *They called him from the pay phone. (objective, singular)*

They called us from the pay phone. (objective, plural)

Possessive case is for pronouns functioning to indicate "belonging to."

Examples   *Gloria Gaynor sang her disco hits. (possessive, singular)*

The Bee Gees sang their hits from Saturday Night Fever. *(possessive, plural)*

Table 5.10 Pronoun Case

Pronoun Type	Subjective Case (Nominative)		Objective Case		Possessive Case	
Personal Pronouns	I you he, she, it	we you they	me you him, her, I	us you them	my, mine your his, hers, theirs its	our, ours yours, their
Relative Pronouns	Who	whoever	whom	whomever	whose	whosever

When you struggle to decide between using *I* and *me*, or *who* and *whom*, you are grappling with pronoun case. The right answer is in the rules above. However, two situations can make pronoun case difficult. One is because we often violate these rules in speech, so much so that the correct use sounds unnatural or pedantic, as in "Whom did he call?" Yet, this is correct because *whom* is the object of the verb call. Second, there are several grammatical formats that cause confusion and make it tricky to determine whether the case we need is the subjective or the objective. Knowing these confusing formats helps you identify the most common problems students have with pronoun case.

Plurals and Possessives

Forming Plurals

Most nouns can be singular or plural. The usual plural form adds *–s* to the end of the word.

    desk   *desks*   *book*   *books*

However, there are exceptions to this guideline. After a *–y* preceded by a consonant, the *–y* changes to *–i* and *–es* is added.

    sky   *skies*   *secretary*   *secretaries*

If the final *–y* is preceded by a vowel, no change is made, and the plural is formed by adding *–s*.

    decoy   *decoys*   *attorney*   *attorneys*

If the last sound in the word is a sibilant—a word ending in –s, –z, –ch, –sh, or –x, or –z –add –es.

> *churches, sashes, masses, foxes, quizzes*

(However, with words ending in –z, it must be doubled before adding the –es.)

> *class*   *classes*   *branch*   *branches*

However, if the –ch is pronounced –k, only –s is added.

> *stomach*   *stomachs*

Often the final –fe or –f in one-syllable words becomes –ves.

> *half*   *halves*
>
> *wife*   *wives*

There are exceptions, of course.

> *chief*   *chiefs*
>
> *roof*   *roofs*

Many nouns have plural forms that are irregular or the same.

> *child*   *children*   *mouse*   *mice*
>
> *woman*   *women*   *series*   *series*

For nouns ending in "o," it depends on the word whether you add –s or –es to form the plural. These spellings must be memorized individually.

> *potato, potatoes*   *hero, heroes*

Possessive nouns (those that own something, or to which something belongs) use apostrophe plus an s (s') as in,

Eleanor Roosevelt's husband was perhaps the most famous president of the twentieth century; or,

The classroom's ceiling is too high to be energy efficient; or,

Charles Manson's behavior has become synonymous with modern psycho-social disorder.

If the noun showing possession is a plural that ends, as most plurals do, with an –s (boys, girls, and engineers), then only an apostrophe is used:

The engineers' computers are left on even during the evening when they are not around.

The girls' attitudes made them a delight to work with.

However, there are nouns that do not use an –s to form their plural. These non –s ending plurals—such as children, men, women—use an apostrophe and an –s to show possession:

The women's hats are all different colors.

The children's playground is across the street.

Joint Possession: In situations where two nouns "possess" something together, add the –s apostrophe (s') to the last noun owner:

John and Mary's Mercedes Benz is frequently borrowed by their son for dates.

Be careful, however, if the subject nouns "own" separate and different things; then, each requires an 's:

Although they are married, John's and Mary's bank accounts are in different banks.

Possessive Pronouns do not use any form of apostrophe s. They are possessive in themselves and require no special sign:

The tree cast its shadow across the field. (Not *it's,* which means *it is.* And not *its':* It's not a word!)

Contractions use an apostrophe to show that letters have been omitted, frequently in auxiliary verb constructions such as do + not = don't, have + not = haven't, and the one often misused as a possessive, it + is = it's.

Quotations and Quotation Marks

Quotation marks are necessary with **direct quotes**, which are words that someone else exactly said or words exactly as they are written or spoken from a source such as a book or film.

> *Mary gave me very precise directions. "Do not," she urged, "enter the kitchen, and do not open the door to the basement."*

> *According to the philosopher, Hannah Arendt, "Evil is banality."*

Indirect quotes are reports of what someone said, summarizing or paraphrasing it. They do not take quotation marks.

> *Sarah said that yesterday had been the worst of her life.*

> *The historian Barbara Tuchman claimed that World War I was an unnecessary mistake.*

Note: The word *that* is generally a sign that you are dealing with an indirect quotation. To indicate someone's exact words, not the writer's, requires quotation marks, as when a character in a short story makes a statement:

> *John turned to Mary and confessed, "I quit my job."*

In essays, however, most quotations are to acknowledge another writer's words on the subject of the essay; and in an argumentative/persuasive essay, we often use quotations as evidence to support our arguments.

Quotation Mechanics and Punctuation

Where and when to capitalize and to place quotation marks and punctuation marks (such as periods, question marks, and exclamation points) is largely dependent upon the position of the quotation.

If it is at the beginning, the quotation starts with a capital and ends with a comma inside the quotation marks. The same is true for question marks and exclamation points.

> *"I have loved you since we were children," Mary admitted to John.*

> *"Did you really love me all along?" John asked. "Yes!" Mary exclaimed.*

If it is at the end of the sentence, place a comma after the source of the quotation, a capital letter for the first word, and the terminal punctuation (if a period, question mark, or exclamation point) inside the quotation marks.

> *Wendell Phillips says, "The Tree of Liberty requires constant pruning to maintain vital and true."*

The **broken quotation** is a bit more complicated. Let's examine the varieties:

> *"The unexamined life," says Socrates, "is not worth living."*

The beginning follows the same format as noted above. The second part, which is a continuation of the first, is not capitalized, needs a comma after the source, and follows the same rules for placing the period inside the quotation marks. If, however, the quotation consists of two sentences with its source in the middle, note the changes:

> *"The unexamined life is not worth living," says Socrates. "It is the life of the beast, not of the man."*

Italics

Word processing has made this font style easier and has thus replaced underlining in many instances. However, there are still some style manuals that encourage underlining of titles.

Major use	Example
books	*Gone with the Wind*
magazines	*Newsweek*
plays	*The Glass Menagerie*
newspapers	*The Boston Globe*
films	*Terminator*
TV shows	*American Idol*
music	*Sentimental Journey*
art works	*Mona Lisa*
web sites	*Google*

Capitalization

A very important element of writing is knowing when to capitalize a word and when to leave it alone. When a word is capitalized, it calls attention to itself. This attention should be for a good reason. There are standard uses for capital letters. In general, capitalize (1) all proper nouns, (2) the first word of a sentence, and (3) the first word of a direct quotation. The following lists outline specific guidelines for capitalization.

What Should Be Capitalized

Capitalize the names of ships, aircraft, spacecraft, and trains:

Examples   *Apollo 13*

Boeing 767

Capitalize the names of divine beings:

Examples   God

Allah

Capitalize the geological periods:

Examples   Cenozoic era

Neolithic age

Capitalize the names of astronomical bodies:

Examples   Big Dipper

Ursa Major

Capitalize personifications:

Examples   Reliable Nature brought her promised Spring.

Bring on Melancholy in his sad might.

Capitalize historical periods:

Examples   the Great Depression

Roaring Twenties

Capitalize the names of organizations, associations, and institutions:

Examples   Harvard University

Pittsburgh Steelers

U.S. House of Representatives

Capitalize the first word of a sentence:

Examples   *Our car would not start.*

When will you leave? I need to know right away.

Let me in! Please!

When a sentence appears within a sentence, start it with a capital letter:

Examples   *We had only one concern, "When would we eat?"*

My sister said, "I'll find the Monopoly game."

He answered, "We can only stay a few minutes."

The most important words of titles are capitalized. Those words not capitalized are conjunctions (*and, or, but*) and short prepositions (*of, on, by, for*). The first and last word of a title must always be capitalized:

Examples   *Of Mice and Men*

Sonata in G Minor

Capitalize newspaper and magazine names:

Examples   *The New York Times*

National Geographic

Capitalize radio and TV network abbreviations or station call letters:

Examples   ABC

CNN

Capitalize regions:

Examples	the Northeast, the South, the West
	Eastern Europe
	but: the south of France, the east side of town

Capitalize political organizations, and in some cases, their philosophies and members:

Example	Democratic Party, the Communist Party

But do not capitalize systems of government or individual adherents to a philosophy:

Example	democracy, communism

Do not capitalize compass directions or seasons:

Examples	north, south, east, west
	spring, summer, winter, autumn

Numbers, the Basics

When to spell out a number and when to use the numeral (ten, or 10)—that's the question! Unfortunately, there's no simple answer because the experts differ: Some say spell out numbers between one and ten, and use numerals for all above ten: *Only 59 students out of 100 passed the test.* Some experts, however, recommend spelling out all the numbers from one to ninety-nine. So choose whichever you like best, but be consistent.

There are some clear-cut guidelines however. Never begin a sentence with a number—it must be spelled out. Percentages, statistics, distances, and money are not spelled out, unless they begin a sentence.

Commonly Misused Words and Phrases

Note that many of the confusions involve parts of speech.

alot/a lot: *A lot* is informally used a lot. But it is incorrect.

> *"A lot" is a much-used informal phrase; do not use it in your writing.*

advice/advise: *Advice* is a noun; *advise*, a verb.

> *I never asked for your advice.*
>
> *The counselor advised me to research the biotechnology field.*

affect/effect: *Affect* is a verb meaning "to influence, or have impact upon." *Effect* is a noun meaning results of; *effect* can also be used to mean influence, or impact, but not as a verb: *The effects of nuclear radiation are radiation sickness, soil contamination, and global pollution.*

> *Poverty affects the incidence of animal neglect. When people are short on cash, they sometimes abandon their pets.*
>
> *My paper concerns the effects of television violence on children's behavior.*

all ready/already: *All ready* means fully prepared; *already* is an adverb meaning previously or before.

> *I was all ready to leave for my trip when I got the surprise cancellation.*
>
> *By the time I arrived home, the family had already eaten.*

bad/badly: *Bad* is an adjective and thus modifies nouns and pronouns; *badly* is an adverb.

> *John looked bad after his accident*
>
> *John was badly hurt in the accident.*

breath/breathe: *Breath* is a noun; *breathe* is a verb.

> *I was all out of breath by the time I reached the summit.*

> *She was so frightened that she couldn't breathe.*

capitol/capital: A *capitol* is a building wherein a legislative body meets. A *capital* is either a political center, as in, *Boston is the capital of Massachusetts*, or it refers to the uppercase letter that must begin all sentences. Capital can also mean goods, assets, or cash.

> *Madoff bilked many investors of their capital.*

complement/compliment: *Complement* means to go along with, to match; *compliment* means to flatter. Both can be either nouns or verbs.

> *The professor complimented the class on its stellar performance.*

> *As one of the class members, I felt honored by his compliment.*

conscience: the part of mind that experiences right and wrong

> *After lying to his girlfriend, Jim's conscience bothered him.*

conscientious: an adjective meaning very careful, attentive to requirements

> *He is a very conscientious teacher; lectures are always well prepared.*

conscious: an adjective meaning aware or deliberate

> *Irena is often not conscious of how alienating her behavior can be.*

continual/continuous: *Continuous* refers to something that never stops; *continual* to something that happens frequently but not always.

> *The continuous force of evolution means that change is inevitable.*

> *Rainfall is the result of the continuous cycle of evaporation and condensation linking the waters of the earth and the clouds of its atmosphere.*

The college students in the apartment above us have frequent parties that continually disturb us in the middle of the night.

council/counsel: *Council* is a noun and signifies a group; *counsel* is either a noun or a verb meaning advice or to advise.

The council debated heatedly before finally deciding to whom the prize was awarded.

The therapist counseled my best friend to leave her relationship.

When I met her partner, I gave her the same counsel.

desert/dessert: *Desert* is an arid land; *dessert* is a delicious, sweet food.

Arizona contains many deserts.

Dessert is the best part of the meal.

Mnemonics: As a desert lacks water, so the word lacks an s.

every day/everyday: *Every day* is a phrase, two words meaning "happening daily"; *everyday* is one word, meaning ordinary or usual.

Every day I go to the gym to work out.

Arguments at dinner are everyday affairs.

farther/further: *Farther* refers to physical distance, while *further* refers to difference in degree or time.

The restaurant is about two miles farther down this road.

His shifting eyes were further proof of guilt.

good/well: *Good* is an adjective; *well* is an adverb. Hence,

I may look good, but I don't feel well.

He cooks very well.

hanged/hung: Unless you are referring to stringing someone up by a rope, use *hung*.

The stockings were hung on the chimney. The clothes hung on the line.

The vigilantes hanged John Dooley for his thievery.

its/it's: *Its* is a possessive form of the pronoun *it; it's is* a contraction of *it is.*

Our town must improve its roads.

It's time to leave the zoo.

like/as: *Like* is a preposition; *as* is a conjunction that introduces a clause. Hence, if a statement has a verb, use *as*; if not, use *like*.

Dorothy drank as heartily as a thirsty camel.

Her muscles were strong and ropey like a weightlifter's.

loose/lose: *Loose* means "not attached," the opposite of tight; *lose* means to misplace.

He has been accused of having loose lips: don't trust him!

If I lose these keys, I'll be in serious trouble.

passed/past: *Passed* is the past tense of the verb, *to pass,* meaning to move by, or succeed; *past* is a noun meaning before the present time.

We passed two hitchhikers on Route 22.

In times past, people enjoyed much richer social lives.

principal/principle: *Principal* means a supervisor or something of major importance; *principle* refers to a value, an idea.

The principal of Sunnyside High was fired for fiscal irresponsibility.

The fired principal was evidently not a man of high principles.

proceed, proceeds, precede: *Proceed* is a verb meaning to carry on, to go forth; *proceeds* is a plural noun, meaning revenue raised; *precede* is a verb, meaning to be ahead or in front of, or earlier than.

"Proceed, counselor," bellowed the judge, "or be fined for stalling."

The proceeds from the raffle are going to the Food Bank.

In the Easter procession, the bishops, priests, and other clergy precede the parishioners.

quote/quotation: *Quote* is a verb; *quotation* is a noun.

I chose a quotation from Karl Marx to summarize the negative effects of capitalism upon family ties.

I quoted Karl Marx to emphasize the adverse effects of capitalism on family ties.

raise/rise: *Raise* means to elevate, or to increase; the past tense is regular, *raised*. *Rise* means to stand up, to get up; the past tense is irregular, *rose*.

The State Department of Education is charged with raising academic standards.

The reform effort has successfully raised student achievement.

"All rise for the benediction," the minister directed.

The congregation rose for the benediction as surely as the sun rises every day.

real/really: *Real* is an adjective; *really* is an adverb.

He is a real artist, in my opinion, contrary to the hacks employed in advertising.

He is a really good artist, despite his large commercial appeal.

set/sit: *Set* means to put down or to adjust; its past tense is also *set*. *Sit* is a verb meaning to place oneself in a sitting position; the past is *sat*.

John set his hat on the bureau.

After setting his hat on the bureau, John sat in his favorite chair.

than/then: *Than* is a comparison word; *then* is an adverb referring to time.

The politics of health care are more complicated than those of public education.

I got up at 8:00 a.m., and then, five minutes later, I was on my way to the office.

their/they're: *Their* is a possessive pronoun; *there're* is a contraction for *they are.*

The Smiths can be annoying; they're always late for dinner.

Their habitual lateness annoys their friends.

used to/use to: *Used to* is the past tense phrase to express a former action/state; *use to* is simply incorrect.

When American artists migrated to France in the 1920s, they used to gather at the Café Metro in Paris.

who/whom: *Who* is the nominative case; *whom* is the objective case.

The first person who reaches the goal post wins the prize.

Ask not for whom the bell tolls: It tolls for thee.

who's/whose: *Who's* is a contraction of *who is*; *whose* is a possessive pronoun.

The student who's voted the most likely to succeed wins a full scholarship.

The student whose GPA is the highest wins a full scholarship for graduate school.

your/you're: *You're* is a contraction of *you are*; *your* is a possessive pronoun.

The neighbors dislike that you're an environmentalist who doesn't cultivate a lawn.

The neighbors dislike your choice of herbs and stones for your front yard.

Spelling

Many of the easily confused words we study are different in spelling, such as *advise/advice*. Many stem from confusing phonetics (how a word sounds) with how it is spelled, a real problem since English contains many words that are spelled very differently from how they sound. There are some rules to help us, for instance, the jingle that many of us learned:

I before e except after c, or when it sounds like "ay" as in neighbor, eighteen, weigh.

Unfortunately, there are exceptions such as *seize, leisure, height*.

Plural formations are another area in which some general rules help. Recall from the section above that discusses nouns that most nouns form plural by adding –s: (flower/flowers; car/cars). However, if a noun ends in a –y that follows a consonant (country), then drop the *y* and substitute *ies*, as in *country/countries* or *story/stories*. However, the *y* is kept if it follows a vowel (*day/days*), or if it ends a proper noun (*Barney/Barneys*).

What's a person to do? Given the many exceptions that characterize English, here are two practical strategies:

- Do not rely on spellcheck alone for there are some words it simply cannot pick up.

- Familiarize yourself with the typical problem situations (such as *ie/ei*). Pay attention to them and look them up in a dictionary if you are not sure. The following are some of the most common words prone to spelling errors:

occurred	becoming	certain	embarrass
heroes	calendar	difference	acceptable
parallel	address	easily	believe
laboratory	definite	describe	schedule
preferred	excellent	argument	separate
preference	finally	familiar	recommend
grievance	achieve	except	occasionally

Skill Factor 2: Essay Writing and Scoring

As we mentioned in the beginning of the chapter, the writing portion of the CBEST assesses your ability to effectively compose two essays. You must write your essays on the two topics printed in the test booklet. One of the essays will require you to analyze a given situation or a particular statement through your writing. The other essay will involve your reflecting on and writing about a personal experience you have had. The readers of the essays will judge your ability to express yourself clearly, to use appropriate language and supporting details, and to demonstrate an understanding of your topics. You will need to rely on your experiences, thoughts, beliefs, and personal knowledge to write these essays. No additional information will be needed for you to express yourself effectively.

An example of the first type of essay topic is:

Topic 1

"Describing how individuals are different is the easier task; discovering how individuals are alike is the more important task."

On the basis of your own experience, explain why you agree or disagree with this idea.

In the second essay, you will be asked to write about a personal experience.

An example of this second type of topic is:

Topic 2

Describe two incidents in your life that significantly influenced your decision to choose the career you are pursuing.

Essay writing demonstrates your ability to think critically and to use language logically and clearly. Your performance on the CBEST writing test will demonstrate your ability to organize and support your ideas within a time limit. This type of writing is illustrative of the kind of thinking all teachers need to effectively present concepts and ideas to their students.

The time limit challenges you to write quickly and to write well. In most writing situations, writers have the luxury of time to organize their thoughts and to polish their work to a professional level; they can work through multiple drafts to increase the subtlety and sophistication of their words. In a timed writing scenario, however, you must recognize that you do not have these optimal conditions.

It is essential, therefore, that you organize your thoughts prior to writing your essay. *Take a few minutes at the outset of this portion of the CBEST to make an outline of your ideas.* Write down a thesis statement, and then brainstorm a few reasons why you believe your thesis statement to be true. For each of these reasons, think of an illustrative example that supports your point of view. Taking a few minutes to write such an outline will help you to organize your thoughts, to develop your essay in a clear and logical manner, and to maintain your thesis throughout the essay. This strategy is the single most effective step you can take to help you write a coherent and compelling essay.

Note the similarities between an analytical essay (given in the first essay topic) and a personal experience essay (given in the second essay topic). In both types of essays, you must articulate a reasonable and interesting thesis, provide reasons why your thesis is an intelligent response to the essay prompt, explore illustrative examples, and end with a conclusion that summarizes the argument and gives a sense of its relevance. Within the parameters of the CBEST, the differences between an analytical essay and a personal experience essay are almost nonexistent because you cannot include relevant research on the given topic for the analytical essay; the test does not allow you time to do library or other types of research to provide the foundation of your analysis. Therefore, for both the analytical and the personal experience essay, concentrate on providing examples and observations from your personal experiences in order to create a compelling thesis that responds to the question put before you by the test.

Six Primary Traits of Good Writing

The CBEST essays are graded holistically, which means that the grader examines your essay as a complete entity unto itself. Essays that do not pass are then scored diagnostically. The diagnostic scoring offers feedback to the test-taker about the weaknesses of the essay. (See the Essay Scoring section for more information on this topic.) The following **Six Primary Traits of Good Writing** are evaluated during diagnostic scoring:

1. **Rhetorical Force:** Can you clearly convey the central idea of your essay? Does your essay exemplify logical reasoning and coherency of argument? Do you maintain a consistent point of view throughout the essay? Is your thesis powerful, interesting, and free of clichés?

2. **Organization:** Do your ideas follow a logical sequence? Do you provide smooth transitions between ideas? Do the introduction, the supporting paragraphs, and the conclusion all work to support the same thesis?

3. **Support and Development:** Do you provide supporting information that helps the reader to understand your thesis? Is the supporting information relevant and meaningful?

4. **Usage:** Do you use words carefully and correctly? Does your writing show close attention to how words work together to build sentences?

5. **Structure and Conventions:** Is your writing free of grammatical errors? Do you spell, punctuate, and capitalize correctly?

6. **Appropriateness:** Do you choose a topic appropriate to your audience? Does the thesis of your essay demonstrate your understanding of the question at hand? Does your style highlight your comprehension of who your audience is?

Paying close attention to these Six Primary Traits of Good Writing will help you polish your writing and, since writing reflects your thought processes, you want your writing to be clear and organized.

Review of Essay Writing Concepts and Skills

An essay is a group of related paragraphs organized around a single topic. This topic should be as fully developed as possible, given the time limitations of the test. All the sentences in each paragraph and all the paragraphs in the essay are focused on this topic. **Essays that tend to receive the highest score on the CBEST (known as a Pass) have five or six relatively short paragraphs.** The structure of a typical five-paragraph essay consists of an opening paragraph that contains a thesis statement, three supporting paragraphs, and a concluding paragraph. Although the five-paragraph format is not the only way to organize your essay, it is a useful template with which to begin.

The opening (introductory) paragraph performs three functions. First, the opening paragraph defines the audience. In other words, it sets the tone or style of your writing for the rest of the essay. Obviously, you would write in a very different style for an audience of children or students; choose an appropriate tone and style for your audience of CBEST graders. Second, the opening paragraph attracts the attention of the readers so that they will want to know what you have to say. Finally, it contains a thesis statement that presents the focus of your essay; it tells the reader your opinion on a given topic and suggests the direction your essay will then take. The thesis statement is often (although not always) the final sentence of the introductory paragraph.

The body of the essay follows the opening paragraph. Here you present several major points to support the thesis statement. Each major point is developed into a supporting paragraph. The number of supporting paragraphs will vary according to the nature of your topic and ideas, but three is a common number of major points in a timed-test exercise of this type. Each supporting paragraph should have a topic sentence and supporting information or statements that expand or explain the topic sentence of the paragraph. Supporting paragraphs are important to the cohesiveness of your essay because they explain, narrate, describe, or argue the key points of the thesis statement in the opening paragraph. Be careful to provide smooth transitions between the body paragraphs; highlight the logical connection between the body paragraphs by telling the reader how these ideas are related.

The concluding paragraph of the essay often summarizes the thesis statement and the topic sentences of the supporting paragraphs; it also rephrases the main idea and explores it in more depth. A conclusion should also give the reader a sense of the importance of the ideas presented in the essay. Although you are writing the essay because it is part of a test, give the reader a sense of why the ideas presented in your essay are important to you and why they should be important to the reader as well.

A summary of this multi-paragraph essay structure follows:

Opening Paragraph: *This includes the thesis statement, sets the style or tone of writing appropriate for the audience, and captures the attention of the reader.*

Supporting Paragraphs: *Each supporting paragraph includes a topic sentence, which is the first major point related to the thesis. Then, an illustrative example is given that demonstrates to the reader the validity of your opinion. (You may include as many supporting paragraphs as you need to set forth your major points. Three or four paragraphs should be sufficient.)*

Concluding Paragraph: *This includes a restatement and/or summary of the essay and an appropriate logical conclusion.*

Strategies for Answering the Essay Questions

Use the strategies described below in order to prepare for the essay section of the CBEST.

Preparing for the Test

1. Practice writing essays about the example topics given in this book. Limit yourself to 30 minutes so that you become accustomed to working under timed conditions.

2. Practice brainstorming and making outlines to help you structure your ideas.

3. Study a list of the most frequently misspelled words so that you can avoid such mistakes.

4. Use the first section of this chapter to review the basic rules of good grammar and mechanics. Also, know your own error patterns and practice editing your own writing. Working with a tutor at a college writing lab can help you both to identify errors you often make and to develop strategies for spotting and correcting them.

On the Day of the Test

1. **Wear a watch** so that you can keep track of the time. If you allot one hour to write two essays, allow 30 minutes to write each one. Give yourself five to seven minutes to write an outline, and spend the remaining time writing the essay. Pace yourself carefully, as no one will make time announcements during the test.

2. **Take two No. 2 soft-lead pencils with good erasers.** You will need two pencils, in case one breaks. You are not allowed to have paper, other than the test booklet, during the test. However, you may make notes at the bottom of the test booklet page on which the assigned topics appear. You should jot notes in the bottom margin as you brainstorm and outline. The CBEST requires that you use a No. 2 pencil, so do not bring a pen.

3. **Make sure that your handwriting is legible!** After graders have looked at many tests, they are tired and possibly grumpy. Do not give them an "incentive" to lower your grade by making them struggle to read your writing.

Writing Strategies

A number of strategies are helpful in writing a clearly reasoned, well-organized, well-developed essay that demonstrates a thorough understanding of the assigned topic.

1. **Read the essay topic carefully.** Read it two or three times. Underline the key ideas and words so that you know exactly what you are being asked by the essay prompt. *An essay on a topic other than the one assigned will not be accepted.*

2. **Form a thesis statement.** Since this statement is critical to the organization of the essay, write it down in rough form at the bottom of the test booklet page where you are allowed to make notes. Then form it into a well-crafted representation of your thoughts on the subject chosen.

3. **Order your major supporting points.** Use the first few minutes of the test to make an outline at the bottom margin of the test booklet after brainstorming several ideas to support your thesis. You can write the essay more easily if you first make an outline to keep your ideas on track.

4. **Take a stand and relate all your points to it.** Do not digress from your thesis! If you do not maintain your thesis, the scorers will think that your writing is unorganized, lacking in focus, and confused. *You may fail if your essay is not well organized.*

5. **Write or print legibly.** Be as neat as possible. Readers like neat writing because it is easier for them to read. Avoid using excessively large handwriting. Do not skip any lines in the test booklet; do not leave margins wider than approximately an inch on each side of the paper. Indent approximately five spaces at the beginning of each new paragraph.

6. **Proofread your writing during the last five minutes for correct spelling, grammar, and punctuation.** Make sure that you did not unintentionally forget to write down an important word. Break any run-on sentences into two or more complete sentences. Correct errors as neatly as possible. Although the appearance of your essay is not graded, too many crossed-out or squeezed-in words can be distracting and make it difficult for the evaluator to follow your train of thought.

Stylistic Tips

In addition to these Writing Strategies, bear in mind the following Stylistic Tips when writing your essay. Style is as important in the construction of a good essay as the subject of the essay itself, so be careful to make your style increase the readability of your writing. Let's quickly review some of the most important mechanical elements.

1. **Only use words that you know how to spell.** The *Oxford English Dictionary* lists approximately 500,000 words in the English language. This tremendous variety of words makes it possible to write with simple, easily spelled words that are synonyms of more complex words, which may be difficult to spell. Study the list of commonly misspelled words in the first section of this chapter. When in doubt about the spelling of a difficult word, substitute a word that has the same meaning but a familiar spelling.

2. **Use an appropriate tone in your writing.** Try to avoid contractions, slang, colloquialisms, and platitudes, all of which indicate an informal tone. Also, avoid repeating words in proximity so that your essay displays an interesting variety in vocabulary.

3. **Try to use the active voice rather than the passive voice.** The active voice enhances your writing by making it more direct and straightforward, whereas the passive voice often suggests evasiveness.

4. **Keep your verbs in the same tense.** If your topic sentence is in the present tense, then each sentence within that paragraph should also be in the present tense.

5. **Use familiar punctuation that you know.** Colons, semicolons, dashes, parentheses, or ellipsis points are confusing to most people who do not write professionally. Do not use them unless you are absolutely certain that you are using them correctly.

6. **Be careful with your word usage.** Be sure to use *I/me, there/they're/their, to/two/too, its/it's* and other easily confused words correctly. If you are unsure how to use a word correctly, rephrase the sentence so that you do not have to use that word.

7. **Use exciting verbs.** Verbs are the key to presenting ideas forcefully and with variety. For example, instead of a simple verb such as "go," use *run, hurry, move,* or *stumble.*

8. **Never use swear words, profanity, or derogatory language.**

Essay Scoring

The evaluators who read your essays are experienced teachers who will score your writing holistically; that is, each of your essays will receive a single score based on its overall quality. Holistic scoring is similar to the scoring of individual ice skaters in the Olympics. The skater's performance is ranked by the judges for its overall artistic appeal; however, the performance must also display technical merit. The overall score takes into account both the skater's artistic qualities and technical skills. Holistic scoring for writing means that the evaluators will judge not only the overall quality of your ideas but also how well and correctly you use language. The organization of your ideas will receive the most weight, just as the judges in the skating competition give more weight to a skater's artistic performance. Nonetheless, it is important to recognize that, just as an excellent artistic performance by an Olympic skater can be hurt by poor technique, a writer with excellent organization and ideas can be hurt by the use of incorrect language. In other words, to receive the highest score on your writing, you must demonstrate good organization and ideas as well as correct and effective use of language. (The following section, **Sample Papers and Grading,** illustrates how the grading rubric functions.)

Your essays will be read under very carefully controlled conditions to ensure fairness and reliability. Two readers will score your first essay; two different readers will score your second essay. The evaluators will rate your essay on the Six Primary Traits of Good Writing (described earlier in this chapter):

- Rhetorical Force

- Organization

- Support and Development

- Usage

- Structure and Conventions

- Appropriateness

Each reader will give your essay a score. Individual readers will not see the other scores given to your writing. *Pass* (a score of 4) is the highest rating. *Marginal Pass* (a score of 3) is the second highest rating. *Marginal Fail* means a score of 2; *Fail* means a score of 1 and is the lowest rating.

A Pass is given to an essay that is well formed and communicates effectively a coherent and meaningful message to its audience. In order to receive a Pass, you must demonstrate your proficiency with the Six Primary Traits of Good Writing. First, you must clearly present your thesis statement and maintain your focus on it throughout the essay (Rhetorical Force). Second, the organization of your essay must display a logical and coherent arrangement (Organization). Third, assertions should be supported with specific examples that fully develop your thesis (Support and Development). Fourth, your word choice should highlight your strong vocabulary, and grammar must be used correctly (Usage). Fifth, the sentences should showcase syntactic complexity and variety; the sentences should combine to form coherent paragraphs (Structure and Conventions). Sixth, the essay should respond to the question at hand, and it should do so in a manner that engages its audience (Appropriateness).

A Marginal Pass essay adequately communicates its thesis to the specified audience, yet it lacks the overall cohesion of a Pass essay. The writer succeeds in presenting a central idea, and the focus of the essay is maintained throughout most of the supporting paragraphs. The organization of ideas is strong and clear, and the meaning of the essay is easy to follow. Assertions are supported with evidence, but the evidence is perhaps not always especially compelling. Word choice and usage are simple and effective; the errors that do exist do not hamper comprehension. If the essay has problems with paragraphing, sentence structure, and/or mechanical conventions, they do not present excessive confusion to the reader. The writer addresses the topic with language and style suitable to the audience.

A Marginal Fail essay inadequately communicates its thesis. Although the writer may declare a thesis in the introductory paragraph, the thesis is lost in the ensuing discussion, and the reasoning is simplistic. The organization and structure of the essay fail to assist the reader in grasping the ideas of the writer. Assertions are presented without clear supporting evidence, and the writer fails to provide meaningful examples. The writer's words are imprecise, and the essay evinces little concern for correct grammar and punctuation. Distracting errors in paragraphing, sentence structure, and/or mechanical conventions result in confusion for the reader. The essay fails to address the question put forth in the assignment; also, it does not communicate to its audience with appropriate language or with an appropriate style.

A failing essay represents an unsuccessful attempt to communicate a message. No central idea or thesis directs the reader's attention. The organization of ideas appears haphazard, and no structure provides support for an overarching argument. Assertions devolve into mere generalizations that cannot be adequately supported and that lack logical meaning. Word choice and usage are too often incorrect, and these errors distract the reader's ability to follow the essay.

Paragraphing, sentence structure, and mechanical conventions are ignored. The response does not appear to engage with the assignment at hand, and the style and language of the essay are inappropriate for its target audience.

Sample Papers and Grading

Analyze the following essays as part of your preparation for the CBEST. As you read each essay, judge it yourself in terms of its Rhetorical Force, Organization, Support and Development, Usage, Structure and Conventions, and Appropriateness. Remember, these Six Primary Traits of Good Writing are the basis for the scoring of an essay.

> **Topic 1:** *Describing how individuals are different is the easier task; discovering how individuals are alike is the more important task.*

On the basis of your own experience, explain why you agree or disagree with this statement.

Sample Essay on Topic 1

When I am asked why Janet, my best friend, and I get along so well, I always tell people it is because we are so different. However, the more I think about our relationship, I realize our differences are not the only things that make our friendship so special. Beneath the obvious variations, there are many similarities which make us even more compatible.

In the middle of my sophmore year, my English teacher, Mrs. Estrada, changed the seating chart and I found myself sitting next to a quiet, but pretty black-haired girl named Janet. Being the loquacious person that I am, I immediately engaged her in a conversation. My lack of shyness, though I did not know it at the time, would create a beautiful friendship.

After I got to know Janet a little better, I became aware that we were very different. She was shy and pretty, and I was forward and gawky. She had a boyfriend and many friends, while I had not yet discovered boys and had few friends. She was from a lower socio-economic class, while I was from an upper socioeconomic class. With all of these differences, I wondered how we could be such good friends.

At first, I thought our friendship was as secure as it was because we contrasted so well. Yet, after we acknowledged that we were best friends and we began to spend more time together, I began to see many similarities. For instance, we both had the same goals and morals. We are both kind, compassionate, and sensitive people, and we both snort when we laugh.

It is very important for individuals to identify how they are different from others, but more difficult and more important is to discover how they are similar. By identifying how I am different from Janet, I was able to keep my individuality and learn about how another person operates, and by discovering our similarities, I was able to form an unbreakable bond with a unique and special individual who I can relate on terms that I understand. Now, when I am asked about why our relationship is so secure, I tell them it is because we are very different yet so very similar.

Analysis of the Essay

The preceding essay, which answers the first topic, fits the Pass criteria. The organization of the essay is very strong. If you superimpose the summary for multi-paragraph essays from earlier in this review, you see that the first topic essay is well structured. The opening paragraph includes the thesis statement: "Beneath the obvious variations, there are many similarities which make us even more compatible." This statement agrees with the essay prompt, which fulfills the assignment of choosing to agree or to disagree with the prompt. The style and tone of the writing are appropriate for an audience of teachers and graders. The illustrations from the area of values, socioeconomic background, physical appearance, and politics support the thesis statement and capture the attention of the reader. The supporting paragraphs each explore a point implied in the introductory paragraph or provide support for the thesis. The first supporting paragraph tells the ways in which the writer and Janet are different. The second supporting paragraph elaborates on how their characteristics differ. The third supporting paragraph emphasizes the importance of recognizing similarities. The concluding paragraph summarizes the importance of such similarities in relating to other people. It also brings in the uniqueness of individuals as a strong link to the topic sentence in the opening paragraph; in this return to the ideas of the introduction, the conclusion expands upon these initial ideas, rather than just repeating the thesis. This essay meets the criteria of a Pass because it is clearly reasoned, well organized, and well developed; it also demonstrates a thorough understanding of the question it is answering.

In addition to the strong presentation of a thesis statement and the superior organization of supporting and concluding paragraphs, the writer also demonstrates familiarity with Usage (the writer's precision in word choice) and Structure and Conventions (the writer's avoidance of errors in syntax and mechanics). Only minor flaws appear in the essay that detract from its readability, such as overusing the word "friendship," failing to hyphenate "socio-economic" in the third paragraph, mistakenly using "a" rather than "an" before "unbreakable" in the fifth paragraph, and writing "individual who" rather than "individual to whom" in the fifth paragraph. These few flaws, however, do not detract from the essay's overall excellent use of language. Furthermore, the sentences are interesting and developed with variety. The verbs are in the active voice and primarily in the present tense. Spelling errors do not handicap the flow of ideas. No run-on sentences impede comprehension, and the punctuation is correct. This essay exhibits the writer's ability to communicate effectively and to construct sentences with precision, variety, and complexity.

This essay completes all the tasks set by the assignment. The writer expressed an opinion in response to the prompt. The writer used personal experience and observations to explain the reasons for agreeing with the quotation. It is important to note that personal experience and observation are useful tools for providing compelling reasons to support your thesis, but one could also cite experiences and observations gained from other sources.

> **Topic 2:** *Describe two incidents in your life that significantly influenced your decision to choose the career you are pursuing.*

Sample Essay on Topic 2

Throughout my life, I have made many decisions concerning my career goals. I wanted to do a variety of things, ranging from engineering to teaching, but certain circumstances and realizations discouraged me from carrying out those plans. My decision to be a psychologist was final after two incidents that occurred during high school.

During my sophomore year, my boyfriend was arrested and sent to a continuation high school. I was a sheltered girl with a high sense of values, and so this bewildered and angered me. Soon this anger was channeled into concern. We remained friends and I tried to be supportive. I discovered many reasons why he was delinquent, but I felt helpless because I couldn't do very much for him. I realized that many people have frustrations and other problems that drive them to hurt themselves. Recognizing this, I wanted to help others with their problems.

In the same year, my mother took me to a psychologist. I was going to see one because I have problems with my friends and I was very depressed and pessimistic about my life. Right away, I felt uncomfortable with the lady. When I explained the situations that were bothering me, she seemed to always tell me that I was feeling as all teenagers do. I felt as though she was citing from a textbook, readily willing to lump me into a stereotypical group. This made me more determined to counsel people. I am a person who can see others as individuals and I learned that this is necessary to work with people.

I have always had an awareness and concern for others and these incidents helped me realize my calling. I love talking and being with people but it is painful and confusing to see the strife people inflict upon themselves and on others. Psychology is a field where I will be working directly with people and actually help them; it also represents a continuing learning process for me and will encourage me to keep growing.

Analysis of the Essay

This essay, which answers the prompt for the second topic, also fits the criteria of a Pass. The organization of this essay is very strong and adheres nicely to the guidelines for multi-paragraph essays, described earlier in this review. The thesis statement, located in the opening paragraph, declares that "My decision to be a psychologist was final after two incidents that occurred during high school." This sentence fulfills the assignment because it speaks of two experiences that changed the writer's perception of career choices. The two supporting paragraphs elaborate on the attitudes and events that support the key statement in the opening paragraph. The second and third paragraphs describe these critical incidents and the impact they had on the writer's career decisions. The fourth paragraph addresses goals in life and the steps in finalizing a career choice; it also summarizes the changes that took place because of the two experiences and again underscores their great influence. Furthermore, the conclusion does not merely restate the thesis; it amplifies upon the thesis and delineates its greater significance. This essay meets the criteria of a Pass score because it is clearly reasoned, solidly organized, and well developed; also, it demonstrates a clear understanding of the assignment.

Note, too, the skilled manner in which the writer handles issues both of Usage and of Structure and Conventions. The sentences are interesting and developed with variety. The verbs use the active voice in the past tense. The writer uses a variety of words. The style, although slightly informal, holds the attention of the reader; if the style had been more casual or conversational, the essay would have been inappropriate for its audience of teachers. There are no run-on sentences, and the punctuation is error-free (although some grammarians would advocate commas to separate clauses both in the last sentence of the third paragraph and the second sentence of the final paragraph). This essay demonstrates that the writer uses language effectively to construct an essay of interest and complexity.

Sample Writing Topic

You should practice some of the strategies and techniques described in this review. Compare your writing to the essays in this review; then analyze your own writing with the Six Primary Traits of Good Writing. For your practice writing, be sure to time yourself and to limit your writing time to 30 minutes.

> **Essay Prompt:** *Describe the major qualities you feel have led to the success of the person you most admire.*

Once you have completed this practice essay, ask another person, preferably an experienced teacher or perhaps a tutor at your college writing lab, to read and criticize your work against the criteria in this review.

Practice Test 1

CBEST

This test is also offered online at the REA Study Center (*www.rea.com/studycenter*). We highly recommend that you take the computerized version of the exam to simulate test-day conditions and to receive these added benefits:

- **Timed testing conditions**—Gauge how much time you can spend on each question.

- **Automatic scoring**—Find out how you did on the test, instantly.

- **On-screen detailed explanations of answers**—Learn not just the correct answers, but also why the other answer choices are incorrect.

- **Diagnostic score reports**—Pinpoint where you're strongest and where you need to focus your study.

ANSWER SHEET – PRACTICE TEST 1

Section 1: Reading

1. (A) (B) (C) (D) (E)
2. (A) (B) (C) (D) (E)
3. (A) (B) (C) (D) (E)
4. (A) (B) (C) (D) (E)
5. (A) (B) (C) (D) (E)
6. (A) (B) (C) (D) (E)
7. (A) (B) (C) (D) (E)
8. (A) (B) (C) (D) (E)
9. (A) (B) (C) (D) (E)
10. (A) (B) (C) (D) (E)
11. (A) (B) (C) (D) (E)
12. (A) (B) (C) (D) (E)
13. (A) (B) (C) (D) (E)
14. (A) (B) (C) (D) (E)
15. (A) (B) (C) (D) (E)
16. (A) (B) (C) (D) (E)
17. (A) (B) (C) (D) (E)
18. (A) (B) (C) (D) (E)
19. (A) (B) (C) (D) (E)
20. (A) (B) (C) (D) (E)

21. (A) (B) (C) (D) (E)
22. (A) (B) (C) (D) (E)
23. (A) (B) (C) (D) (E)
24. (A) (B) (C) (D) (E)
25. (A) (B) (C) (D) (E)
26. (A) (B) (C) (D) (E)
27. (A) (B) (C) (D) (E)
28. (A) (B) (C) (D) (E)
29. (A) (B) (C) (D) (E)
30. (A) (B) (C) (D) (E)
31. (A) (B) (C) (D) (E)
32. (A) (B) (C) (D) (E)
33. (A) (B) (C) (D) (E)
34. (A) (B) (C) (D) (E)
35. (A) (B) (C) (D) (E)
36. (A) (B) (C) (D) (E)
37. (A) (B) (C) (D) (E)
38. (A) (B) (C) (D) (E)
39. (A) (B) (C) (D) (E)
40. (A) (B) (C) (D) (E)

41. (A) (B) (C) (D) (E)
42. (A) (B) (C) (D) (E)
43. (A) (B) (C) (D) (E)
44. (A) (B) (C) (D) (E)
45. (A) (B) (C) (D) (E)
46. (A) (B) (C) (D) (E)
47. (A) (B) (C) (D) (E)
48. (A) (B) (C) (D) (E)
49. (A) (B) (C) (D) (E)
50. (A) (B) (C) (D) (E)

PRACTICE TEST 1

Section 1: Reading

DIRECTIONS: One or more questions follow each statement or passage in this test. The question(s) are based on the content of the passage. After you have read a statement or passage, select the best answer to each question from among the five possible choices. Your answers to the questions should be based on the stated (literal) or implied (inferential) information given in the statement or passage. Mark all answers on your answer sheet. Note: You will encounter some passages with numbered sentences, blank spaces, or underscored words and phrases. These cues are provided on the CBEST for your reference in answering the questions that follow the relevant passages.

Questions 1 and 2 refer to the following passage:

America's national bird, the mighty bald eagle, is being threatened by a new menace. Once decimated by hunters and loss of habitat, this newest danger is suspected to be from the intentional poisoning by livestock ranchers. Authorities have found animal carcasses injected with restricted pesticides. These carcasses are suspected to have been placed to attract and kill predators such as the bald eagle in an effort to preserve young grazing animals. It appears that the eagle is being threatened again by the consummate predator, humans.

1.   One can conclude from this passage that

    A.   the pesticides used are beneficial to the environment.

    B.   ranchers believe that killing the eagles will protect their ranches.

    C.   ranchers must obtain licenses to use illegal pesticides.

    D.   poisoning eagles is good for livestock.

    E.   pesticides help to regulate bird populations.

2.   The author's attitude is one of

   A.   uncaring observation.

   B.   concerned interest.

   C.   uninformed acceptance.

   D.   suspicion.

   E.   unrestrained anger.

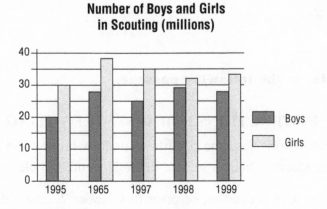

Number of Boys and Girls in Scouting (millions)

Questions 3 and 4 refer to the graph above:

3.   In what year was the involvement in scouting closest to being equal between girls and boys?

   A.   1999

   B.   1995

   C.   1996

   D.   1998

   E.   1997

4.   How much of a difference was there between the number of boys and the number of girls involved in scouting in 1997?

   A.   10 million

   B.   1 million

   C.   5 million

   D.   .1 million

   E.   100 million

Question 5 refers to the following statement:

The <u>disparaging</u> remarks about her performance on the job made Alice uncomfortable.

5.   The word <u>disparaging</u> is closest in meaning to

   A.   congratulatory.
   B.   immoral.
   C.   whimsical.
   D.   tantalizing.
   E.   insulting.

Questions 6–8 refer to the following passage:

INSTRUCTIONS FOR ABSENTEE VOTING

These instructions describe conditions under which voters may register for or request absentee ballots to vote in the November 5 election.

(1)   If you have moved on or prior to October 7, and did not register to vote at your new address, you are not eligible to vote in this election.

(2)   If you move after this date, you may vote via absentee ballot or at your polling place, using your previous address as your address of registration for this election.

(3)   You must register at your new address to vote in further elections.

(4)   The last day to request an absentee ballot is October 29.

(5)   You must be a registered voter in the county.

(6)   You must sign your request in your own handwriting.

(7)   You must make a separate request for each election.

(8)   The absentee ballot shall be issued to the requesting voter in person or by mail.

6.   A voter will be able to participate in the November 5 election as an absentee if he or she

   A.   planned to register for the next election.

   B.   requested an absentee ballot on November 1.

   C.   voted absentee in the last election.

   D.   moved as a registered voter on October 13.

   E.   moved on October 7, 2010.

7.   On October 21, Mr. Applebee requested an absentee ballot for his daughter, a registered voting college student, to enable her participation in the election process. Mr. Applebee will not be successful because of which of the following instructions?

   A.   3

   B.   2

   C.   6

   D.   7

   E.   5

8.   You can vote in future elections if you

   A.   register at your new address.

   B.   registered at your previous address.

   C.   request a registration form in your own handwriting.

   D.   moved after October 29.

   E.   registered as a Republican.

Questions 9 and 10 refer to the following passage:

   The atrophy and incapacity that occurs when a broken bone is encased in plaster and immobilized clearly demonstrates what a sedentary lifestyle can do to the human body.

9.   In the passage above, atrophy refers to

   A.   a strengthened condition brought about by rest.

   B.   a decrease in size and strength.

   C.   a type of exercise and rehabilitation.

   D.   rest and recuperation.

   E.   the effects of convalescence.

10. Which of the following statements best paraphrases the author's view of sedentary living?

   A. It's good to relax and take it easy.

   B. A sedentary lifestyle is a healthy lifestyle.

   C. A body responds well to a sedentary lifestyle.

   D. Sedentary living increases mobility.

   E. Mobility is affected by lifestyle.

Questions 11–15 refer to the following passage:

Frederick Douglass was born Frederick Augustus Washington Bailey in 1817 to a white father and a slave mother. Frederick was raised by his grandmother on a Maryland plantation until he was eight. It was then that he was sent to Baltimore by his owner to be a servant to the Auld family. Mrs. Auld recognized Frederick's intellectual acumen and defied the law of the state by teaching him to read and write. When Mr. Auld warned that education would make the boy unfit for slavery, Frederick sought to continue his education in the streets. When his master died, Frederick, who was only sixteen years of age, was returned to the plantation to work in the fields. Later, he was hired out to work in the shipyards in Baltimore as a ship caulker. He plotted an escape but was discovered before he could get away. It took five years before he made his way to New York City and then to New Bedford, Massachusetts, eluding slave hunters by changing his name to Douglass.

At an 1841 anti-slavery meeting in Massachusetts, Douglass was invited to give a talk about his experiences under slavery. His impromptu speech was so powerful and so eloquent that it thrust him into a career as an agent for the Massachusetts Anti-Slavery Society.

Douglass wrote his autobiography in 1845, primarily to counter those who doubted his authenticity as a former slave. This work became a classic in American literature and a primary source about slavery from the point of view of a slave. Douglass went on a two-year speaking tour abroad to avoid recapture by his former owner and to win new friends for the abolition movement. He returned with funds to purchase his freedom and to start his own anti-slavery newspaper. He became a consultant to Abraham Lincoln and throughout Reconstruction fought doggedly for full civil rights for freedmen; he also supported the women's rights movement.

11.   According to the passage, Douglass's writing of his autobiography was motivated by

A.   the desire to make money for the anti-slavery movement.

B.   his desire to become a publisher.

C.   his interest in authenticating his life as a slave.

D.   his desire to educate people about the horrors of slavery.

E.   his desire to promote the Civil War.

12.   The central idea of the passage is that Douglass

A.   was instrumental in changing the laws regarding the education of slaves.

B.   was one of the most eminent human rights leaders of the nineteenth century.

C.   was a personal friend and confidant to a president.

D.   wrote a classic in American literature.

E.   was an advocate of women's rights.

13.   According to the author of this passage, Mrs. Auld taught Douglass to read because

A.   Douglass wanted to go to school like the other children.

B.   she recognized his natural ability.

C.   she wanted to comply with the laws of the state.

D.   he needed to be able to read so that he might work in the home.

E.   she was obeying her husband's wishes regarding education.

14.   The title that best expresses the ideas of this passage is

A.   The History of the Anti-Slavery Movement in America.

B.   The Outlaw Frederick Douglass.

C.   Reading: A Window to the World of Abolition.

D.   Frederick Douglass's Contributions to Freedom.

E.   Frederick Douglass's Oratorical and Literary Brilliance.

15. In the context of the passage, <u>impromptu</u> is the closest in meaning to

   A. unprepared.

   B. nervous.

   C. angry.

   D. loud.

   E. elaborate.

Questions 16 and 17 refer to the following passage:

   Acupuncture practitioners, those who use the placement of needles at a strategic location under the skin to block pain, have been tolerated by American physicians since the 1930s. This form of Chinese treatment has been used for about 3,000 years and until recently has been viewed suspiciously by the West. New research indicates that acupuncture might provide relief for sufferers of chronic back pain, arthritis, and recently, pain experienced by alcoholics and drug addicts as they kick the habit.

16. According to the passage, acupuncture has been found to help people suffering from all of the following EXCEPT

   A. arthritis.

   B. recurring back pain.

   C. alcoholics in withdrawal

   D. liver disease.

   E. drug addicts in withdrawal.

17. According to the passage, acupuncture has

   A. been enthusiastically embraced by American physicians.

   B. been used to alleviate chronic migraine headaches.

   C. always been available only in the Far East.

   D. been used since the 1930s.

   E. received tepid support from American physicians.

Question 18 refers to the following passage:

Commercial enterprises frequently provide the backdrop for the birth of a new language. When members of different language communities need to communicate or wish to bargain with each other, they may develop a new language through a process called "pidginization." A pidgin language, or pidgin, never becomes a native language; rather, its use is limited to business transactions with members of other language communities. Pidgins consist of very simple grammatical structures and small vocabularies. They have tended to develop around coastal areas where seafarers first made contact with speakers of other languages.

18.   The passage suggests which of the following about pidgins?

A.   We could expect to hear pidgins along the coast of Africa and in the Pacific Islands.

B.   Pidgins are a complex combination of two languages.

C.   Pidgins develop in inland mountain regions.

D.   Pidgins become native languages only after several generations of use.

E.   Pidgins are the language of the seafarer.

Question 19 refers to the following passage:

There are two ways of measuring mass. One method to determine the mass of a body is to use a beam-balance. By this method, an unknown mass is placed on one pan at the end of a beam. Known masses are added to the pan at the other end of the beam until the pans are balanced. Since the force of gravity is the same on each pan, the masses must also be the same on each pan. When the mass of a body is measured by comparison with known masses on a beam-balance, it is called the gravitational mass of the body.

The second method to determine the mass of a body is distinctly different; this method uses the property of inertia. To determine mass in this way, a mass is placed on a frictionless horizontal surface. When a known force is applied to it, the magnitude of the mass is measured by the amount of acceleration produced upon it by the known force. Mass measured in this way is said to be the inertial mass of the body in question. This method is seldom used because it involves both a frictionless surface and a difficult measurement of acceleration.

19. Which of the following statements can best be supported from the passage?

   A. The gravitational and inertia mass methods measure different properties of the object.

   B. The masses are equal when the weights are equal and cause the beam to be balanced.

   C. Gravitational inertial measurements do not give the same numerical value for mass.

   D. The same result for a beam-balance method cannot be obtained at higher altitudes.

   E. The mass of a body depends on where it is located in the universe.

Question 20 refers to the following passage:

   Her introductory remarks provided a <u>segue</u> into the body of the speech.

20. In the context of this passage, the word <u>segue</u> means

   A. rendition.

   B. performance.

   C. transition.

   D. plausible.

   E. critique.

Questions 21–23 refer to the following passage:

   One of the many tragedies of the Civil War was the housing and care of prisoners. The Andersonville prison, built by the Confederates in 1864 to accommodate 10,000 Union prisoners, was not completed when prisoners started arriving. Five months later, the total number of men incarcerated there had risen to 31,678.

   The sounds of death and dying were not diminished by surrender of weapons to a captor. Chances of survival for prisoners in Andersonville were not much better than in the throes of combat. Next to overcrowding, inadequate shelter caused unimaginable suffering. The Confederates were not equipped with the manpower, tools, or supplies necessary to house such a population of captives. The prisoners themselves gathered lumber, logs, anything they could find to construct some sort of protection from the elements. Some prisoners dug holes in the ground, risking suffocation from cave-ins, but many hundreds were left exposed to the wind, rain, cold, and heat.

The sheer numbers of prisoners exhausted daily food rations, and this situation resulted in severe dietary deficiencies for the incarcerated men. The overcrowding, meager rations, and deplorable unsanitary conditions resulted in rampant disease and high mortality rates. The consequences of a small scratch or wound could result in death in Andersonville. During the prison's 13-month existence, more than 12,000 prisoners died and were buried in the Andersonville cemetery. Most of the deaths were caused by diarrhea, dysentery, gangrene, and scurvy that could not be treated due to inadequate staff and supplies.

21. What is the central idea of the passage?

    A.   The major problem for the Confederates was finding proper burial spaces in the cemetery.

    B.   The prison was never fully completed.

    C.   Prison doctors were ill-equipped to handle emergencies.

    D.   Andersonville prison was not adequate to care for three times as many prisoners as it could hold.

    E.   Many prisoners died as a result of shelter cave-ins.

22. From this passage, the author's attitude toward the Confederates is one of

    A.   endorsement.

    B.   objectivity.

    C.   scorn.

    D.   insensitiveness.

    E.   contradiction.

23. The first sentence of the second paragraph of this passage can best be described as

    A. an homage.

    B. a deviation.

    C. a tentative assumption.

    D. an anecdote.

    E. an irony.

Questions 24–27 refer to the following passage:

When William Wordsworth implies that the "mind [is] an aesthetic object," he is validating the human narcissistic capacity to impose such a judgment in the first place. And if this is so, then is romantic poetry merely self-serving, or is it responding to social, political, economic, and theological anxieties, tensions, and issues?

24. What does the term narcissistic mean?

    A. Naïveté

    B. Intelligent

    C. Self-centered

    D. Foolish

    E. Impulsive

25. What does Wordsworth mean when he implies that the mind is "an aesthetic object"?

    A. It is lovely to look at.

    B. It creates beauty.

    C. It wants beauty.

    D. It lacks beauty.

    E. It smells funny.

26. The passage suggests which of the following about romantic poetry?

    A. It is art for art's sake.

    B. It is beauty, and beauty is truth.

    C. It can represent and/or encompass significant contemporary issues.

    D. It is only about love and love lost.

    E. It has the capacity to impose judgment.

27. What does the term <u>aesthetic</u> mean?

    A. Thoughtful

    B. Intelligent

    C. Empty

    D. Artistic

    E. Arrogant

Questions 28–30 refer to the following index sample:

Gloves, 59
Goggles, 59
Grinders, portable, 66
Grinding operations, 126–140
Grinding wheels, 126–129
    selecting and using the wheel, 129–140
Grinding wheel selection and use, 129–140
    center punch sharpening, 133
    chisel head grinding, 135
    grinding metal stock, 131–133
    hand sharpening twist drills, 138
    installing the wheel, 130
    markings and composition, 127
    screwdriver tip dressing, 133
    sharpening a twist drill by machine, 139
    sharpening a twist drill for drilling brass, 139
    sharpening metal-cutting chisels, 136–138
    sizes and shapes, 127
    thinning the web of a twist drill, 139
    tin snips sharpening, 134
    truing and dressing the wheel, 131

28. To which page(s) would one turn for information on how to install a grinding wheel?

   A. 126–140
   B. 136–138
   C. 130
   D. 126–129
   E. 129–140

29. Which of the following best describes the organizational scheme used to index the section dealing with grinding wheel selection and use?

   A. by type of wheel
   B. by physical characteristics
   C. by task
   D. by type of drill
   E. by order of appearance

30. On which page(s) would you find information on grinding a rounded edge on metal stock?

   A. 136–138
   B. 131–133
   C. 126–129
   D. 126–140
   E. 127

Questions 31–35 refer to the following passage:

   Jonathan Edwards's lineage was comprised of a prestigious line of clergymen. His parents were the Rev. Timothy Edwards, pastor of the Congregational Church of East Windsor for 64 years, and his mother was Esther Stoddard, daughter of the Rev. Solomon Stoddard, pastor of the Congregational Church of Northampton for more than 50 years. Edwards received his Master of Arts from Yale in 1723. In 1727 he became his grandfather's colleague in the church at Northampton, whereby, "upon the death of his grandfather, Edwards became the sole proprietor of the Northampton pulpit." Edwards soon became renowned for a series of powerful sermons. Enthusiastic sermonizing such as Justification by Faith

Alone (1734), contributed to a great spiritual <u>grassroots revival</u>, known throughout the colonies as the Great Awakening. In the winter and spring of 1734-35, Edwards's subsequent report, A Faithful Narrative of the Surprising Works of God (1737) made a profound impression in America and Europe. Needless to say, Edwards <u>correlated the nuances</u> of religious discourse, politics, and rhetoric fluently.

31. What does the phrase "grassroots revival" mean?

    A.   People spoke to one another outside, in parks and squares, instead of meeting halls and other public buildings.

    B.   People brought their concerns to the politician and he was able to address their needs.

    C.   It personifies Jonathan Edwards as a natural outdoorsman, thereby making him easier for the common man to relate to.

    D.   It is a social resurgence of philosophical values that stems from the common man upward.

    E.   It suggests that public figures like Edwards plant the philosophical seeds and their agendas grow from there.

32. The author's attitude toward the subject is

    A.   angry.

    B.   impartial.

    C.   apologetic.

    D.   lamenting.

    E.   propitious.

33. From the information provided by the passage, it can be inferred that Jonathan Edwards was

    A.   gregarious and debonair.

    B.   prominent and devoted.

    C.   auspicious and adamant.

    D.   ancillary and dejected.

    E.   deceitful and hypocritical.

34. In the context of the passage, what does <u>correlated the nuances</u> mean?

    A.   Connected the differences

    B.   Ordered the similarities

    C.   Utilized the subtleties

    D.   Deplored the differences

    E.   Assimilated the correlations

35. According to the passage, Edwards made a profound impact on both Europe and America after the release of a report published in

    A.   1737.

    B.   1734.

    C.   1735.

    D.   1723.

    E.   1727.

Questions 36–40 refer to the following passage:

Life in seventeenth-century England was <u>tempestuous</u> indeed. It was a time of religious and secular confrontations resulting in new social abstractions, symbolism, paradoxes, and ironies. Explorers such as Galileo Galilei (1564–1642), the Italian astronomer and physicist, challenged the formal dogma of the day by mindfully watching the heavens and questioning conventional reality, thereby threatening established theological doctrine. Galileo was the first person to use a telescope to study the constellations in 1610. He was an outspoken advocate of Copernicus's theory, which states that the sun, and not the earth, forms the center of the universe. This blasphemy led to Galileo's persecution and finally to his imprisonment by the Inquisition of 1633.

_____ , philosophers, essayists, courtiers, clergymen, scholars, laborers, and statesmen such as Francis Bacon (1561–1626) were "pleading for science in an age dominated by religion," while their counterparts such as Sir Thomas Browne were "pleading for religion in an age which was beginning to be dominated by science."

The age of religious sovereignty was coming to a close. Protestant reformers began to challenge sovereign sacrament during the reign of

Queen Elizabeth I, 1558–1603, and those responsible for instigating the friction came to be known as Puritans. These "non-conformists" wanted greater reorganization and simplicity within the Episcopal and Anglican branches of the Church of England, ostensibly to purify it from "elaborate ceremony" and "regal formalities," which they saw as major distractions from religious meditations and moral purity. Moral purity was closely linked with the practice of ritual purity, that is, ritual free from ostentatious display. _____ , ritual purity from this perspective precipitated Puritan conceptions of human impurity connected with disorder, since they involve uncontrolled bodily emissions, fluids, and death.

36. From the information in the above passage it can be deduced that the seventeenth century was a time of

    A.   anger and resentment due to economic hierarchy.

    B.   social tranquility due to religious and scientific conflicts.

    C.   social agitation due to scientific and religious conflicts.

    D.   social controversy due to a woman on the throne.

    E.   peace, prosperity, and social harmony due to scientific advancements.

37. What is the meaning of the word tempestuous?

    A.   Jocund

    B.   Disinterested

    C.   Impoverished

    D.   Turbulent

    E.   Progressive

38. According to the information in the passage, Galileo went to prison because he

    A.   used a new invention to see something he shouldn't have.

    B.   did not pay his taxes at the appropriate time.

    C.   questioned contemporary scientific and religious doctrine.

    D.   questioned the authority of the monarchy.

    E.   wrote a pamphlet that some thought to be propaganda.

39. Which of these grouped words or phrases, if inserted in order into the passage's blank lines, would address the logical sequencing of the narrative?

    A. Nonetheless; However

    B. Concomitantly; Thus

    C. However; Consequently

    D. Therefore; Disturbingly

    E. Meanwhile; Interestingly

40. The central idea of the passage is that the seventeenth century was a time of

    A. artistic expression.

    B. religious freedom.

    C. religious and scientific controversy.

    D. social oppression.

    E. legal maneuvering.

Questions 41–44 refer to the following passage:

In order to categorize the fourteenth-century narrative verse "The Alliterative Morte Arthure (AMA)" as an epic, one must first determine the criteria by which the piece is to be evaluated. Therefore, for the purposes of this argument, when referring to the conventions of the epic, I refer to a long narrative poem on a serious subject matter, told in a formal or elevated style. Concurrently, epic conventions include adventure. Adventure centered around a heroic protagonist or quasi-divine figure of great national or cosmic significance; a figure upon whose decisions and actions hinged the fate of a clan, tribe, nation, or even (as in the case of Milton's "Paradise Lost") the entire human race.

The topography plays an important role in epic narrative. It is usually of a grand scale, as in the Iliad. The epic territory can be worldwide, or even larger, as in the representation of Mt. Olympus or purgatory. It might well include ancient worlds personified as real (i.e., Camelot as an entity or a haunted house as an antagonist), surreal (as in the domain of Grendel's mother), or completely imaginary (as in Dante's Divine Comedy). The topography is relevant because it provides the adventurer with both physical and emotional challenges, as well as establishing a stylized ambiance.

41. According to the passage, an <u>epic</u> is defined as

    A. a long narrative poem, on a monotonous subject matter, told in an elevated or formal style.

    B. a long narrative poem, on a serious subject matter, told in an elevated or formal style.

    C. a long alliterative poem, on a lyrical subject matter, told in an elevated or formal style.

    D. a long poem, on any subject, told any way the poet feels appropriate.

    E. a poem that talks about the topography in an elevated or formal manner.

42. What does <u>topography</u> mean?

    A. Terrain

    B. Alchemy

    C. Language

    D. Heroics

    E. Movement

43. The topography is important because it provides the adventurer with

    A. a difficult challenge that he must overcome to become king.

    B. both physical and emotional challenges, as well as establishing a stylized atmosphere.

    C. rewards both physical and emotional, as well as establishing social status.

    D. a long road which must be traversed in order for the hero to succeed.

    E. makes for a more believable atmosphere.

44. The meaning of <u>protagonist</u> is

    A. the landscape.

    B. a villain.

    C. the central character.

    D. a quest.

    E. the lust for adventure.

Use the table of contents below from an English textbook to answer the Questions 45, 46, and 47 that follow.

45. In which part of the book would information about writing a narrative essay most likely be found?

A. Beginning to Write
B. Course 1
C. Course 2
D. Course 3
E. Appendix

46. A reader is looking for the definitions of composition and voice. The reader could probably find this information most readily by looking in which of the following sections of the book?

    A. Bibliography

    B. Glossary

    C. Rules of syntax

    D. Training in composition

    E. Elementary expression

47. Which of the following best matches the number of pages dedicated to Narrating?

    A. 10

    B. 13

    C. 20

    D. 23

    E. 39

Questions 48–50 refer to the following passage:

Christina Rossetti's "Goblin Market" is actually a traveling farmer's market, selling an abundance of "orchard [fresh] fruits, nuts" and produce. The caravan is owned and operated by grotesque and unscrupulous businessmen or "merchant men," who impose their wares of "orchard fruits" upon the female inhabitants of a rural community. Despite the conspicuous absences of fellow residents, the poem's insistence on consumerism, with its resounding commercial <u>mantra</u> of "come buy, come buy" is indicative of the dilemma faced by burgeoning market towns and provincial communities that grew in relationship to England's industrial economy. Urban commercialism brought domestic convenience and leisure, as well as vice and corruption, to traditionally established rural communities.

48. What does the author feel is the overall idea of the poem?

   A.   Urban commercialism brought both convenience and wealth to traditionally established rural communities.

   B.   Urban commercialism brought both produce and textiles to traditionally established rural communities.

   C.   Merchants brought affordable wares to traditionally established rural communities.

   D.   Urban commercialism brought both convenience and vice to traditionally established rural communities.

   E.   Urban commercialism brought businessmen and farmers to traditionally established rural communities.

49. What is meant by the term mantra?

   A.   Profiteering

   B.   Redundancy

   C.   Shopkeepers

   D.   Indebtedness

   E.   Incantation

50. The author's tone in writing the passage is

   A.   aggressive.

   B.   laughable.

   C.   promiscuous.

   D.   assertive.

   E.   impartial.

Answer Key

Section 1: Reading

1.	B	14.	D	27.	D	40.	C
2.	B	15.	A	28.	C	41.	B
3.	D	16.	D	29.	C	42.	A
4.	A	17.	E	30.	B	43.	B
5.	E	18.	A	31.	D	44.	C
6.	D	19.	B	32.	B	45.	C
7.	C	20.	C	33.	B	46.	B
8.	A	21.	D	34.	C	47.	D
9.	B	22.	B	35.	A	48.	D
10.	E	23.	E	36.	C	49.	E
11.	C	24.	C	37.	D	50.	E
12.	B	25.	B	38.	C		
13.	B	26.	C	39.	E		

PRACTICE TEST 1 – Detailed Explanations of Answers

Section 1: Reading

1. **B**

   The ranchers believe that killing the eagles will protect their ranches. This is understood by the implication that "attract[ing] and kill[ing] predators . . . in an effort to preserve young grazing animals" will protect their ranches.

2. **B**

   The author's use of words such as "mighty bald eagle" and "threatened by a new menace" supports concern for the topic. For the most part, the author appears objective; thus, concerned interest is the correct answer.

3. **D**

   In 1998, the difference between boys and girls was a slim half of a percentage point.

4. **A**

   In 1997, the difference between the two was 10 million: 25 million for boys and 35 million for girls.

5. **E**

   Insulting is the correct definition. The other terms are either antonyms or incorrect interpretations.

6. **D**

   Answer (D) fulfills the requirements stated in rules 2 and 4 of the instructions for absentee voting. All other choices do not.

7. **C**

   Mr. Applebee's daughter must sign the request in her own handwriting, as stated in instruction (6).

8. **A**

    You can only vote in future elections if you are registered at your new address, as explained in instruction (3).

9. **B**

    "Atrophy" means "to decrease in size and strength." Answer choices (A), (C), (D), and (E) do not fit this meaning.

10. **E**

    The passage suggests that mobility is directly affected by lifestyle.

11. **C**

    The passage suggests that Douglass was concerned with raising social consciousness about slavery. His interest in refuting those who doubted his claims was for the sake of authenticity.

12. **B**

    Douglass was one of the most eminent human rights leaders of the nineteenth century. All the other choices, while true, are irrelevant to the question and are not supported by the text.

13. **B**

    The passage states "Mrs. Auld recognized Frederick's intellectual acumen." A synonym for "acumen" is "intelligence, insight, or natural ability." The other choices are inaccurate.

14. **D**

    Choices (A), (B), and (C) are too vague or ill-defined. Choice (E) is too finite and limited in its relevance to the entire passage. Thus, choice (D) is correct.

15. **A**

    An "impromptu" speech is one given extemporaneously, or off the cuff.

16. **D**

    Liver disease is never mentioned. All the other choices are.

17. **E**

   The passage states that American physicians "have...tolerated" acupuncture.

18. **A**

   The passage tells us to expect to hear pidgins in coastal communities. All the other statements are contradicted by the passage.

19. **B**

   None of the other statements is supported by the text.

20. **C**

   Although musical in origin, a segue has now come to refer to a transition between two information and/or reference points.

21. **D**

   The passage tells us that Andersonville prison was built to accommodate 10,000 prisoners; upon completion there were 31,678—over three times as many prisoners as it was designed to hold. All other choices are discussed, but the main focus of the passage is the overcrowding and its tragic results.

22. **B**

   The author remains objective (impartial) rather than (D) insensitive. Answers (A), (C), and (E) are contradictory by definition.

23. **E**

   One definition of irony is "a result that is the opposite of what might be expected, anticipated, or appropriate." Thus, "the sounds of death and dying were not diminished by surrender," as one might expect them to be. That is, surrender was no guarantee of survival.

24. **C**

   Based upon the Greek mythological figure Narcissus, who fell in love with his own reflection, the word "narcissistic" means self-centered.

25. **B**

By definition, the adjective "aesthetic" suggests something beautiful, cultured, or artistic. Thus, Wordsworth is suggesting that the mind is able to create beauty, rather than (A) looks beautiful, (C) wants beauty, (D) lacks beauty, or (E) smells funny.

26. **C**

Because the passage asks us if romantic poetry is capable of "responding to social, political, economic, and theological issues," there is an implied sense that (C) it can represent and/or encompass significant contemporary issues.

27. **D**

The word "aesthetic" means "artistic."

28. **C**

Choice (A), "Grinding operations, 126–140," would be expected to discuss how the grinders are operated, but "grinding wheels" is too general in the context of the question posed. Choice (E), pages 129–140 ("Grinding wheel selection and use"), essentially suffers from the same weakness as Choice (A). Pages 136–138 (B) describe an unrelated function. Choice (D), "Grinding wheels,126–129," is overly broad, particularly when considered alongside choice (C), which proves to be the best choice because it specifically uses the phrase "installing the wheel."

29. **C**

While the extract is surely arranged alphabetically, there is another pattern that emerges—one governed by task. This is clear by the preponderance of task-oriented descriptors (e.g., "grinding," "sharpening," "truing and dressing," etc.). Choice (B), "Physical characteristics," addresses a level of detail that does not figure to any appreciable extent in the passage. Thus, choice (C) is the best answer.

30. **B**

Choice (A) is incorrect because finding information on grinding a rounded edge is not relevant to the idea of sharpening a chisel. Choice (C),"grinding wheels," gives no particular indication of holding the answer. Choice (D), while pointing generally to the answer, proves inferior when juxtaposed with choice (B) because the latter contains some of the specific language sought in the extract (i.e., "grinding metal stock"). Choice (E), of course, is completely irrelevant.

31. **D**

   The term "grassroots" is synonymous with the common people, especially those of rural or non-urban areas, thought of as best representing essential political interests or fundamental sources of support.

32. **B**

   The author's attitude toward the subject is impartial, stating facts as facts without excessive emotional intrusions.

33. **B**

   From the information provided by the passage, such as the "profound impression [Edwards made] in America and Europe" and prolific spiritual writings, it can be determined that he was both prominent (eminent) and devoted (dedicated).

34. **C**

   Edwards, we are told, utilized or incorporated the subtleties of discourse and rhetoric fluently. (A), (B), (D), and (E) suggest similar discourse techniques but they are not the definition suggested by the passage.

35. **A**

   The passage tells us that after *A Faithful Narrative* was published in 1737, it "made a profound impression in America and Europe."

36. **C**

   The declaration in the second paragraph of the passage states that a variety of seventeenth-century socio-political figures were "pleading for science in an age dominated by religion" and vice versa. Thus, social agitation was predicated on the conflicts between those two disciplines. Answers (A), (B), (D), and (E) are erroneous.

37. **D**

   The meaning of "tempestuous" is "turbulent."

38. **C**

   The passage states that Galileo supported Copernicus's theory, which was considered blasphemy at the time. Thus, answer (C), "questioned contemporary scientific and religious dogma (doctrine)," is the correct answer.

39. **E**

   Only choice (E) properly addresses the logic and flow of the passage. All the other responses are appropriate to only one of the blank lines or to neither.

40. **C**

   The overall theme of the passage states that the social controversy of the period raged over religious and scientific conflicts.

41. **B**

   The passage tells us that an epic is a long narrative poem, on a serious subject, told in an elevated or formal style. While answers (A), (C), (D), and (E) contain components of the formula, only (B) contains all three elements.

42. **A**

   "Topography" refers to the terrain.

43. **B**

   The last sentence of the passage states that the topography is relevant (important) because "it provides . . . both physical and emotional challenges, as well as establishing a stylized ambiance." Thus, (B) is the correct answer.

44. **C**

   A "protagonist" is (C), the central character.

45. **C**

   Course 2 (C) provides a section on writing a narrative essay.

46. **B**

   A glossary of terms is where one will find definitions.

47. **D**

   The best match is "23 pages," which is answer (D).

48. **D**

   The passage tells us that the paradox of commercialism is that it "brought domestic convenience and leisure, as well as vice and corruption, to traditionally established rural communities." Answers (A), (B), (C), and (E) allude to individual components brought about by the advent of consumerism, but only answer (D) states both the pros and cons.

49. **E**

   The term "mantra" means song, chant, or incantation.

50. **E**

   The author's tone is one of impartiality. (A), aggressive, suggests hostility, (B), laughable, suggests humor, and (C), promiscuous, implies indiscretion, while (D), assertive, suggests a sense of moderate aggression.

ANSWER SHEET – PRACTICE TEST 1

Section 2: Mathematics

1. Ⓐ Ⓑ Ⓒ Ⓓ Ⓔ
2. Ⓐ Ⓑ Ⓒ Ⓓ Ⓔ
3. Ⓐ Ⓑ Ⓒ Ⓓ Ⓔ
4. Ⓐ Ⓑ Ⓒ Ⓓ Ⓔ
5. Ⓐ Ⓑ Ⓒ Ⓓ Ⓔ
6. Ⓐ Ⓑ Ⓒ Ⓓ Ⓔ
7. Ⓐ Ⓑ Ⓒ Ⓓ Ⓔ
8. Ⓐ Ⓑ Ⓒ Ⓓ Ⓔ
9. Ⓐ Ⓑ Ⓒ Ⓓ Ⓔ
10. Ⓐ Ⓑ Ⓒ Ⓓ Ⓔ
11. Ⓐ Ⓑ Ⓒ Ⓓ Ⓔ
12. Ⓐ Ⓑ Ⓒ Ⓓ Ⓔ
13. Ⓐ Ⓑ Ⓒ Ⓓ Ⓔ
14. Ⓐ Ⓑ Ⓒ Ⓓ Ⓔ
15. Ⓐ Ⓑ Ⓒ Ⓓ Ⓔ
16. Ⓐ Ⓑ Ⓒ Ⓓ Ⓔ
17. Ⓐ Ⓑ Ⓒ Ⓓ Ⓔ
18. Ⓐ Ⓑ Ⓒ Ⓓ Ⓔ
19. Ⓐ Ⓑ Ⓒ Ⓓ Ⓔ
20. Ⓐ Ⓑ Ⓒ Ⓓ Ⓔ

21. Ⓐ Ⓑ Ⓒ Ⓓ Ⓔ
22. Ⓐ Ⓑ Ⓒ Ⓓ Ⓔ
23. Ⓐ Ⓑ Ⓒ Ⓓ Ⓔ
24. Ⓐ Ⓑ Ⓒ Ⓓ Ⓔ
25. Ⓐ Ⓑ Ⓒ Ⓓ Ⓔ
26. Ⓐ Ⓑ Ⓒ Ⓓ Ⓔ
27. Ⓐ Ⓑ Ⓒ Ⓓ Ⓔ
28. Ⓐ Ⓑ Ⓒ Ⓓ Ⓔ
29. Ⓐ Ⓑ Ⓒ Ⓓ Ⓔ
30. Ⓐ Ⓑ Ⓒ Ⓓ Ⓔ
31. Ⓐ Ⓑ Ⓒ Ⓓ Ⓔ
32. Ⓐ Ⓑ Ⓒ Ⓓ Ⓔ
33. Ⓐ Ⓑ Ⓒ Ⓓ Ⓔ
34. Ⓐ Ⓑ Ⓒ Ⓓ Ⓔ
35. Ⓐ Ⓑ Ⓒ Ⓓ Ⓔ
36. Ⓐ Ⓑ Ⓒ Ⓓ Ⓔ
37. Ⓐ Ⓑ Ⓒ Ⓓ Ⓔ
38. Ⓐ Ⓑ Ⓒ Ⓓ Ⓔ
39. Ⓐ Ⓑ Ⓒ Ⓓ Ⓔ
40. Ⓐ Ⓑ Ⓒ Ⓓ Ⓔ

41. Ⓐ Ⓑ Ⓒ Ⓓ Ⓔ
42. Ⓐ Ⓑ Ⓒ Ⓓ Ⓔ
43. Ⓐ Ⓑ Ⓒ Ⓓ Ⓔ
44. Ⓐ Ⓑ Ⓒ Ⓓ Ⓔ
45. Ⓐ Ⓑ Ⓒ Ⓓ Ⓔ
46. Ⓐ Ⓑ Ⓒ Ⓓ Ⓔ
47. Ⓐ Ⓑ Ⓒ Ⓓ Ⓔ
48. Ⓐ Ⓑ Ⓒ Ⓓ Ⓔ
49. Ⓐ Ⓑ Ⓒ Ⓓ Ⓔ
50. Ⓐ Ⓑ Ⓒ Ⓓ Ⓔ

Section 2: Mathematics

DIRECTIONS: Each of the 50 questions in this section is a multiple-choice question with five answer choices. Read each question carefully and choose the one best answer.

1. In a class of 25 students, there are 15 girls and 10 boys. On the first history test of the semester, 80% of the girls and 60% of the boys earned a passing grade. What percent of the entire class earned a passing grade on this test?

    A. 60%

    B. 66%

    C. 70%

    D. 72%

    E. 80%

2. A farmer has five pumpkins which weigh 26, 28, 26, 39, and 36 pounds, respectively. What is the average weight of the pumpkins?

    A. 28 pounds

    B. 29 pounds

    C. 30 pounds

    D. 31 pounds

    E. 32 pounds

3. Which of the following is the most appropriate unit of measure for expressing the length of a spoon?

    A. gallons

    B. inches

    C. miles

    D. pounds

    E. yards

4.   Jose drinks 2 gallons of water every three days. Approximately how much water does Jose drink during 2 weeks?

    A.   6 gallons

    B.   8 gallons

    C.   10 gallons

    D.   12 gallons

    E.   14 gallons

5.   The scale of the diagram is 1 inch equals 36 feet. What is the approximate height of the tree?

    A.   27 feet

    B.   36 feet

    C.   72 feet

    D.   81 feet

    E.   120 feet

6.   Nine girls are wrapping gifts for a birthday party. Each girl needs 8 feet plus 9 inches of ribbon to wrap her gifts. What is the total length of ribbon that the nine children need?

    A.   72 feet 9 inches

    B.   76 feet 9 inches

    C.   78 feet 9 inches

    D.   81 feet 1 inch

    E.   87 feet

7. Each side of each square of the grid has length equal to 10 yards. What is the perimeter of the playground?

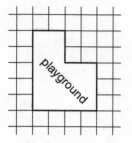

   A. 100 yards

   B. 180 yards

   C. 200 yards

   D. 220 yards

   E. 230 yards

8. Tanya uses two bottles of soap to wash 15 cars. At this rate, how many bottles of soap will Tanya need to wash 135 cars?

   A. 7.5 bottles

   B. 9 bottles

   C. 12.5 bottles

   D. 18 bottles

   E. 21.5 bottles

9. There are 8 black, 10 blue, and 12 white socks in a box. A sock is randomly chosen from this box. What is the probability that the chosen sock is not blue?

   A. $\dfrac{2}{15}$

   B. $\dfrac{4}{15}$

   C. $\dfrac{2}{5}$

   D. $\dfrac{1}{2}$

   E. $\dfrac{2}{3}$

10. Which of the following is the best estimate for 66126 ÷ 18?

    A.   70,000
    B.   35,000
    C.   30,000
    D.   7,000
    E.   3,500

11. A farmer wants to enclose a rectangular field with a fence and also use fencing to subdivide the field into three equal parts as shown below. How much fencing will the farmer need?

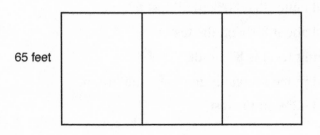

65 feet

150 feet

    A.   215 feet
    B.   345 feet
    C.   430 feet
    D.   560 feet
    E.   690 feet

12. At Almond Creek Elementary School, approximately 3 out of 5 students buy their lunch in the cafeteria each day. If there are 450 students at this school, how many students would be expected to buy their lunch in the cafeteria each day?

    A.   30 students
    B.   90 students
    C.   225 students
    D.   250 students
    E.   270 students

13. There are 2,435,102 people living in Springview and 876,004 in Westfield. Which of the following is the best estimate of how many fewer people live in Westfield than in Springview?

A. 1,500,000
B. 1,400,000
C. 1,300,000
D. 1,200,000
E. 1,100,000

14. Jill's stanine score on this year's standardized reading test is an 8. This indicates that:

A. Jill scored better that 80% of all test takers.
B. Jill scored about 80% on the test.
C. Jill's reading level is 8th grade.
D. Jill scored in the second highest stanine group.
E. Jill scored 92% on the test.

15. Joel has 16 white, 14 brown, 7 grey, and 13 black rocks in a bag. Joel randomly removes a rock from the bag and does not return it to the bag. He then randomly chooses another rock from the bag. What is the probability that the first rock is brown and the second rock is white?

A. $\dfrac{56}{625}$

B. $\dfrac{16}{175}$

C. $\dfrac{16}{50}$

D. $\dfrac{16}{49}$

E. $\dfrac{3}{5}$

16. Stu has debts totaling $12,650 while Christine has $27,013 in debts. Which of the following best estimates the total amount of debt that Stu and Christine have together?

    A. $39,000

    B. $40,000

    C. $41,000

    D. $42,000

    E. $43,000

17. The expression $-46 + 111 - (-29)$ simplifies to which of the following?

    A.   36

    B.   94

    C.   106

    D.   144

    E.   186

18. A farmer collected 4 baskets of apples from his trees. One basket had 118 apples, the second had 142 apples, the third basket had 202 apples, and the fourth held 186 apples. If the farmer put all the apples in 12 boxes so that the boxes contained the same number of apples, how many apples were in each box?

    A.   54

    B.   74

    C.   114

    D.   248

    E.   648

19. What is the hundreds digit in the dividend of the problem shown below?

$$16\ \overline{)\ 3\ \square\ 4\ 7}\qquad 2\ 1\ 5\ \text{Remainder} = 7$$

    A.   8

    B.   6

    C.   4

    D.   2

    E.   0

20. Mickey has three bags of candy. The first weighs $2\frac{2}{3}$ pounds, the second weighs $3\frac{1}{4}$ pounds, and the third bag weighs $5\frac{5}{6}$ pounds. What is the total weight of candy that Mickey has in the three bags?

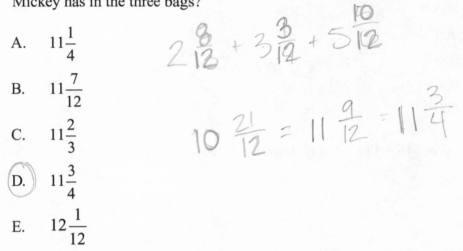

A. $11\frac{1}{4}$

B. $11\frac{7}{12}$

C. $11\frac{2}{3}$

D. $11\frac{3}{4}$

E. $12\frac{1}{12}$

21. The Schmit family went hiking at Yellowstone National Park one day last winter. They recorded the temperature throughout the day. This data is shown in the chart below. What is the difference between the highest temperature of the day and the lowest?

6 am	9 am	12 pm	2 pm	4 pm	6 pm
−11° F	16° F	37° F	28° F	33° F	−3° F

A. 48°

B. 44°

C. 38°

D. 26°

E. 24°

22. A committee started its meeting at 10 a.m. At 11 a.m. one-third of the committee members left to attend a different meeting. At 12 noon half of the remaining members of the committee departed for lunch. If there were eight committee members remaining, how many committee members were present at the beginning of the meeting?

A. 18

B. 24

C. 30

D. 36

E. 42

23. The Axle Car Rental Company rents compact cars at a daily basic rate of $29.99. If a customer is offered a 20% discount on the daily basic rate what will a customer's total basic rate be for a three day rental of a compact car at Axle Car Rental Company?

    A. $17.98
    B. $21.81
    C. $71.97
    D. $74.97
    E. $75.98

24. Samantha works 30 hours per week. If Samantha's hourly wage is increased by $0.75 so that her gross weekly pay becomes $277.50, what was her hourly wage before the raise?

    A. $10.25
    B. $10.00
    C. $ 9.50
    D. $ 8.50
    E. $ 8.00

25. Solve the following equation for x:

    $$2(x - 3) = 18 - x$$

    A. $x = 32$
    B. $x = 27$
    C. $x = 20$
    D. $x = 13$
    E. $x = 8$

26. Brandon mowed lawns to earn money to buy a bicycle. His total earnings for five days work are shown in the table below. If the bicycle's total cost is $186.99 then how much more money does Brandon need to buy the bicycle?

Day	Money Earned from Mowing Lawns
Saturday	$30.50
Monday	$45.00
Tuesday	$20.00
Thursday	$12.50
Friday	$32.75

A. $38.75

B. $46.24

C. $56.24

D. $65.75

E. $140.75

27. This month Jenny bought six less than twice the number of gallons of gasoline for her car than she did last month. If the total number of gallons of gasoline that Jenny bought this month and last month is 150, how many gallons of gasoline did Jenny buy this month?

A. 54 gallons

B. 83 gallons

C. 89 gallons

D. 98 gallons

E. 104 gallons

28. Read the problem below, then answer the question that follows.

> Lana went shopping. On her first trip she bought six pairs of shoes, all at the same price, and three pairs of socks, also all at the same price (shoes and socks are not necessarily the same price) for a total of $195. On her second trip, Lana went to the same store and bought ten more pairs of the same socks at the previous price and returned one pair of the shoes she bought on the first trip. How much did one pair of the shoes cost?

What single piece of additional information is required to solve this problem?

A. the amount of money that Lana spent on her second shopping trip

B. the total time spent shopping

C. the amount of money Lana took with her each time she shopped

D. whether she paid by cash or credit card

E. the types of shoes Lana bought

29. Read the information below, and then answer the question that follows.

> Phillip sold tickets for the student musical. The cost of a student ticket was $5 and the cost of an adult ticket was $8. Phillip sold 6 student tickets and 11 adult tickets.

Which of the following facts can be determined from the information given above?

A. the total number of people who went to see the musical

B. the total amount of money Phillip collected for tickets

C. the profit for putting on the musical

D. the total number of student tickets that were sold

E. where the musical was performed

30. Read the problem below, and then answer the question that follows.

> Gerry drove his car from Summit to Newton. He drove at a constant speed of 50 miles per hour for the first half of the driving time and then he increased his speed to a constant 60 miles per hour for the second half of the trip. How far did Gerry drive?

What single piece of additional information is required to solve this problem?

A. the time Gerry began his trip

B. the total time of the trip

C. the time Gerry arrived in Newton

D. Gerry's average speed over the entire trip

E. the type of car Gerry drove

31. Lisa bought two shirts, one priced at $19.99 and the other $26.95. The sales tax was 9.5%, so Lisa calculated the cost of the two shirts by using the following expression:

$$(19.99 + 26.95) + .095 \times (19.99 + 26.95)$$

Which of the following expressions could Lisa have also used?

A. $0.195 \times (19.99 + 26.95)$

B. $0.905 \times (19.99 + 26.95)$

C. $1.095 \times (19.99 + 26.95)$

D. $(19.99 + 26.95) + 0.195$

E. $(19.99 + 26.95) + 1.095$

32. Madeline wants to buy a $45 purse at a discount of 25% off. She calculates her discounted price in the following way:

$$45 \times \frac{75}{100}$$

Which of the following methods could Madeline also use to correctly calculate her discounted price?

   A. $(45 \times .25) - 45$

   B. $(45 \times .25) + 45$

   C. $45 - (45 \times .25)$

   D. $(45 \times .75) + 45$

   E. $45 - (45 \times .75)$

33. Which of the following mathematical statements is correct?

   A. $2.362 < 2.354 < 2.326$

   B. $2.326 > 2.362 > 2.354$

   C. $2.354 > 2.362 > 2.326$

   D. $2.326 < 2.362 < 2.354$

   E. $2.362 > 2.354 > 2.326$

34. This table represents a linear function with input value x and output value y.

x	y
0	5
1	4.25
2	3.5
3	
4	2
5	1.25

What is the missing value of y?

A. 3.75

B. 3

C. 2.75

D. 2.5

E. 2.25

35. Consider the inequality:

$$\frac{3}{4} < p < \frac{8}{9}$$

For which of the following values of p will the given inequality be true?

A. $p = \dfrac{9}{10}$

B. $p = \dfrac{7}{10}$

C. $p = \dfrac{1}{2}$

D. $p = \dfrac{7}{8}$

E. $p = \dfrac{6}{8}$

36. Which of the following expressions is equivalent to $\frac{1}{2}(b_1 + b_2) \times h$?

 A. $\frac{1}{2}b_1 + b_2 \times h$

 B. $\frac{b_1 + b_2}{2h}$

 C. $\frac{1}{2} + b_1 + b_2 \times h$

 D. $(b_1 + b_2) \times \frac{h}{2}$

 E. $(b_1 + b_2) \div \frac{h}{2}$

37. Which of the following numbers is between $\frac{1}{3}$ and $\frac{1}{2}$?

 A. $\frac{3}{5}$

 B. $\frac{6}{11}$

 C. $\frac{5}{19}$

 D. $\frac{9}{23}$

 E. $\frac{11}{34}$

38. If the value of m is between 3,265,190 and 3,248,333, which of the following could be m?

 A. 3,258,386

 B. 3,266,376

 C. 3,488,981

 D. 3,490,902

 E. 3,268,060

39. Julie spends $8.94 on coffee drinks each work day. If her daily coffee drink expenses are rounded to the nearest dollar, which of the following is the best estimate of her total coffee drinks expenses for the five-day work week?

   A. $40
   B. $43
   C. $44
   D. $45
   E. $48

40. Judy scored double digit points in six consecutive basketball games. Her scores for these games were 12, 26, 22, 18, 27, and 32, respectively. If each of her scores is rounded to the nearest tens place, what is the estimate of her average scoring for the six games rounded to the nearest integer?

   A.   22
   B.   23
   C.   24
   D.   25
   E.   26

41. Last year Cynthia sold 80 houses. How many houses would Cynthia have to sell this year to increase her sales by 15%?

   A.   95
   B.   92
   C.   89
   D.   88
   E.   84

42. Use the table below to answer the question that follows.

Homework Average	Quiz Average	Test Average
66%	84%	92%

The table shows Kyle's grades for his Spanish class. To compute the overall grade for the class, the homework and quiz average count the same but the test average counts twice as much as the quiz average. Which of the following can be used to find Kyle's overall average grade?

A. $[66 + 84 + 2(92)] \div 4$

B. $[66 + 84 + 92] \div 3$

C. $[2(66) + 2(84) + 92] \div 5$

D. $66 + 84 + .5(92)$

E. $66 + [84 + 2(92)] \div 4$

43. Use the information below to answer the question that follows.

- Mike lives two houses away from Sam.

- Ginny lives 4 houses away from Sam.

Which of the following statements is true? Assume all three houses lie in a straight line.

A. Ginny lives farther from Mike than from Sam.

B. Ginny lives farther from Sam than from Mike.

C. Mike lives farther from Ginny than from Sam.

D. Sam lives farther from Mike than from Ginny.

E. Sam lives farther from Ginny than from Mike.

44. Use the information below to answer the question that follows.

- If Ricky earned more than $50 but less than $100 last week at his job then he will buy a pair of jeans.

- If Ricky earned more than $100 but less than $150 last week at his job then he will buy a sweater.

- If Ricky earned more than $150 last week at his job then he will buy a leather jacket.

If Ricky buys only a sweater this week, which of the following could be true?

A. Ricky earned less than $100 last week at his job.
B. Ricky earned exactly $150 last week at his job.
C. Ricky earned exactly $75 last week at his job.
D. Ricky earned exactly $120 last week at his job.
E. Rickey earned more than $200 last week at his job.

45. Use the information below to answer the question that follows.

- All eighth graders study algebra.

- Jim is in eighth grade.

If Sara studies algebra, which of the following statements must be true?

A. Sara is in eighth grade.
B. Sara is in high school.
C. Sara and Jim are in the same algebra class.
D. Jim studies algebra.
E. Jim likes algebra.

46. Use the following pie chart to answer the question that follows.

Kali's Household Budget

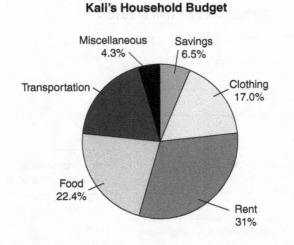

Kali's household budget shows the percentage allocated for each category except *transportation*. What percentage of Kali's budget is allocated for *transportation*?

A. 18.0%

B. 18.8%

C. 20.0%

D. 21.8%

E. 22 .0%

Use the graph below to answer the two questions that follow.

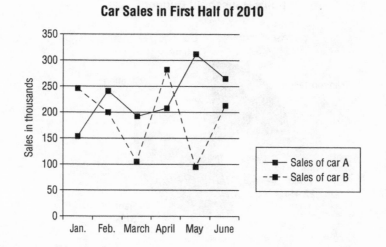

Car Sales in First Half of 2010

47. According to the graph, in how many months were more car A's sold than car B's?

   A. 2
   B. 3
   C. 4
   D. 5
   E. 6

48. According to the graph, what was the approximate maximum difference in any one month between the sales of car A and the sales of car B?

   A. 200,000
   B. 160,000
   C. 130,000
   D. 90,000
   E. 40,000

49. Use the graph to answer the following question.

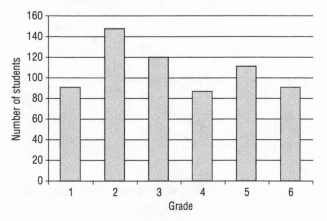

Students at Lincoln Elementary School

Between what two consecutive grade levels is the greatest difference in numbers of students?

A. between grades 2 and 1

B. between grades 3 and 2

C. between grades 4 and 3

D. between grades 5 and 4

E. between grades 6 and 5

50. Use the graph below to answer the following question.

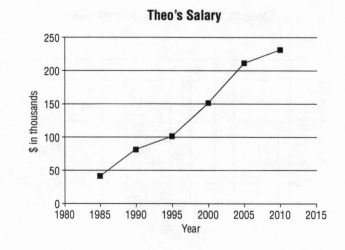

Theo's Salary

In what period did Theo's salary have the greatest percentage increase?

A.   from 1985 to 1990

B.   from 1990 to 1995

C.   from 1995 to 2000

D.   from 2000 to 2005

E.   from 2005 to 2010

Answer Key

Section 2: Mathematics

1. D	14. D	27. D	40. B
2. D	15. B	28. A	41. B
3. B	16. B	29. B	42. A
4. C	17. B	30. B	43. E
5. D	18. A	31. C	44. D
6. C	19. C	32. C	45. D
7. B	20. D	33. E	46. B
8. D	21. A	34. C	47. C
9. E	22. B	35. D	48. A
10. E	23. C	36. D	49. A
11. D	24. D	37. D	50. A
12. E	25. E	38. A	
13. A	26. B	39. D	

PRACTICE TEST 1 – Detailed Explanations of Answers

Section 2: Mathematics

1. **D**

    80% of the 15 girls earned a passing grade on the test. 80% of 15 is $.8 \times 15 = 12$, so 12 girls in this class earned a passing grade. Also 60% of the 10 boys earned a passing grade of the test. 60% of 10 is $.6 \times 10 = 6$, so 6 boys in this class earned a passing grade. Thus, a total of $12 + 6 = 18$ students out of 25 in the class earned a passing grade on this test. But 18 out of 25 is $\dfrac{18}{25} = \dfrac{4 \times 18}{4 \times 25} = \dfrac{72}{100} = 72\%$. (D) is the correct answer.

2. **D**

    The average weight of the 5 pumpkins is $\dfrac{26 + 28 + 26 + 39 + 36}{5} = \dfrac{155}{5} = 31$ pounds. The correct answer is (D).

3. **B**

    The gallon is a measure of liquid capacity and the pound is a measure of weight. A spoon is not a long object and its length can easily be determined by a standard 12-inch ruler. So the most appropriate unit of measure for expressing the length of a spoon is the inch. So, (B) is the correct answer.

4. **C**

    Jose drinks 2 gallons of water every three days. There are 14 days or approximately 15 days in two weeks. There are 5 blocks of three days in 15 days. So Jose will drink 2 gallons in each of these 5 blocks of time for a total of 10 gallons. Therefore, (C) is the correct answer.

5. **D**

    The tree measures about 2.25 inches of the ruler. We can set up a proportion as follows: $\dfrac{1 \text{ inch}}{36 \text{ feet}} = \dfrac{2.25 \text{ inches}}{y \text{ feet}}$. To solve for the unknown y, which represents the height of the tree, we use the following property of proportions: $\dfrac{a}{b} = \dfrac{c}{d}$ is equivalent to $ad = bc$. Using this we have $1 \times y = 36 \times 2.25$ or $y = 81$. Thus, (D) is the correct answer.

6.   **C**

Each girl needs 8 feet plus 9 inches of ribbon and there are 9 girls. The total length of ribbon needed is 9 × (8 feet + 9 inches) = (9 × 8 feet) + (9 × 9 inches) = 72 feet + 81 inches. There are 12 inches in a foot, so dividing 81 by 12 we get 6 with remainder 9; this means that 81 inches is equal to 6 feet and 9 inches. So the total ribbon needed is 72 + 6 = 78 feet plus 9 inches. The correct answer is (C).

7.   **B**

Consider the playground as labeled on the right.

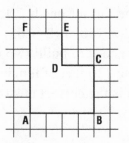

The perimeter of the playground is the sum of the lengths of the sides of the polygon ABCDEF. The lengths: AB = 40, BC = 30, CD = 20, DE = 20, EF = 20, and FA =50. The total length of the perimeter is 40 + 30 + 20 + 20 + 20 + 50 = 180 yards. Thus, (B) is the correct answer.

8.   **D**

Tanya uses two bottles of soap to wash 15 cars. To find how many bottles of soap Tanya will need to wash 135 cars we can set up a proportion as follows: $\frac{2\text{ bottles}}{15\text{ cars}} = \frac{z\text{ bottles}}{135\text{ cars}}$. Again we turn to the property that $\frac{a}{b} = \frac{c}{d}$ is equivalent to $ad = bc$ to arrive at 2 × 135 = 15 × z or 270 = 15 × z. Solve for z by dividing 270 by 15 to arrive at z = 18. (D) is the correct answer.

9.   **E**

There are 30 total socks in the box. The probability that a randomly chosen sock is not blue is $\frac{\text{number of non blue socks in the box}}{\text{total number of socks in the box}} = \frac{8+12}{30} = \frac{20}{30} = \frac{2}{3}$. Thus, (E) is the correct answer.

10. **E**

To estimate the quotient we first round off the dividend, 66126 and the divisor, 18, each to its highest digit: $66126 \approx 70000$ since the thousands digit, 6, is greater than or equal to 5, and $18 \approx 20$ since the units digit, 8, is greater than or equal to 5. Then to approximate we compute the division using the approximations: $\frac{66126}{18} \approx \frac{70000}{20} = \frac{7000}{2} = 3,500$. The correct answer is (E).

11. **D**

We consider the length of the field to be 150 feet, and the width of the field to be 65 feet. To build the fence, the farmer needs 2 lengths and 2 widths (perimeter of a rectangle is $2l + 2w$). This is $(2 \times 150) + (2 \times 65) = 300 + 130 = 430$. To subdivide the field into three equal parts he needs to build two more pieces of fence with the same length as the 65 ft. width, using 130 feet of fencing. So the farmer needs $430 + 130 = 560$ feet of fencing. Thus, (D) is the correct answer.

12. **E**

Three out of five is 60%, so about 60% of the 450 students eat lunch in the cafeteria each day. This is $.6 \times 450 = 270.0$ students. Therefore, (E) is the correct answer.

13. **A**

To approximate the difference of the two populations we subtract the rounded populations, rounding both populations to the nearest hundred thousands place: since the ten thousands place, 3, is less than 5, $2,435,102 \approx 2,400,000$, and $876,004 \approx 900,000$ since the ten thousands place, 7, is greater than or equal to 5. Subtracting the two approximations we have $2,400,000 - 900,000 = 1,500,000$. Therefore, (A) is the correct answer.

14. **D**

The word "stanine" means STAndard NINE and is a method of scaling test scores so that the mean is five and standard deviation is two. The scale ranks scores from 1 to 9 with 1 being the lowest score and 9 being the highest. The lowest 4% of scores are assigned the stanine 1, the next 7% are assigned the stanine 2, the next 12% are assigned the stanine score 3, the next 17% are assigned a 4, the middle 20% are assigned a 5, and so on as shown in this table:

grouped ranking	4%	7%	12%	17%	20%	17%	12%	7%	4%
stanine score	1	2	3	4	5	6	7	8	9

A stanine score of 8 on a standardized reading test indicates that she scored in the second highest stanine group. The correct answer is (D).

15. **B**

There are 50 rocks in Joel's bag. The probability that the first randomly chosen rock will be brown is $\dfrac{\text{number of brown rocks in bag}}{\text{number of rocks in bag}} = \dfrac{14}{50} = \dfrac{7}{25}$. Next we compute the probability that the second rock will be white when we choose from the bag of 49 rocks: $\dfrac{\text{number of white rocks in bag}}{\text{number of rocks in bag}} = \dfrac{16}{49}$. When we are making consecutive choices (called "events" in probability) we must use the Multiplication Principle and multiply these probabilities to get the probability of the second event following the first event. In this problem we have: $\dfrac{7}{25} \times \dfrac{16}{49} = \dfrac{16}{175}$. Thus (B) is the correct answer.

16. **B**

Stu has debts totaling $12,650 while Christine has $27,013 in debts. We round off Stu's debt to the nearest ten thousand to get $10,000 since the 2 in the thousands place is less than 5, and we round Christine's debt off to $30,000 since the 7 in the thousands place is greater than or equal to 5. Adding these estimates together gives us $40,000, giving the correct answer as (B).

17. **B**

The expression $-46 + 111 - (-29) = -46 + 111 + 29$ because subtracting a negative is the same as adding a positive. Then adding the two positive numbers gives the following: $-46 + 111 + 29 = -46 + 140$. Next, using the rules that the order of addition does not matter and $a + (-b) = a - b$, we have: $-46 + 140 = 140 + (-46) = 140 - 46 = 94$. Thus, (B) is the correct answer.

18. **A**

The total number of apples collected by the farmer is $118 + 142 + 202 + 186 = 648$. Dividing 648 by 12 we see that there are 54 apples in each of the 12 boxes. Thus, (A) is the correct answer.

19. **C**

The Remainder Theorem tells us that when $(a \times b) + r = c$ then $c \div a = b$ with remainder r. For example, $(4 \times 3) + 2 = 14$ so $14 \div 4 = 3$ with remainder 2. Therefore our given division problem can be rewritten as a multiplication problem: (215×16)

$+ 7 = 3m47$ where m represents the missing digit. So, $(215 \times 16) + 7 = 3440 + 7 = 3447$ so that m equals 4. (C) is the correct answer.

20. **D**

$2\dfrac{2}{3} + 3\dfrac{1}{4} + 5\dfrac{5}{6} = (2+3+5) + \left(\dfrac{2}{3} + \dfrac{1}{4} + \dfrac{5}{6}\right) = 10 + \left(\dfrac{2}{3} + \dfrac{1}{4} + \dfrac{5}{6}\right)$. To add the fractions we need a common denominator. The numbers 3, 4, and 6 are all divisors of 12 so we will use 12 as our common denominator: $\left(\dfrac{2}{3} + \dfrac{1}{4} + \dfrac{5}{6}\right) = \dfrac{8}{12} + \dfrac{3}{12} + \dfrac{10}{12} = \dfrac{21}{12} = \dfrac{7}{4} = 1\dfrac{3}{4}$. Adding this to 10 gives us $11\dfrac{3}{4}$. Therefore, (D) is the correct answer.

21. **A**

The highest temperature of the day was 37 degrees and the lowest −11 degrees, so the difference is $37 - (-11) = 37 + 11 = 48$. Hence, (A) is the correct answer.

22. **B**

Let C be the number of committee members present at the beginning of the meeting. At 11 a.m., one-third left the meeting leaving two-thirds of C remaining. Then half of these members left at noon, leaving $\dfrac{1}{2}$ of $\dfrac{2}{3}C = \dfrac{1}{3}C$ or 8 members. Solving $\dfrac{1}{3}C = 8$ by multiplying both sides of the equation by 3 gives $C = 24$. Therefore, (B) is the correct answer.

23. **C**

The daily basic rate is $29.99. If the company offers a 20% discount then the customer will pay 80% of the rate, so multiplying by 80% we obtain $.8 \times \$29.99 = \$23.992$ which rounds to $23.99 per day. For three days the cost would be $3 \times \$23.99 = \$71.97$. So, (C) is the correct answer.

24. **D**

Samantha now earns $277.50 for 30 hours of work. Divide 277.50 by 30 to find her current hourly wage, $\$277.50 \div 30 = \$9.25$. If she has just received a 75 cent raise, then her former hourly wage was $9.25 - 0.75 = \$8.50$. The correct answer is (D).

25. **E**

To solve the equation $2(x - 3) = 18 - x$ for x, first distribute to get rid of the parenthesis on the left side of the equation. $2(x - 3) = 18 - x \Leftrightarrow 2x - 6 = 18 - x$. Next gather all the terms with the variable x on the left side and those which are constant on the right by using the Addition Property of Equality: $2x - 6 = 18 - x \Leftrightarrow 2x - 6 + x + 6 = 18 - x + x + 6 \Leftrightarrow 3x = 24$.

Then divide both sides of the equation by 3 to arrive at $x = 8$. Thus, (E) is the correct answer.

26. **B**

First add the five days earnings: $30.50 + 45 + 20 + 12.50 + 32.75 = 140.75$ so that Brandon still needs $186.99 - \$140.75 = \$46.24$. (B) is the correct answer.

27. **D**

Let x be the number of gallons of gasoline that Jenny bought this month. Since the total number of gallons that Jenny bought in 2 months is 150, then the number of gallons she bought last month is $y = 150 - x$. The sentence, "This month Jenny bought six less than twice the number of gallons of gasoline for her car than she did last month," can be translated into a mathematical sentence as follows: $x = 2y - 6$. Then substituting $150 - x$ for y we arrive at the equation $x = 2(150 - x) - 6$, which we must solve. To solve, first distribute the 2 through the parentheses on the right to get $x = 300 - 2x - 6$ or $x = 294 - 2x$. Then add $2x$ to both sides of the equation: $x + 2x = 294 - 2x + 2x$ which reduces to $3x = 294$. Lastly divide both sides of the equation by 3 to arrive at $x = 98$ and a correct answer of (D).

28. **A**

If we let x represent the price of one pair of shoes and y be the price of one pair of socks, then the first shopping trip's expenses can be represented by $6x + 3y = 195$ or, after simplifying by dividing each term by 3, $2x + y = 65$. This can be solved for y: $y = 65 - 2x$. The second trip can be represented by $10y - x = $ total spent on 2nd trip, and substituting in for y we have: $10(65 - 2x) - x = 650 - 20x - x = 650 - 21x = $ total spent on 2nd trip. Hence, if we knew the amount of money that Lana spent on the second trip we could solve the problem. Thus, (A) is the correct answer.

29. **B**

We know that Phillip sold 6 student tickets at $5 each for a total of $30 and 11 adult tickets at $8 each for a total of $88. Adding these together we compute that Phillip collected $30 + 88 = \$118$ for the tickets. Therefore, (B) is the correct answer.

30. **B**

> Distance equals rate times time. This problem asks for distance, and the rate for each half of the trip is given, so we need the time. The correct answer is (B).

31. **C**

> $(19.99 + 26.95) + .095 \times (19.99 + 26.95) = 1 \times (19.99 + 26.95) + .095 \times (19.99 + 26.95)$, so that first you are multiplying 1 times the sum $19.99 + 26.95$, and then you are multiplying 0.095 times the same sum. This is the same thing as multiplying 1.095 times the sum. Thus, (C) is the correct answer.

32. **C**

> Another way to find the discounted price is to calculate the discount and then subtract it from the original price; this would be: $45 - (45 \times .25)$. Hence, (C) is the correct answer.

33. **E**

> Each of the three numbers in each possible answer have the same units digit 2 (the place to the left of the decimal point) and the same tenths digit 3 (the place to the right of the decimal point). So in comparing the hundredths digit (two places to the right of the decimal point) we see that (A), (C), and (D) must be incorrect since 5 is less than 6 and so 2.362 cannot be less than 2.354. Also, since 2 is less than 6 answer (B) is incorrect as the hundredths digit in 2.326 is less than 2.362. Answer (E) is the correct answer.

34. **C**

> According to the table, for every 1-unit increase in the x value there is a 0.75 decrease in the y value. So as x increases from 2 to 3, the y value must decrease from 3.5 to 2.75. The correct answer is (C).

35. **D**

> To compare these fractions we can find equivalent decimals. $\frac{3}{4} = 0.75$ and $\frac{8}{9} = 0.888...$ Then considering the decimal equivalents of the possible answers: $\frac{9}{10} = 0.9$, $\frac{7}{10} = 0.7$, $\frac{1}{2} = 0.5$, $\frac{7}{8} = 0.875$, and $\frac{6}{8} = 0.75$ we see that the only possible correct answer is (D).

36. **D**

The parentheses in the expression $\frac{1}{2}(b_1 + b_2) \times h$ means that the addition $b_1 + b_2$ may be done first; then h will be multiplied by the result. In addition this second result must be either multiplied by one-half or divided by 2. The correct answer is (D).

37. **D**

$\frac{3}{5}$ and $\frac{6}{11}$ are both greater than $\frac{1}{2} = 50\%$ which can be seen by looking at $\frac{3}{5}$ as "3 out of 5," and $\frac{6}{11}$ as "6 out of 11." Also, $\frac{5}{19}$ is less than $\frac{5}{15} = \frac{1}{3}$; similarly, $\frac{11}{34}$ is less than $\frac{11}{33} = \frac{1}{3}$. $\frac{9}{23}$ is clearly less than $\frac{1}{2} = 50\%$ when considered as "9 out of 23," and $\frac{9}{23}$ is greater than $\frac{9}{27} = \frac{1}{3}$ so $\frac{9}{23}$ is greater than $\frac{1}{3}$. Therefore, the correct answer is (D).

38. **A**

Note that 3,248,333 is less than 3,265,190 and that they both have "three million two hundred thousand" as part of them; i.e., their millions and hundred thousands places are the same. Their ten thousands places are 6 and 4 respectively, so for m to be between 3,265,190 and 3,248,333 the ten thousands place must be 4, 5, or 6; this eliminates answers (C) and (D). Also note that answer (A) has 5 as its ten thousands digit which means that (A) must be the correct answer. Answer (B) has the same ten thousands digit as the higher number 3,265,190 but its thousands digit is greater ($6 > 5$) so it cannot be between the two numbers. Answer (E) is larger than both given numbers since its ten thousands place is 6 and thousands place is 8. The correct answer is (A).

39. **D**

Julie's daily coffee drink expense rounded to the nearest dollar is $9, so for five days this would be $45. The correct answer is (D).

40. **B**

Judy's scores rounded to the tens place are: 10, 30, 20, 20, 30, and 30, respectively. The average of these numbers is $\frac{10 + 30 + 20 + 20 + 30 + 30}{6} = \frac{140}{6} = \frac{70}{3} = 23\frac{1}{3} \approx 23$. Hence, the correct answer is (B).

41. **B**

Fifteen percent of 80 is $.15 \times 80 = 12.0$, so Cynthia would have to sell $80 + 12 = 92$ houses this year to increase her sales by 15%. Therefore, (B) is the correct answer.

42. **A**

Since the test average counts twice as much as the quiz average, there are effectively four grades that need to be averaged: 66, 84, 92, and 92. $\dfrac{66+84+92+92}{4} = (66+84+2(92)) \div 4$. The correct answer is (A).

43. **E**

From the information in the box, we can conclude that either (i) Sam lives in the middle with Mike 2 houses away on one side and Ginny 4 houses away on the other, or (ii) Mike lives in the middle with Sam's house 2 away on one side and Ginny's house 2 away on the other as shown below:

(i) Mike X Sam X X X Ginny or (ii) Sam X Mike X Ginny

Ginny lives farther from Mike than from Sam only in case (i). Ginny lives farther from Sam than from Mike only in case (ii) Mike lives farther from Ginny than from Sam only in case (i). Sam lives farther from Mike than from Ginny in neither case. Sam lives farther from Ginny than from Mike in both cases, so the correct answer is (E).

44. **D**

The fact that Ricky bought only a sweater this week must follow from his earning more than $100 but less than $150 last week. Only answer (D) could be true since $120 is greater than $100 and less than $150.

45. **D**

Since Jim is an eighth grader and all eighth graders study algebra, then it must follow that Jim studies algebra; the correct answer is (D).

46. **B**

The total of the percentages for all categories except transportation is: $4.3 + 6.5 + 17.0 + 31.0 + 22.4 = 81.2\%$. Then transportation must be $100 - 81.2 = 18.8\%$. Thus, the correct answer is (B).

47. **C**

Sales of car A are indicated with the solid line while sales of car B are indicated with the dotted line. Sales of car A are higher in February, March, May, and June, so answer (C) is correct.

48. **A**

The maximum difference between sales of car A and car B occurs in May. Car A sales in May were about 300,000 while car B's sales were approximately 100,000 so that the difference in sales in May was about 200,000. (A) is the correct answer.

49. **A**

The number of students in each grade level, according to the graph, is approximately: grade 1 = 90, grade 2 = 144, grade 3 = 120, grade 4 = 82, grade 5 = 110, grade 6 = 90.

The greatest difference between consecutive grades is clearly between 1 and 2 and this is equal to $144 - 90 = 54$. The correct answer is (A).

50. **A**

Percentage increase is calculated using the formula: $\dfrac{\text{change in amount}}{\text{original amount}}$.

The percent increase from 1985 to 1990 is $\dfrac{80000 - 40000}{40000} = \dfrac{40000}{40000} = 1 = 100\%$

The percent increase from 1990 to 1995 is $\dfrac{100000 - 80000}{80000} = \dfrac{20000}{80000} = 0.25 = 25\%$

The percent increase from 1995 to 2000 is $\dfrac{150000 - 100000}{100000} = \dfrac{50000}{100000} = .5 = 50\%$

The percent increase from 2000 to 2005 is $\dfrac{210000 - 150000}{150000} = \dfrac{60000}{1500000} = \dfrac{2}{5} = 40\%$

The percent increase from 2005 to 2010 is $\dfrac{230000 - 210000}{210000} = \dfrac{20000}{2100000} = \dfrac{2}{21} \approx \dfrac{2}{20} = 10\%$
The correct answer is (A).

Section 3: Writing

DIRECTIONS: Carefully read the two writing topics below. Plan and write an essay on each, being sure to cover all aspects of each essay. Allow approximately 30 minutes per essay.

Topic 1

The minimum wage in America has been the subject of debate for many years. Many people argue that we should be careful about sharp increases in the minimum wage because of the resulting inflation (higher labor costs equal higher consumer prices) and layoffs. Others believe the minimum wage is too low to support a family and should be raised to keep up with the cost of living.

Write an essay analyzing and evaluating these opposing views on the minimum wage. You may include personal experience, knowledge, or observations.

Topic 2

Popular psychology tells us that "habit" is a powerful force, compelling us to live out our lives with basically the same behaviors we learned as we grew up. Write an essay in which you discuss a significant habit of yours that you'd like to change. Speculate on why this may be difficult for you.

Section 3: Writing

Sample Scored Essays With Explanations

Topic 1 Sample Answers

Essay #1—Pass (Score = 4)

There is no doubt that minimum wage laws are necessary for the well-being of workers and their families. It had always been the policy for most businesses to pay laborers less than they deserve. Minimum wage laws are one of the only ways workers can be protected from management; without them they are fair game to whatever exploitation the employer can manage.

Many argue against the minimum wage, protesting that it is too high. The fact is, even with raises in the rate, it still does not meet the needs of the laborers because of the increases in inflation and the basic cost of living. At present, it would be extremely difficult, or even impossible, to support a family on a salary as low as $5.00 an hour. There is no person (or family) in my experience who survives on minimum wage; teenagers who have financial help from their parents, might find a minimum wage adequate, but no "head of a household" would. If anything, the current minimum wage rate is too low.

Another argument against minimum wage, especially sharp increases, is the possibility of inflation due to higher labor costs which might cause higher consumer prices. The problem with this is management. Workers do not cause inflation, businesses and corporations do. If the leaders of these companies were not so money hungry, workers could have higher salaries without causing an increase in the price of goods and services. It is quite possible to do this because products are extremely overpriced. Most businesses, however, look to short-term, easy money instead of long-term stability. A raise in the minimum wage would actually help the business in the long-run because workers would be happier and thus, productivity would be increased. The only way a raise in the minimum wage would cause inflation would be if the companies themselves let it.

The final point made by those opposed to minimum wage is the possibility of inflationary pressures resulting in worker lay-offs. As was discussed earlier, inflation in this situation is not a given. For the moment however, let's just theorize on the possibilities of workers being fired. Those most likely to be laid off are the teenagers, minorities, seniors, and the disabled. Although this seems like the course of action many businesses would take, it is not if the companies are smart. First, firing workers would not be tolerated by unions. Next, even in non-union companies, laying off workers would cost the business money in the long run; with less workers, productivity is diminished and when there is a need for more workers they will have to be paid at the same wage as were the ones who were fired. There is little chance that businesses would make decisions that would cost them money.

It would be ridiculous to say that minimum wage is a panacea for the laborers of the world. It barely makes a dent, even with the recent increases in their bills. What it does do, though, is give the worker a guarantee that he will get paid no less than is mandated; this, in many cases, is enough.

Scoring Explanation for Essay #1—Pass

This essay is thoughtful and well-organized, and it introduces several interesting arguments supporting the minimum wage. The author obviously has some knowledge about and experience with the effect that minimum wage legislation bears on businesses and their employees. The essay attempts to debunk arguments that a minimum wage necessarily entails inflation, higher costs, and layoffs. The writer presents his/her views straightforwardly and clearly, although the opinions may not be popular (or accurate) from an employer's perspective.

Still, the author systematically addresses the most typical arguments against the minimum wage and reaches a realistic conclusion. In other words, he/she does not argue that the minimum wage is a panacea; rather, the position advanced is that it is a valuable support to low-wage workers. In addition, the syntax assists the flow of the argument, and the text is easy to follow. The few grammatical mistakes do not markedly distract from the writer's ideas. Considering the time constraints of the exam, the essay pursues its thesis consistently, answers all aspects of the prompt, and develops its argument with lucid prose. For these reasons, the essay earns a "4."

Essay #2—Marginal Pass (Score = 3)

The issue of minimum wage for American workers is definitely a controversial one. Since there are so many aspects of this issue, many conflicting opinions are held concerning what constitutes a fair minimum wage. Because the cost of living changes so frequently in society, minimum wage should definitely change with it.

Some people argue that raising minimum wage constantly will harm, rather than benefit society. They believe that "higher labor costs would be reflected in higher consumer prices," thereby causing unnecessary inflation. They feel that many workers would be needlessly laid off, due to the fact that their employers would not be able to pay higher wages to many workers. Consequently, there are some people who vehemently oppose the raising of minimum wage and cannot see how it would benefit society.

While these arguments are somewhat understandable, the fact still remains that living conditions change over the years, and the average cost of living only continues to grow.

Although people may have survived on a lower salary many years ago, it is entirely unrealistic to think that this same salary will be adequate for those living in the 1990's. For those who are raising a family, it is crucial that they receive a reasonable salary so that their family can function and survive today's standards. Minimum wage should be raised whenever necessary, for people cannot be expected to manage properly unless they are receiving wages which reflect the current cost of living.

The minimum wage for American workers has consistently risen, so it is evident that Congress had seen the changes in society and raised the minimum wage accordingly. It becomes more expensive daily to live comfortably by today's standards. It is obvious that many people feel the need to earn more money, since the cost of living today is so high.

In order for society to continue functioning efficiently, it must adequately meet the growing needs of its people. One such need is to provide a fair minimum wage for workers which coincides with their cost of living.

Scoring Explanation for Essay #2—Marginal Pass

This essay is generally coherent and satisfactorily written, but it offers much less specific information than most typical passing essays. It relies on the repetition of its points rather than their full explication. Thus, the writer's chief problem lies in his/her development of the argument. The essay does more asserting than analyzing; it assumes the reader will accept, without question, its assertions.

The writer concludes, in reasonable fashion, that the cost of living continues to rise and that the minimum wage should correspondingly increase. Rather than presenting specific evidence that it is difficult for workers to keep up with inflation or demonstrating that the minimum wage should periodically increase, the writer merely asserts that these things are true. A personal anecdote or observation could help to illustrate this key point. Nevertheless, the essay reads well and shows an acceptable command of written English. Although it suffers from many distracting problems, they are not sufficiently detrimental to the essay to earn it a score of marginal fail, and thus the essay marginally passes.

Essay #3—Marginal Fail (Score = 2)

The baby begins to cry as the father enters the run-down apartment. He dodges the dripping ceiling and proceeds over to help his wife who is caught between the bargain dinner and the crying child. After soothes the child he goes onto explain that on account of his low wage, there will not be any hot water for a while. We can't have everything, it was either that or the streets.

I don't believe that the minimum wage is high. It is not fair, some people should be expected to live such a low standard. The Adult work force should be given a more fair and reliable wage to support themselves. Then they would gain a better self esteem and, in turn, give their children a better outlook on life.

The minimum wage does not have to be raised for the teenagers. I believe there should be separate minimums for minors and adults. This way a business owner does not have to pay extra for a teenagers incompetence, and the adult worker who is struggling to support a family is much better.

The poverty levels of this country is increasing more and more. If the minimum wages would be lifted for adults it may aliviate some of the poverty. It may also solve some problems for many struggling families who are going homeless, and once your homeless, the minimum wage doesn't matter any more.

Scoring Explanation for Essay #3—Marginal Fail

This essay begins with a compelling vignette that describes the human difficulties of surviving while earning the minimum wage. The writer gives his/her essay a unique and personal feel which interests the reader in the argument. Unfortunately, the rest of the essay does not maintain the promise of the introductory paragraph.

The organization and development of the remainder of the essay lack focus. The author jumps from topic to topic, arguing that the minimum wage is too low, that teenage workers do not need to have the minimum wage raised, and that poverty is increasing throughout the land. None of these topics is adequately explored to support an argument for raising the minimum wage. For example, the essay should address the potential difficulties of having two separate minimum wages, one for teenagers and the other for adults.

Many errors in punctuation and syntax hinder the reader from readily understanding the writer's ideas. Capital letters and spelling provide problems for the writer, and sentences such as "We can't have everything, it was either that or the streets" highlight the writer's difficulty with combining sentences correctly. The writer displays a clear sense of style in this essay, but inadequate development and frequent grammatical errors result in a failing grade.

Essay #4—Fail (Score = 1)

Todays american economy and cost of-living index has change dramatically within the past years. For the value of the dollar has weaken compared to what it was worth in the early 1900 's; thus making the cost of living for low income and disabled people much more difficult than what it was already. Minimum wage law was created to prevent Americans form becoming poor and homeless by raising the minimum wage for to coincid with todays living standards. But now, the standards of living are very difficult and the minimum wage law has become controversial. People feel the law might enuse inflation and consumer prices. But this is not so.

The minimum wage does not pose a threat and should be raise. We live in a low income society. But since minimum wage was raised more have a chance for college.

Minimum wage gives us americans a chance to live a better and enjoyible life; one of the things that makes this country so great. It makes us americans feel as though we are here to live a life, not just survive and never expand beyond what our life could be.

Many people claim that the raise in minimum wage might cause inflation. But before the minimum increased the prices and inflation were at a high. That is why many of us americans demanded a increase.

Scoring Explanation for Essay #4—Fail

This essay does not adequately support its thesis that the minimum wage should be raised. The author reiterates this point several times but never provides compelling reasons why the current minimum wage is too low. The author should develop his premise that raising the minimum wage would allow more people to attend college or to enjoy a better life; as it now stands, the essay's analysis of this complex issue is too simplistic to warrant a passing score. Thus, because the essay makes many claims that are awkward, confusing, and poorly supported, we never get a full view of the issue's true significance.

Furthermore, the essay teems with grammatical and syntactic errors that cause a great deal of difficulty for the reader. Spelling errors abound, and the writer experiences real difficulty in attempting to write complex sentences. Problems with verb tenses are evident. Due to the serious weaknesses in the essay's organization and development, as well as its problems with grammar and syntax, the essay receives a failing score.

Topic 2 Sample Answers

Essay #1—Pass (Score = 4)

As people grow older, they begin to look at themselves and examine who they are. They look at their life and how they go about living it. These introspections can be very reassuring for a person, revealing many strong qualities that provide them with much comfort. However, some people are able to go further and examine every aspect of their lives—including the things they are uncomfortable with.

As I reflect on my life, I am able to discover many positive qualities which I can be very proud of. On the other hand, I am also able to realize some things about myself which I am not comfortable with and would like to change. One such thing is a bad habit I developed in my youth. Ever since I can remember, I've had trouble letting people know what it is I want to do.

Many times I've let people get away with things just because I'm afraid to tell them how I feel or what I want. For some reason, it's always been hard for me to speak my mind.

This inability to communicate my inner feelings has led to many difficulties. In many situations I have wanted to tell someone how I feel but was afraid to. For example, I ended up attending a party where drugs were being used because I wasn't strong enough to tell my friends I didn't want to go. I didn't want to be thought of as a "nerd." Fortunately, I was able to leave the party without incident.

At times dealing with my parents has been difficult because I won't always let them know what I'm thinking. The same thing occurs in relations with teachers, friends and members of the opposite sex. Perhaps if I could be more open, future difficulties could be avoided.

It's difficult to ascertain the source of this problem. Maybe it's because I grew up under the impression that "real men" don't show emotions. Maybe it's just because I'm a quiet person. Whatever the reason, I'd like to change it, and I have been trying. Lately, I've been more able to tell people how I feel and not hold back. I may have finally realized that people aren't going to laugh at me when I tell them how I feel. It's becoming easier to express myself, but it's still difficult. Perhaps as I grow older the problem will disappear. That is my hope, but I intend to continue my periodic, introspective self-analysis to make sure I don't slip.

Scoring Explanation for Essay #1—Pass

The writer begins this essay by speculating about the value of examining one's life and concludes on a similar note. In the body of the essay, the writer explores a habit that he is uncomfortable with and would like to change. The discussion of this problematic habit is well developed and specific, offering both generalizations and illustrations of the ways in which the habit manifests itself.

The writer also attempts to address the origin of the habit, providing several possible reasons for its existence. The essay prompt asks the writer to speculate why changing the habit might be difficult, and the author addresses this topic in the concluding paragraph. In sum, the writer offers a reasonable response that is also a sincere investigation of a personal issue. Few grammatical errors appear, and the sentence structure is relatively complex at times. For all of its positive features, the essay earns a passing score.

Essay #2—Marginal Pass (Score = 3)

In developing habitual behaviors or tendencies one may find himself limited or restrained. One's habits limit the diversity he is able to experience and develop. They, habits, limit your ability to change, learn and experience novelties by always acting in one particular manner.

I find I have various habits that limit my growth as an individual. One specific habit is that of not speaking my thoughts or opinions amongst family and friends. This habit, although its seemingly minor, often limits the capacity and development of a relationship. All the burdens and pressures of planning, "what we should do," are thrown on the shoulders of the individual. The burdens I create can easily be eased by my own input or opinion. No matter how insignificant the input may be, it still causes more of a "mutual agreement."

This habit will be difficult to break since it takes all the pressure off me. Forcing another to decide everything may make my part of the relationship easier. I have grown so accustomed to not giving input that it will be hard for me to start deciding because of the added pressure. However, I believe if I take some pressure, my relationships will develop fully and concretely.

Scoring Explanation for Essay #2—Marginal Pass

This essay contains elevated diction and sophisticated, complex sentences. Although these features often characterize good writing, this writer uses them to mask the weaknesses of his essay. Pompous phrasings attempt to conceal a discussion that is too abstract to make its points clearly.

The author's implied promise to discuss the habit of "not speaking [his] thoughts or opinions amongst family and friends" is never completely fulfilled. The reader is offered few specific examples of the habit, so the writer's speculations about the burdens he creates are less powerful than if they were well illustrated with specific cases in point. The reader is left wondering what precisely is meant by the "burdens and pressures of planning" and how these burdens create problems for the writer.

Similarly, the writer mentions the difficulty involved in altering the habit (because it's easier not to), but this section is obtuse and generalized. The writer has a firm grip on grammar and syntax, and this strength in communication saves the essay from losing its grounding entirely. The ideas suffer from being overly abstract, but they are presented with sufficient clarity to earn a marginally passing score.

Essay #3—Marginal Fail (Score = 2)

Popular psychology tell us that "habit" is a powerful force, compelling us to live out our lives with basically the some behaviors we learned as we grew up. Reassurance in decision making is a significant habit, I'd like to change. In this essay, I will discuss why this may be difficult.

Since the time I could remember, I would always ask my mother or sister, Alex, to help me. In making a decision; for example, clothes I bought, the University I wanted to attend or whether to cut my hair or not. Some of these decision makings, life did not depended on, but asking for their advice-in trying to make my decision—I was assured that I was right.

I know I need to break this habit, but it is difficult for me. Many times I tell myself that I need to make my own decisions. Because Alex and my mother are not going to be there all the time. One of the reasons it is difficult for me is because I always need someone to approve. Someone to say, "yes, you're making the right choice."

Now in college I am begin to make my own decisions without their consents; but I still need to work on it. I am beginning to force myself to do what I want to do whether someone likes it or not. Although I am trying to break away from this habit, it will take a long time to break completely from it. This is because, although I am making some decisions with out their consent, there are other decisions I make in which I feel I need reassurance.

Scoring Explanation for Essay #3—Marginal Fail

The writer reiterates the question to open this rather ordinary response. A specific example is offered to illustrate the difficulty the writer has in making decisions, but it appears in the middle of a sentence wracked with various grammatical errors. The writer has difficulty with punctuation and syntax, and she/he inadvertently creates many awkward and incomplete sentences. In paragraph two, the reader must struggle with a sentence like, "In making a decision; for example, clothes I bought, the University I wanted to attend or whether to cut my hair or not." Still, the writer does attempt to address the question and mentions his/her need for approval as the impediment to change. Rather than exploring this issue, however, the writer merely reasserts it as the conclusion to the essay. The combination of a superficial response with little development and numerous grammatical errors results in a marginally failing essay.

Essay #4—Fail (Score = 1)

A habit becomes a heartbeat that lets us live on. By this, I mean, that it becomes voluntary; once we start that habit until we end it. A habit that I have and I would like to change is massaging and cracking my nuckles when I am nervous.

It is a significant habit because I start massaging my hand and once I finished, it feels relaxed, but what I realized is that it makes my hand shake more. Sometimes I am so nervous, for example when I am about to give speech in Public Speaking class, that I massage my hand so hard—it turns red and swollen. I cause myself a lot of pain!

I finished massaging my hand, Well, what can I do now? I then start cracking my nuckles(fingers). I know one day I am going to end up with arthritus if I keep on doing this! Sometimes when I do it, it feels good, but other times I over do it. I usually over do it by cracking my fingers so much that they don't want to crack no more. Then they start hurting very much.

I guess I don't realize what pain I am causing myself with this habit. For me it has become a heartbeat. I can't stop it This is how this habit works. Maybe I forget about being nervous. Because I am feeling pain—That is what I think, maybe.

Somehow I think it will be difficult to stop this habit. I don't think when I massage and crack my fingers It just happens. It became—something to do when I am nervous. A painful Heartbeat that will probably go on forever until I die. By then the doctors would of cut of my hands or maybe I cut them of. Who knows what will happen with this habit of mine.

Scoring Explanation for Essay #4—Fail

This essay describes a habit of the author; beyond this surface gesture, however, it does not engage with the essay prompt. The essay is confusing and does not develop any thesis other than describing the author cracking his/her knuckles. Since the thesis itself is so trivial, the author cannot develop a compelling response to the topic at hand.

Frequent grammatical mistakes make the essay very difficult to follow. Sentences such as, "By then the doctors would of cut of my hands or maybe I cut them of," make very little sense and do not contribute to building an effective piece of writing. In the frequent metaphoric comparisons between cracking knuckles and a heartbeat, the author repeatedly attempts to bring a poetic style into the essay, but the endless repetitiveness of this move stifles any life it would allow the essay. A poor thesis, little development, and excessive grammatical mistakes result in a failing grade.

Practice Test 2

CBEST

This test is also offered online at the REA Study Center (*www.rea.com/studycenter*). We highly recommend that you take the computerized version of the exam to simulate test-day conditions and to receive these added benefits:

- **Timed testing conditions**—Gauge how much time you can spend on each question.

- **Automatic scoring**—Find out how you did on the test, instantly.

- **On-screen detailed explanations of answers**—Learn not just the correct answers, but also why the other answer choices are incorrect.

- **Diagnostic score reports**—Pinpoint where you're strongest and where you need to focus your study.

ANSWER SHEET – PRACTICE TEST 2

Section 1: Reading

1. Ⓐ Ⓑ Ⓒ Ⓓ Ⓔ
2. Ⓐ Ⓑ Ⓒ Ⓓ Ⓔ
3. Ⓐ Ⓑ Ⓒ Ⓓ Ⓔ
4. Ⓐ Ⓑ Ⓒ Ⓓ Ⓔ
5. Ⓐ Ⓑ Ⓒ Ⓓ Ⓔ
6. Ⓐ Ⓑ Ⓒ Ⓓ Ⓔ
7. Ⓐ Ⓑ Ⓒ Ⓓ Ⓔ
8. Ⓐ Ⓑ Ⓒ Ⓓ Ⓔ
9. Ⓐ Ⓑ Ⓒ Ⓓ Ⓔ
10. Ⓐ Ⓑ Ⓒ Ⓓ Ⓔ
11. Ⓐ Ⓑ Ⓒ Ⓓ Ⓔ
12. Ⓐ Ⓑ Ⓒ Ⓓ Ⓔ
13. Ⓐ Ⓑ Ⓒ Ⓓ Ⓔ
14. Ⓐ Ⓑ Ⓒ Ⓓ Ⓔ
15. Ⓐ Ⓑ Ⓒ Ⓓ Ⓔ
16. Ⓐ Ⓑ Ⓒ Ⓓ Ⓔ
17. Ⓐ Ⓑ Ⓒ Ⓓ Ⓔ
18. Ⓐ Ⓑ Ⓒ Ⓓ Ⓔ
19. Ⓐ Ⓑ Ⓒ Ⓓ Ⓔ
20. Ⓐ Ⓑ Ⓒ Ⓓ Ⓔ

21. Ⓐ Ⓑ Ⓒ Ⓓ Ⓔ
22. Ⓐ Ⓑ Ⓒ Ⓓ Ⓔ
23. Ⓐ Ⓑ Ⓒ Ⓓ Ⓔ
24. Ⓐ Ⓑ Ⓒ Ⓓ Ⓔ
25. Ⓐ Ⓑ Ⓒ Ⓓ Ⓔ
26. Ⓐ Ⓑ Ⓒ Ⓓ Ⓔ
27. Ⓐ Ⓑ Ⓒ Ⓓ Ⓔ
28. Ⓐ Ⓑ Ⓒ Ⓓ Ⓔ
29. Ⓐ Ⓑ Ⓒ Ⓓ Ⓔ
30. Ⓐ Ⓑ Ⓒ Ⓓ Ⓔ
31. Ⓐ Ⓑ Ⓒ Ⓓ Ⓔ
32. Ⓐ Ⓑ Ⓒ Ⓓ Ⓔ
33. Ⓐ Ⓑ Ⓒ Ⓓ Ⓔ
34. Ⓐ Ⓑ Ⓒ Ⓓ Ⓔ
35. Ⓐ Ⓑ Ⓒ Ⓓ Ⓔ
36. Ⓐ Ⓑ Ⓒ Ⓓ Ⓔ
37. Ⓐ Ⓑ Ⓒ Ⓓ Ⓔ
38. Ⓐ Ⓑ Ⓒ Ⓓ Ⓔ
39. Ⓐ Ⓑ Ⓒ Ⓓ Ⓔ
40. Ⓐ Ⓑ Ⓒ Ⓓ Ⓔ

41. Ⓐ Ⓑ Ⓒ Ⓓ Ⓔ
42. Ⓐ Ⓑ Ⓒ Ⓓ Ⓔ
43. Ⓐ Ⓑ Ⓒ Ⓓ Ⓔ
44. Ⓐ Ⓑ Ⓒ Ⓓ Ⓔ
45. Ⓐ Ⓑ Ⓒ Ⓓ Ⓔ
46. Ⓐ Ⓑ Ⓒ Ⓓ Ⓔ
47. Ⓐ Ⓑ Ⓒ Ⓓ Ⓔ
48. Ⓐ Ⓑ Ⓒ Ⓓ Ⓔ
49. Ⓐ Ⓑ Ⓒ Ⓓ Ⓔ
50. Ⓐ Ⓑ Ⓒ Ⓓ Ⓔ

PRACTICE TEST 2

Section 1: Reading

DIRECTIONS: One or more questions follow each statement or passage in this test. The question(s) are based on the content of the passage. After you have read a statement or passage, select the best answer to each question from among the five possible choices. Your answers to the questions should be based on the stated (literal) or implied (inferential) information given in the statement or passage. Mark all answers on your answer sheet. Note: You will encounter some passages with numbered sentences, blank spaces, or underscored words and phrases. These cues are provided on the CBEST for your reference in answering the questions that follow the relevant passages.

Questions 1–3 refer to the following passage:

The teaching apprentice initiated the discussion in a clear and well-prepared manner. To _____ the lecture topic the teaching apprentice utilized overhead transparencies of both lexicon and abstract representation to better _____ the theories behind various pedagogical concepts. The class culminated whereby students established enthymemes extrapolated from the class discussion. The class maintained integrity and continuity.

1. Which of these grouped words, if inserted *in order* into the passage's blank lines, would address the logical sequencing of the narrative?

    A. refute; criticize

    B. conflate; discern

    C. laud; consider

    D. support; illustrate

    E. undermine; explain

2. The definition of the term pedagogical as used in the sentence means

    A. intelligent.

    B. abstract.

    C. meaningless.

    D.   obtuse.

    E.   academic.

3.   The passage suggests that the author's classroom experience was

    A.   a needless waste of time and energy.

    B.   intelligible and pragmatic.

    C.   haphazard and disorderly.

    D.   too advanced and complicated.

    E.   superfluous and derogatory.

Questions 4–6 refer to the following passage:

To receive an "A" on a paper in this class one must write sophisticated prose. The criteria will be based on the complexity of both content and expression. The grade will require a demonstration of obvious familiarity with primary texts, as well as additional readings of the course and secondary materials and research sources. An effective combination of personal opinion and outside sources will also be required. Proficiency in organizational skills, format, rhetoric, grammar, syntax, and sentence structure is a must. An additional requirement is a thoroughly proofread essay resulting in no distracting mechanical errors with the possible exception of occasional arguable usage.

4.   To receive an "A" grade in the above class, the student must

    A.   turn in a proofread paper with no punctuation errors and demonstrate an understanding of the reading material.

    B.   write an effective paper without mistakes and with an abundance of secondary source materials.

    C.   turn in a thoughtful paper with no corrections as well as demonstrate a proficiency of organizational skills, such as format, rhetoric, and grammar.

    D.   write an intelligent paper without regard for grammar, syntax, or rhetorical strategies, with the possible exception of occasional arguable usage.

    E.   write about arguable strategies and demonstrate an understanding of secondary source materials and research sources.

5. What does the author mean by "sophisticated prose"?

    A. A readable text that does not make sense.

    B. A readable text made up of knowledgeable or thoughtful language.

    C. A readable text consisting of pompous or ostentatious language.

    D. A readable text made up of poetic metaphor.

    E. A readable text that reflects the author's antecedents.

6. When the author of the passage refers to the "primary texts," he means

    A. the reference materials, such as the dictionary, encyclopedia, thesaurus, etc.

    B. the primary note pages, works cited page, or preliminary rough draft page.

    C. the source or principal text in the assignment.

    D. the first text written about a certain subject.

    E. the beginning text in a numbered series of texts.

Questions 7–10 refer to the following passage:

Language not only expresses an individual's ideology, it also sets parameters while it persuades and influences the discourse in the community that hears and interprets its meaning. Therefore, the language of failure should not be present in the learning environment (i.e., the classroom) because it will have a prohibitive impact on the students' desire to learn as well as a negative influence on the students' self-esteem.

The *Oxford English Dictionary* defines *failure* as a fault, a shortcoming, a lack of success, a person who turns out unsuccessfully, becoming insolvent, etc. We as educators might well ask ourselves if this is the sort of doctrine that we want to permeate our classrooms. Perhaps our own University axiom, *mens agitat molem* (the mind can move mountains), will help us discover if, indeed, the concepts of failure are really the types of influences we wish to introduce to impressionable new students. Is the mind capable of moving a mountain when it is already convinced it cannot?

One must remain aware that individuals acquire knowledge at independent rates of speed. Certainly no one would suggest that one infant "failed" the art of learning to walk because she acquired the skill two months behind her infant counterpart. Would anyone suggest that infant number one *failed* walking? Of course not. What would a mentor project to either toddler were he to suggest that a slower acquisition of walking skills implied failure? Yet we as educators feel the need to suggest student A failed due to the slower procurement of abstract concepts than student B. It is absolutely essential to shift the learning focus from failure to success.

7.   Which of the following statements best conveys the meaning of the passage?

    A.   Learning is something that happens at different speeds and is, therefore, natural.

    B.   Instructors need to be sensitive to students' individual needs.

    C.   Instructors need to shift the educational focus from failure to success in learning environments.

    D.   Failure is a potential hazard in the classroom and should be avoided at all costs.

    E.   Too much emphasis is placed on grades and not enough on education.

8.   As stated in the context of the passage, what does <u>University axiom</u> mean?

    A.   University Latin

    B.   University motto

    C.   University rhetoric

    D.   University sophomore

    E.   University legend

9.   According to the passage, what will have a negative effect on student self-esteem?

    A.   The rhetoric of diction

    B.   The slower procurement of abstract concepts

    C.   The learning focus from failure to success

    D.   The language of failure

    E.   The *Oxford English Dictionary*

10. According to the passage, what does language do besides aid individual expression?

    A. It establishes individual thought and tells of individual philosophies.

    B. It paints visual images and articulates individual declaration.

    C. It suggests individual axioms and community philosophy.

    D. It persuades and influences the discourse in the community that hears and interprets its meaning.

    E. It manipulates the truisms and reiterates ideologies.

Questions 11–13 refer to the following passage:

Life in seventeenth-century England was tempestuous indeed. It was a time when religious and secular confrontations resulted in new social abstractions, paradoxes, and ironies. The poet-pastor Robert Herrick (1591-1674) illustrates the ability of lyric poetry to serve not only as an adornment of the era, but as social communiqué, as well. Herrick's Mayday celebration poem, "Corinna's Going A-Maying," serves as both an argument against conservative religious dogma and as a response to specific Puritan manifestos. Herrick incorporates abundant Greco-Roman <u>tropes</u> into "Corinna" in order to construct a stylized response to Puritanism based upon traditional structure, symmetry, and thematic representation.

11. The author's attitude toward the subject is one of

    A. lethargy.
    B. apathy.
    C. objectivity.
    D. intensity.
    E. synergy.

12. The passage fundamentally suggests that

    A. Puritanism is based upon a traditional structure, symmetry, and thematic representation.

    B. lyric poetry has the ability to serve not only as an adornment of an era, but also as social communiqué.

    C. life in seventeenth-century England was tempestuous indeed.

D.   the seventeenth century was a time of religious and secular confrontations, resulting in new social abstractions, paradoxes, and ironies.

E.   the poet-pastor Robert Herrick was a critic of Puritanism.

13. As used in the passage, the word <u>trope</u> means

A.   a group of people, animals, etc., such as a herd, a flock, a band, and so on.

B.   a style of writing in the Greek or Roman language.

C.   a desire to travel to Greece or Rome.

D.   the use of a word in a figurative sense; a figure of speech; figurative language.

E.   Italian philosophy, ideology, heritage, culture, etc.

Questions 14–17 refer to the following passage:

A Critic can be equivalent to "a person who pronounces judgement; especially a *Censurer*." Since the late sixteenth century, the title of Critic has embodied implied meanings such as "professionalism" and "a person *skilled* in textual criticism." Thereby, the title insinuates a distinction of hierarchy among laborers, craftsmen, and the "working class" in general. "Censure" has <u>etymological</u> connotations that date back to the late Middle Ages, "critical recension or revision (along with) expression(s) of disapproval, to give opinion, assess critically, find fault, reprove, blame, pronounce sentence," and "condemnatory (especially ecclesiastical) judgement, opinion, correction," which all furthermore suggest a rather antagonistic posture in relationship to the Humanities. The position of critic is tenuous, as they can serve both as censure or social analyst and commentator. Subsequently, the word is loaded with negative innuendoes, but also innuendoes that denote authority, repression, and judicial propriety. In essence, the Critic who chooses to take the point-of-view of the Censure, sits on the mountaintop, not for a better view of literature, but to establish a false sense of superiority over it in relationship to the Author (as well as the reader for that matter).

14. The passage suggests that

    A. critics are good for the social order.

    B. the position of critic is tenuous as they can serve both as censure or social analyst and commentator.

    C. critics attempt to establish a false sense of superiority over the author and the reader as well.

    D. humanitarians do not make good critics as they are too emotional and not callous or impartial enough.

    E. critics do not serve any valuable social function and, therefore, the position should be eliminated.

15. The passage indicates that the art of criticism

    A. is a modern phenomenon.

    B. is a socially destructive force.

    C. is a thought-provoking entity.

    D. began at around the same time as the Civil War.

    E. dates back to the Middle Ages.

16. Which of the following would make the best title for the passage you just read?

    A. Critical Analysis Ruins Literature for the Rest of Us

    B. Critics Assume a False Superiority Thereby Rendering Critical Judgement Null and Void

    C. The Implications and Connotations of the Critic as Author

    D. Criticism is Synonymous with Censorship

    E. The Critic as Both Judge and Jury

17. What does the term <u>etymological</u> mean as it is used in the passage?

    A. The history of the Middle Ages

    B. The history of a word

    C. The history of critical analysis

    D. The history of literature

    E. The history of censorship

Questions 18–20 refer to the following passage:

The early decades of the fifteenth century was a period in our history when English took a "great (linguistic) vowel shift" by redistributing the vowel pronunciation and configuration. Each vowel changed its sound quality, but the distinction between one vowel and the next was maintained. There was a restructuring of the sounds and patterns of communication, as well. One has to conclude that a concurrent stress and exhilaration was occurring within the parameters of the literate society as well. Musicians, artists, poets, and authors all must have relished the new freedom and experimentation that was now possible with the new-found linguistic shifts.

18. The passage tells about

   A. a shift in vowel pronunciation and configuration.

   B. a fifteenth-century renaissance for musicians, artists, poets, and authors.

   C. a newfound linguistic freedom from conventional sound and linguistic structure.

   D. various vowel stresses and their effect on artistic expression.

   E. the early decades of the fifteenth century.

19. What is the meaning of the word linguistic as used in the passage?

   A. Artistic freedom

   B. Verbal or rhetorical

   C. Social or expressive

   D. Vowel configuration

   E. Historical or archaic

20. Because "each vowel changed its sound quality"

   A. there was a restructuring of the sounds and patterns of communication.

   B. language could never be spoken in the same way again.

   C. artists had to develop new means of expression.

   D. communication went through a divergent change of status and culture.

   E. Shakespeare could write sonnets in Middle English and not Old English.

Questions 21–24 refer to the following passage:

Lead poisoning is considered by health authorities to be the most common and devastating environmental disease of young children. According to studies, it affects 15% to 20% of urban children and from 50% to 75% of inner-city, poor children. As a result of a legal settlement in July 1991, all California MediCal-eligible children, ages one through five, will now be routinely screened annually for lead poisoning. Experts estimate that more than 50,000 cases will be detected in California because of the newly mandated tests. This will halt at an early stage a disease that leads to learning disabilities and life-threatening disorders.

21. Lead poisoning among young children, if not detected early, can lead to

    A.   physical disabilities.
    B.   heart disease.
    C.   liver disease.
    D.   social disease.
    E.   learning disabilities and death.

22. The new mandate to screen all young children for lead poisoning is required of

    A.   all young children in California.
    B.   all children with learning disabilities.
    C.   all MediCal-eligible children, ages one through five, in California.
    D.   all minority children in inner cities.
    E.   all school-age children.

23. The percentages suggest that more cases of lead poisoning are found among

    A.   children in rural areas.
    B.   inner-city children.
    C.   immigrant children.
    D.   upper-middle class children.
    E.   adopted children.

24. The ultimate goal of the newly mandated tests is to

    A.   bring more monies into inner-city medical programs.

    B.   bring more health-care professionals into California's inner cities.

    C.   alleviate over-crowding in California's public schools.

    D.   screen more test subjects to develop more accurate statistical data.

    E.   halt at an early stage a disease that leads to learning disabilities and life-threatening disorders.

Questions 25 and 26 refer to the following passage:

The social ostracizing of male hairdressers and ballet dancers, versus the female mechanic or construction worker, presents the case that society classifies individuals by gender. But are these boundaries really changing? That is, what are the implications of a woman in a traditionally male career, who is "surprised" by another female in a traditional male career? What does that say about gender roles?

25. The passage asks the reader to

    A.   ostracize various individuals who step outside conventional gender roles.

    B.   change social boundaries by taking on non-traditional jobs.

    C.   accept people who take on jobs traditionally occupied by the opposite sex.

    D.   classify individuals by gender.

    E.   question whether traditional gender boundaries are changing or not.

26. As it is used in the passage, what does social ostracizing mean?

    A.   Social acceptance

    B.   Social pressure

    C.   Social traditions

    D.   Social alienation

    E.   Social examination

Questions 27 and 28 refer to the following passage:

The paradigm of a universal rational mind implies a form of stagnation, rigidity or at the very least, an intellectual elitist form of hierarchy. It suggests that everyone in a discourse community is of an equal mind, or should be. If members of a rhetorical community are not of the same equal mind, then there is an implication that their thinking is skewed by the clutter of culture, politics, and commitment. Additionally, it insinuates a discourse community predicated upon a single universal agenda. Because, after all, rhetoric is argumentation with an agenda.

27. The passage implies that

    A. discourse communities allow for individual thought and freedom of expression.

    B. everyone in a discourse community is of a similar mind, and is, therefore, suspect.

    C. members of a rhetorical community are more liberal than those of a discourse community.

    D. rhetoric is argumentation with an agenda and is, therefore, valuable.

    E. rhetoric is void of agenda and is biased.

28. What does the term paradigm mean?

    A. Model or standard

    B. Group or community

    C. Language or rhetoric

    D. Apathy or agenda

    E. Social order or intellectual

Questions 29 and 30 refer to the following passage:

A 150-million-year-old allosaurus skeleton that appears to be intact was found on September 9, 1991, by a Swiss team in north-central Wyoming. This Zurich-based company sells fossils to museums. They were digging on private property, but the fossil actually showed up on federal land.

Immediately, the federal government sealed off the site along the foot of the Big Horn Mountains in Wyoming and deployed rangers from the Bureau of Land Management to prevent vandalism. Paleontologists believe that this discovery could lead them to a vast dinosaur graveyard.

29. The passage you just read can best be utilized by a classroom teacher in

    A.   reading.

    B.   mathematics.

    C.   biology.

    D.   zoology.

    E.   literature.

30. The main idea of the passage is

    A.   government intervention into private matters.

    B.   world communities working together in a chosen field.

    C.   private versus public ownership of historical artifacts.

    D.   dinosaurs once lived in Wyoming.

    E.   this discovery could lead to a vast dinosaur graveyard.

Questions 31–33 refer to the following passage:

Looking specifically at animal symbols and what they represent allows one to see a diversified menagerie of animal representations as social commentary, along with their implications of metaphors, like the aristocratic lion, the perfunctory alley cat, and the domesticated dog. Each creature in its own way serves as a metaphor for British imperialistic progressions and colonial expansion. That is, *imperialism* as capitalistic encroachment and *colonialism* as territorial usurpation with governmental despotic autonomy.

31. The main idea of the passage is

   A. literary animal representations can serve as social symbols.

   B. animal symbols are British in nature and are, therefore, aristocratic.

   C. government organizations manifest themselves in literature as a pack of animals.

   D. literary lions are metaphors for perfunctory alley cats.

   E. colonial expansion and imperialism are mainly terms that apply to dogs and cats.

32. What is a metaphor?

   A. A sentence that ends in a question

   B. A theory of colonialism

   C. A figure of speech containing an implied comparison

   D. Two words that mean the same thing

   E. An abstract sentence where the verb comes before the noun

33. In the passage, imperialism and colonialism are defined, respectively, as

   A. territorial arrangement and economic organization.

   B. economic wealth and territorial abundance.

   C. financial infringement and territorial confiscation.

   D. financial freedom and territorial generosity.

   E. land development and economic liberation.

Questions 34 and 35 refer to the following passage:

San Francisco was named the world's favorite travel destination in the prestigious 1991 *Condé Nast Traveler* magazine poll. It was considered the best city in the world that year, beating out Florence, Italy (No. 2), and London and Vienna, which tied for No. 3. A red-carpet gala in the City Hall rotunda is planned in which Mayor Agnos will laud the city's 60,000 tourism-industry workers, including hotel maids, taxi drivers, bellhops, and others in the local hospitality industry.

34. An appropriate title for the preceding passage might be

    A. San Francisco: The World's Favorite Travel Destination

    B. A Celebration for Tourism Workers

    C. San Francisco Mayor to Applaud Industry Workers

    D. San Francisco's Tourism Industry Workers are the Best in the World

    E. London, Florence, and Vienna: Favorite Travel Destinations

35. A paraphrase of the above passage might be

    A. industry workers are better in San Francisco than in London or Italy.

    B. tourism is more popular in U. S. cities than in European cities.

    C. San Francisco's mayor is sensitive to the needs of industry workers.

    D. industry workers are responsible for San Francisco's increase in tourism.

    E. every year *Condé Nast Traveler* magazine polls tourists and selects a favorite destination spot based upon the result of those polls.

Questions 36–38 refer to the following passage:

Enrollment figures show that by 2005, the majority of California's high school graduates were non-white and that by 2006, one-third of all the nation's students came from minority groups. Nationally, the total non-white and Hispanic student population for all grade levels increased from 10.4 million in 2005–2006 to 13.7 million in 2006–2007. The figures suggest that now, more than ever, equal educational opportunity for all students must be our nation's top priority.

36. The preceding passage suggests that

   A. the nation's educational system is working just fine.

   B. something needs to be done to reduce the growing numbers of minority students in the school system.

   C. urgent educational reform is needed to provide equal opportunity for all students.

   D. a single language system is necessary.

   E. students require additional help with studies outside the classroom.

37. The passage suggests that

   A. if the trend continues, most students will be native speakers of English by the year 2020.

   B. if the trend continues, most students will want to speak English as their language of choice.

   C. English will not be spoken in the California public school system.

   D. all minority groups will absorb English.

   E. English and English as a Second Language programs will need to be implemented accordingly.

38. What does the passage suggest the "number one priority" facing schools must be?

    A. More minority students and more classrooms

    B. More qualified teachers to deal with the influx of minority students

    C. More bilingual teachers to deal with the influx of minority students

    D. Equal time spent on bilingual and multicultural education and instruction

    E. Equal educational opportunities for all students

Questions 39–41 refer to the following passage:

John W. Quinney's speech is a declaration not of independence but a declaration of reproach seeking recompense. Quinney's oratory style is as concise as his language is <u>laconic</u>. He leaves no room for misinterpretation as he opens his address referring to the constituents as a race "of people, who occupy by conquest, or have usurped the possession of the territories of my fathers, and have laid…a train of terrible miseries."

Articulate and powerful, *Quinney's Speech* is not only a caustic political editorial upon the state of the Americas circa 1854, it is also poignant and dignified commentary on the effort put forth by the assimilated Native Americans to preserve their land, their nations, their heritage, and their traditions.

39. The author's style in addressing the issues in the passage is

    A. biased.

    B. acrimonious.

    C. impertinent.

    D. dulcet.

    E. objective.

40. The passage suggests Quinney's speech is about

   A. Americans preserving their lands, their nations, their heritage, and their traditions.

   B. American's caustic political views.

   C. an assertion of condemnation seeking compensation.

   D. Americans helping indigenous native peoples.

   E. a series of speeches given to appease and explain America's usurpation of territories.

41. What does laconic mean?

   A. Depressed

   B. Concise

   C. Apologetic

   D. Sentimental

   E. Incensed

Questions 42–44 refer to the following passage:

The Matsushita Electric Industrial Company in Japan has developed a computer program that can use photographs of faces to predict the aging process and, also, how an unborn child will look. The system can show how a couple will look after 40 years of marriage and how newlyweds' future children will look. The computer analyzes facial characteristics from a photograph based on shading and color difference, and then creates a three-dimensional model in its memory. The system consists of a personal computer with a program and circuit board and will soon be marketed by the Matsushita Company.

42. The main idea in the passage is

   A. a computer will be able to show the aging process.

   B. a computer program will choose the right mate.

   C. a computer program will predict the number of children a couple will spawn.

   D. a computer program will predict the look of unborn children and the aged look of their parents.

   E. a computer program will analyze photographs accurately.

43. The program works by

    A. darkening shaded areas of a photograph.

    B. creating a three-dimensional model in the computer's memory.

    C. clairvoyantly predicting the future.

    D. circuit boards and chips.

    E. understanding concepts of aging via color shading.

44. What will result from this new computer system developed in Japan?

    A. The U.S. will follow up by developing an even more sophisticated digitally enhanced computer scanning program.

    B. Competition among computer manufactures will become even more intense.

    C. Japan's economy will skyrocket.

    D. Law enforcement agencies will incorporate this new computer technology into their crime-fighting techniques.

    E. The passage does not suggest any information about what effects this technology will have.

Questions 45 and 46 refer to the following:

On September 17, 1991, a communications power failure brought New York's three major airports to a virtual stop for several hours. Air traffic control centers communicate with planes through a network of radio towers linked to them by telephone. _____ this power failure, local air traffic control centers could not communicate properly amongst themselves or with other U.S. airports.

45. Which of these grouped words or phrases, if inserted into the passage's blank lines, would address the logical sequencing and progression of the narrative?

    A. Despite

    B. Notwithstanding

    C. Because of

    D. In lieu of

    E. Vis-à-vis

46. What is the main idea of the passage?

    A. Air traffic control centers could not communicate properly, thus disrupting airport operations.

    B. Air traffic control centers are high-stress environments, thus leading to frequent airport disruptions.

    C. Airports cannot function properly without assistance from air traffic control centers.

    D. Airports can be shut down at any moment, so allow for alternate means of transportation.

    E. Airports can be shut down for hours, so allow for extra time when making air travel plans.

Questions 47–50 refer to the following passage:

New health research shows that regular <u>vigorous</u> exercise during the middle and late years of life not only keeps the heart healthy, but may also protect against colon cancer, one of the major killers in the United States. The researchers in the study compared the rate of colon cancer among those who were physically inactive with those who were either active or highly active. The study covered 17,148 men age 30 to 79. Among the men judged to be inactive, there were 55 cases of colon cancer; among those moderately active, there were 11; and only 10 cases of colon cancer were found among the very active ones.

47. Which of the following would make an appropriate title for the passage?

    A. Colon Cancer, the Deadly Killer

    B. Findings on Colon Cancer: Bleak at Best

    C. Regular Exercise May Prevent Colon Cancer

    D. Latest Results of Colon Cancer Research

    E. Various Ways to Prevent Colon Cancer

48. What is the main idea of the passage?

    A. American men do not exercise enough.

    B. Americans are overweight, and that leads to heart disease.

    C. Regular vigorous exercise should be limited to the later stages of the adult male's life.

    D. Regular vigorous exercise is only beneficial after the age of 30.

    E. Vigorous exercise during the middle and late years of life may protect against colon cancer.

49. What is the meaning of the term <u>vigorous</u>?

    A. Energetic

    B. Constant

    C. Burning

    D. Lethargic

    E. Languorous

50. What major component is excluded from the study?

    A. It does not clearly define what "vigorous exercise" is.

    B. It does not address other forms of cancer.

    C. It does not include diseases outside the United States.

    D. It does not include women of the same age group.

    E. It does not include ways of living with cancer.

Answer Key

Section 1: Reading

1.	D	14.	B	27.	B	40.	C
2.	E	15.	E	28.	A	41.	B
3.	B	16.	C	29.	D	42.	D
4.	A	17.	B	30.	E	43.	B
5.	B	18.	A	31.	A	44.	E
6.	C	19.	B	32.	C	45.	C
7.	C	20.	A	33.	C	46.	A
8.	B	21.	E	34.	A	47.	C
9.	D	22.	C	35.	E	48.	E
10.	D	23.	B	36.	C	49.	A
11.	C	24.	E	37.	E	50.	D
12.	B	25.	E	38.	E		
13.	D	26.	D	39.	E		

PRACTICE TEST 2 – Detailed Explanations of Answers

Section 1: Reading

1. **D**

   A teaching assistant would be expected to lay the foundation for her lecture and then present greater detail by way of example, or as the passage puts it, "illustration." Someone in this position, having set this task for herself, would not be prone to refuting her own lecture notes (A), attempting to cause confusion (B), reciting praise (C), or perhaps least of all, working to subvert the lecture topic she herself had elected to teach.

2. **E**

   The definition of the term "pedagogical" is (E) "academic." The answers (A) "intelligent," (B) "abstract," (C) "meaningless," and (D) "obtuse" are incorrect.

3. **B**

   The author's classroom experience was (B) intelligible (understandable) and pragmatic (practical or utilitarian). The passage gives credence to this by the author's use of phrases like "clear and well prepared." Answers (A), (C), and (E) suggest the opposite of a positive experience, and there is no evidence given that the experience was too advanced or complicated (D).

4. **A**

   The last sentence in these instructions tells the student that the paper must be proofread with no "mechanical" (punctuation) errors. The third sentence states that an understanding of the reading material is required. Answers (B) and (C) contain only a portion of the needed requirements, while (D) and (E) are completely inaccurate. Thus, (A) is the correct answer.

5. **B**

   As used in the passage, the term "sophisticated prose" means that the student must write a readable paper using thoughtful language, thereby demonstrating a familiarity with the primary text. Answers (A), (C), (D), and (E) all contain language that suggests the opposite of a readable paper.

6. **C**

A primary text is the source material, main, or principal text used in an assignment. The remaining answers (A), (B), (D), and (E) refer to either secondary materials or reference sources.

7. **C**

The passage suggests that education is primarily based on failure as negative reinforcement and that, in order to create a more productive and positive learning environment, the emphasis must shift to success. While answers (A), (B), and (E) may be correct, they are not the main idea of the passage. (D) is simply a statement that is not based upon any factual evidence whatsoever. Therefore, (C) is the correct answer.

8. **B**

An "axiom" in this case is another word for "motto." It can also mean an accepted truism or principle, which would also apply here. Answers (A), (C), (D), and (E) are erroneous definitions and, therefore (B), University motto or principle is the correct answer.

9. **D**

The passage states that "the language of failure…will have a prohibitive impact on the students' self-esteem," and, thus, (D) is the correct answer. Answers (A), (B), (C), and (E) do not apply in this case.

10. **D**

The first paragraph of the passage tells the reader that, in addition to personal expression, language also has the power to "persuade and influence." While answers (A), (B), (C), and (E) may indeed be attributes of language, they are not focused upon in the passage.

11. **C**

The author remains objective throughout the passage. That is, he remains impartial and factual. Answer (A), "lethargy," means "sluggish," (B), "apathy" means "unconcerned." (D), "intensity" means "vehement" or "fierce," and (E), "synergy" means "fellowship" or "union," and thus, these definitions do not apply.

12. **B**

   The third sentence suggests that poetry has the ability to serve both as an adornment or embellishment of an era and as a social commentary. The passage fundamentally suggests that poetry is more than just lyrical fluff, it is a means of social analysis, protest, and interpretation. While (A), (C), (D), and (E) are components of the passage, they are not the passage's main topic.

13. **D**

   The word <u>trope</u> means that a word is used in a figurative sense. That is, it conjures images of Greco-Roman representations. Answer (A) is a troop; (B), (C), and (E) are types of terminology that do not apply.

14. **B**

   The passage suggests that a critic is a viable political force that serves both as a censure and a social commentator. Answers (A), (C), (D), and (E) are subjective answers and are, therefore, inappropriate.

15. **E**

   The passage states that the etymology of the word "censure" dates to the Middle Ages, suggesting that it was in use at that time. The passage also states that a critic can also be equivalent to a censurer. It, therefore, could not be (A), a modern phenomenon or (D), developed around the time of the Civil War. Answers (B) and (C) are not addressed in the passage, leaving (E) as the best answer.

16. **C**

   The passage addresses both the implications (indications) and the connotations (meaning) associated with the role of the critic as author. Answers (B), (D), and (E) are only alluded to, while (A) is a supposition. Thus, (C) is the correct answer.

17. **B**

   <u>Etymology</u> is the study of the history and/or origin of a word. This definition renders the remaining answers false.

18. **A**

   The passage tells of the "great (linguistic) vowel shift" of the early fifteenth century. While the passage speaks of (B) an artistic renaissance, (C) new linguistic freedoms, (D) effects on artistic expression, and (E) the early decades of the century, these are all results of the shift and not the shift itself. The shift is what the passage is about. Thus, (A) is the correct answer.

19. **B**

In this case, <u>linguistic</u> refers to "speaking, talking, verbiage, and/or the act of oration." (A), (C), (D), and (E) are not acceptable definitions for the word "linguistic." Consequently, (B) "verbal or rhetorical" is the correct answer.

20. **A**

Answers (B), (C), and (D) are generalized answers resulting from the vowel shift, while (E) is simply extraneous. (A) is a direct result of the shift and is quoted directly from the passage. Therefore, (A) is the correct answer.

21. **E**

The passage states that lead poisoning leads to learning disabilities and possibly even death. Choice (A) is too broad, (B) and (C) are not directly addressed, and (D) is inappropriate, leaving (E) as the correct answer.

22. **C**

The passage states that "all California MediCal-eligible children, ages one through five, will now be routinely screened." Answer choices (A) children in California, (B) children with learning disabilities, (D) minority children, and (E) school-age children are generalities not stated in the passage. Only (C) is clearly stated in the passage.

23. **B**

The statistics suggest that inner-city children are at the greatest risk from lead poisoning. The statistics do not support answers (A), (C), (D), and (E), leaving (B) as the only legitimate answer.

24. **E**

The last sentence of the passage suggests that testing will catch the disease "at an early stage" and prevent serious disorders. Answers (A), (B), (C), and (D) do not address this ultimate goal of the testing program. Only answer (E) reiterates the program's ultimate purpose.

25. **E**

    The passage asks the reader to question traditional gender issues. The punctuation at the end of the passage affirms this. (A), (B), (C), and (D) do not assert questions. Rather, they suggest a declarative action or stance to be taken regarding social gender issues. Only (E) addresses the passage's questioning of gender roles; therefore, (E) is the correct answer.

26. **D**

    To "ostracize" is "to alienate, exile, or banish." (A) "acceptance," (B) "pressure," (C) "traditions," and (E) "examination" are false definitions and are incorrect.

27. **B**

    The passage states that discourse communities are of similar mindsets, thus making them suspect. (A), (C), (D), and (E) do not address this issue directly. Only (B) reiterates the second sentence of the passage; therefore, it is the correct answer.

28. **A**

    The definition of the noun <u>paradigm</u> is that it is "a model, criterion, or standard that others follow or by which they are measured." Thus, (A), model or standard, is the correct answer.

29. **D**

    While the issues surrounding the allosaurus can be applied to several academic disciplines, including (A) reading, (E) literature, and (C) biology, the scientific study of living organisms, (D) zoology, is the appropriate answer.

30. **E**

    Answers (A), (B), (C), and (D) are part of, but not the main idea, of the passage. Only (E) encompasses the complete or "main idea" of the passage.

31. **A**

    The opening sentence of the passage tells the reader what one might see by "looking specifically at animal symbols and [deciphering] what they represent." With this precept in mind, answer (A) is the only one that restates the idea.

32. **C**

The definition of "metaphor" is that it is "a figure of speech that contains an implied comparison." Only answer (C) provides the proper definition. The remaining answers are inaccurate.

33. **C**

The last sentence of the passage states that "imperialism [is] capitalistic encroachment and colonialism [is] territorial usurpation." Another word for "encroachment" is "infringement, or intrusion." Another word for "usurpation" is "confiscation, or appropriation, or taking over." Answer (A), arrangement and organization, and (E), development and liberation, would not suffice. Answer (B), wealth and abundance, and (D), freedom and generosity, are the opposite meanings, leaving (C), financial infringement and territorial confiscation, as the correct answer.

34. **A**

The article declares the 1991 winner of the travel magazine poll to be San Francisco. While the other answers are mentioned in the passage, only (A) suggests San Francisco is the year's best travel destination. Therefore, (A) is the appropriate answer.

35. **E**

Answers (A), (B), (C), and (D) are inferences (i.e., suppositions) drawn from the passage's information, while (E) restates the factual information presented by the passage. Since a paraphrase is a restatement, a rephrasing, or an interpretation of the original, (E) is the correct answer.

36. **C**

This is an interesting passage, because while the information suggests that multicultural numbers are on the rise, it simultaneously demonstrates how urgently educational reform is needed to accommodate students of every ethnic background. (C) is the only answer that addresses this agenda. Answers (A), (B), (D), and (E) are simply erroneous.

37. **E**

The passage does not suggest that (A), all students will speak English; its thrust is quite the opposite. Answers (B) and (D) suggest a false choice on the part of students to abandon their native language for English, and again, this is not stated in the passage. (C) is simply untrue, leaving answer (E), which suggests accommodation, as the only correct answer.

38.   **E**

The answer to this question is stated in the last sentence of the passage: "equal educational opportunity for all students must be our nation's top priority." Answer (E) is the only answer that states this idea in its entirety.

39.   **E**

The author's style in addressing the passage is one of (E) objectivity. Answer (A), "biased," means "prejudiced," and (D), "dulcet," means "melodious," so neither of these is correct. Answer (C), "impertinent" (impolite), and (B), "acrimonious" (sarcastic), clearly have negative connotations which are not present in the passage, thus (E), "objective," is the correct answer.

40.   **C**

The opening sentence declares Quinney's speech to be one of "reproach seeking recompense." Another word for "reproach" is condemnation and a synonym for "recompense" is compensation. Answers (A), (B), (D), and (E) do not include these definitions; therefore, (C) is the correct answer.

41.   **B**

The word "laconic" means (B) "concise." The other answers are erroneous.

42.   **D**

The passage states that the program's function is to "predict the aging process and [show how] an unborn child will look." While answer (A) does say "show the aging process," it does not address the issue of the projection of the unborn child. (B), (C), and (E) are misleading notions, leaving only (D) as the complete answer.

43.   **B**

The passage tells the reader that the program "creates a three-dimensional model in its memory." Answer (E) does address the issue of color shading, as does (A), but neither of them contain the complete answer, (B), which reiterates the passage exactly.

44. **E**

    The question asks for information that is not supplied by the passage. Answers (A), (B), (C), and (D) all attempt to provide information that is not in the passage. This is called supposition. Only (E) correctly states that the passage does not give the facts required; thus, (E) is the correct answer.

45. **C**

    Air traffic controllers' inability to communicate was directly linked to the power failure, making choice (C) the only logical, accurate response.

46. **A**

    The main idea of the passage is the loss of airport operation time due to a communications failure. This precept is stated in the first sentence of the passage. Answers (B), (C), (D), and (E) state assertions not addressed in the passage. Therefore, (A) is the correct answer.

47. **C**

    Answers (A) and (B) use exaggerated language to restate the passage. Answers (D) and (E) are too general. This leaves only (C) as the appropriate answer.

48. **E**

    Answers other than (E) are inferences or assumptions, while answer (E) is taken directly from the passage.

49. **A**

    The definition of the word "vigorous" is "energetic, dynamic, or enthusiastic." Thus, (A) is the correct definition.

50. **D**

    While the passage looks at various aspects of middle-age male health issues (see Sentence 3), it does not address those of women. While one could argue that (C) is the correct answer, the passage states that it was a test conducted on and by U.S. subjects. (A), (B), and (E) are not questions at issue for the study, so (D) is the correct answer.

ANSWER SHEET – PRACTICE TEST 2

Section 2: Mathematics

1. Ⓐ Ⓑ Ⓒ Ⓓ Ⓔ
2. Ⓐ Ⓑ Ⓒ Ⓓ Ⓔ
3. Ⓐ Ⓑ Ⓒ Ⓓ Ⓔ
4. Ⓐ Ⓑ Ⓒ Ⓓ Ⓔ
5. Ⓐ Ⓑ Ⓒ Ⓓ Ⓔ
6. Ⓐ Ⓑ Ⓒ Ⓓ Ⓔ
7. Ⓐ Ⓑ Ⓒ Ⓓ Ⓔ
8. Ⓐ Ⓑ Ⓒ Ⓓ Ⓔ
9. Ⓐ Ⓑ Ⓒ Ⓓ Ⓔ
10. Ⓐ Ⓑ Ⓒ Ⓓ Ⓔ
11. Ⓐ Ⓑ Ⓒ Ⓓ Ⓔ
12. Ⓐ Ⓑ Ⓒ Ⓓ Ⓔ
13. Ⓐ Ⓑ Ⓒ Ⓓ Ⓔ
14. Ⓐ Ⓑ Ⓒ Ⓓ Ⓔ
15. Ⓐ Ⓑ Ⓒ Ⓓ Ⓔ
16. Ⓐ Ⓑ Ⓒ Ⓓ Ⓔ
17. Ⓐ Ⓑ Ⓒ Ⓓ Ⓔ
18. Ⓐ Ⓑ Ⓒ Ⓓ Ⓔ
19. Ⓐ Ⓑ Ⓒ Ⓓ Ⓔ
20. Ⓐ Ⓑ Ⓒ Ⓓ Ⓔ

21. Ⓐ Ⓑ Ⓒ Ⓓ Ⓔ
22. Ⓐ Ⓑ Ⓒ Ⓓ Ⓔ
23. Ⓐ Ⓑ Ⓒ Ⓓ Ⓔ
24. Ⓐ Ⓑ Ⓒ Ⓓ Ⓔ
25. Ⓐ Ⓑ Ⓒ Ⓓ Ⓔ
26. Ⓐ Ⓑ Ⓒ Ⓓ Ⓔ
27. Ⓐ Ⓑ Ⓒ Ⓓ Ⓔ
28. Ⓐ Ⓑ Ⓒ Ⓓ Ⓔ
29. Ⓐ Ⓑ Ⓒ Ⓓ Ⓔ
30. Ⓐ Ⓑ Ⓒ Ⓓ Ⓔ
31. Ⓐ Ⓑ Ⓒ Ⓓ Ⓔ
32. Ⓐ Ⓑ Ⓒ Ⓓ Ⓔ
33. Ⓐ Ⓑ Ⓒ Ⓓ Ⓔ
34. Ⓐ Ⓑ Ⓒ Ⓓ Ⓔ
35. Ⓐ Ⓑ Ⓒ Ⓓ Ⓔ
36. Ⓐ Ⓑ Ⓒ Ⓓ Ⓔ
37. Ⓐ Ⓑ Ⓒ Ⓓ Ⓔ
38. Ⓐ Ⓑ Ⓒ Ⓓ Ⓔ
39. Ⓐ Ⓑ Ⓒ Ⓓ Ⓔ
40. Ⓐ Ⓑ Ⓒ Ⓓ Ⓔ

41. Ⓐ Ⓑ Ⓒ Ⓓ Ⓔ
42. Ⓐ Ⓑ Ⓒ Ⓓ Ⓔ
43. Ⓐ Ⓑ Ⓒ Ⓓ Ⓔ
44. Ⓐ Ⓑ Ⓒ Ⓓ Ⓔ
45. Ⓐ Ⓑ Ⓒ Ⓓ Ⓔ
46. Ⓐ Ⓑ Ⓒ Ⓓ Ⓔ
47. Ⓐ Ⓑ Ⓒ Ⓓ Ⓔ
48. Ⓐ Ⓑ Ⓒ Ⓓ Ⓔ
49. Ⓐ Ⓑ Ⓒ Ⓓ Ⓔ
50. Ⓐ Ⓑ Ⓒ Ⓓ Ⓔ

Section 2: Mathematics

DIRECTIONS: Each of the 50 questions in this section is a multiple-choice question with five answer choices. Read each question carefully and choose the one best answer.

1. Which of the following is the most appropriate unit of measure for expressing the weight of a horse?

   A.   pounds

   B.   ounces

   C.   centimeters

   D.   liters

   E.   yards

2. Lisa builds 3 birdfeeders every two days. At this rate, approximately how many birdfeeders can Lisa build in 3 weeks?

   A.   25 birdfeeders

   B.   27 birdfeeders

   C.   29 birdfeeders

   D.   31 birdfeeders

   E.   33 birdfeeders

3. The scale of the diagram is 1 inch equals 7.2 feet. What is the approximate height of the stop sign?

A. 7.2 feet

B. 9.4 feet

C. 12.6 feet

D. 14.8 feet

E. 17.6 feet

4. At a local teen soccer game there were 180 spectators. One hundred of the spectators came to cheer for Team Tigers, while the rest came to support Team Angels. About what percent of the spectators came to cheer for Team Angels?

A. 34%

B. 44%

C. 56%

D. 60%

E. 80%

5. Alex has four puppies which weigh 8, 14, 16, and 22 pounds, respectively. What is the average weight of the puppies?

A. 12 pounds

B. 13 pounds

C. 14 pounds

D. 15 pounds

E. 16 pounds

6. Jay bought nine boxes of candy each weighing one pound five ounces. What is the total amount of candy that Jay bought?

A. 9 pounds 5 ounces

B. 11 pounds 5 ounces

C. 11 pounds 13 ounces

D. 13 pounds 5 ounces

E. 13 pounds 13 ounces

7. Which of the following is the best estimate for 5762 × 22?

    A.   120,000

    B.   100,000

    C.   12,000

    D.   10,000

    E.   1,500

8. Approximately 5 out of 7 employees at TPR Electronics buy life insurance through the TPR Electronics company plan. If there are 613 employees at TPR Electronics, how many employees buy their life insurance through the company plan?

    A.   410 employees

    B.   440 employees

    C.   460 employees

    D.   510 employees

    E.   550 employees

9. A family is planning to buy a wall-to-wall rug for their living room. The room has been drawn on graph paper below with each square of the grid representing a 2 foot by 2 foot square area of the living room floor. What will be the area of the purchased rug?

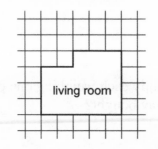

living room

    A.   18 square feet

    B.   24 square feet

    C.   36 square feet

    D.   48 square feet

    E.   72 square feet

10. Phillip's stanine score on this year's standardized mathematics test is a 7. This indicates that:

    A.   Phillip scored 93% on the test.

    B.   Phillip's mathematics level is 8th grade.

    C.   Phillip scored 70% on the test.

    D.   Phillip scored higher that 70% of all test takers on this exam.

    E.   Phillip scored in the third highest stanine group.

11. Cary used 7 lemons to make 3 quarts of lemonade. At this rate, how many lemons will Cary need to make 16 quarts of lemonade?

    A.   12 lemons

    B.   20 lemons

    C.   32 lemons

    D.   38 lemons

    E.   46 lemons

12. There are 10 brown, 6 white, and 12 speckled marbles in a box. A marble is randomly chosen from this box. What is the probability that the chosen marble is speckled?

    A. $\dfrac{3}{7}$

    B. $\dfrac{5}{11}$

    C. $\dfrac{2}{5}$

    D. $\dfrac{1}{2}$

    E. $\dfrac{2}{3}$

13. Dana has 12 yards of rope. She needs to use 3.5 feet to secure each of her new trees in her yard to a metal stake. If Dana has 9 new trees in her yard, how much rope will be left over?

    A.   0 yards

    B.   1 yard

    C.   1.5 yards

    D.   7.5 yards

    E.   10.5 yards

14. The seven people in the shopping club have the following amounts to spend on the next shopping trip: $75, $128, $180, $203, $93, $100, and $173. What is the median value of money that the club members have to spend on the next shopping trip?

    A. $128

    B. $136

    C. $140

    D. $152

    E. $173

15. There are 10 diamond earrings and 6 pearl earrings in a jewelry box. If two earrings are randomly chosen from the box, one after the other, what is the probability that both earrings are pearl earrings?

    A. $\dfrac{1}{8}$

    B. $\dfrac{3}{11}$

    C. $\dfrac{5}{12}$

    D. $\dfrac{9}{64}$

    E. $\dfrac{2}{3}$

16. Tim estimates that he will need $800 to buy two motorcycles. If Tim earns $14.50 per hour and worked 30 hours last week, approximately how much more money will he need to buy his motorcycles?

    A. $545
    B. $435
    C. $385
    D. $365
    E. $295

17. Toni has $352.58 and Jen has $479.83. Which of the following best estimates the difference in the amount of money Toni and Jen have to the nearest dollar?

    A. $120
    B. $123
    C. $127
    D. $133
    E. $137

18. The expression $16 - 20(5 + 7)$ simplifies to which of the following?

    A. 36
    B. 48
    C. −48
    D. −198
    E. −224

19. Sherry, Paul, and Jan sold 186, 244, and 189 tickets, respectively, for the auction party. What is the approximate average number that each of them sold?

    A. 192
    B. 200
    C. 206
    D. 212
    E. 220

20. Nina interviewed 240 college students about their favorite snacks. One hundred eighty-eight said they ate pizza and one hundred sixty-two admitted to snacking on popcorn. If twenty-five said they did not eat either popcorn or pizza, how many students ate both popcorn and pizza?

   A. 64
   B. 135
   C. 162
   D. 188
   E. 215

21. What is the tens digit in the dividend of the problem shown below?

   $$\begin{array}{r} 2\ 2\ 4 \text{ Remainder} = 3 \\ 21\overline{)4\ 7\ \Box\ 7} \end{array}$$

   A. 8
   B. 6
   C. 4
   D. 2
   E. 0

22. Jordan has three pet chickens. The first chicken weighs $3\frac{2}{5}$ pounds, the second weighs $2\frac{1}{4}$ pounds, and the third one weighs $5\frac{5}{8}$ pounds. What is the total weight of Jordan's chickens?

   A. $10\frac{3}{4}$
   B. $10\frac{17}{20}$
   C. $11\frac{11}{40}$
   D. $11\frac{3}{5}$
   E. $12\frac{1}{12}$

23. Peter took 4 exams in his Latin class. His scores are shown in the chart below. What is the difference between his highest score and his lowest score on the Latin exams?

Exam	1	2	3	4
Score	65	87	72	85

    A. 2
    B. 13
    C. 15
    D. 22
    E. 25

24. Tina spent half of her money on a dress. Next she paid $15 for a purse. After buying the purse Tina spent one fourth of her remaining money on lunch. If Tina had $12 left over when she finished her shopping trip, how much money did Tina start her shopping with?

    A. 38
    B. 44
    C. 50
    D. 56
    E. 62

25. Lena bought 20 boxes of the same brand of frozen pizza for a party. She had a 20% discount on her purchase and paid $72 total for all the pizza. What was the original price per box of the pizza?

    A. $4.50
    B. $5.00
    C. $5.25
    D. $5.75
    E. $6.00

26. Solve the following equation for x:

$$16 - 2x = 110 - (4x - 2)$$

A. $x = 48$

B. $x = 42$

C. $x = 40$

D. $x = 36$

E. $x = 32$

27. Kayla scored in the 72 percentile on an English Standardized Exam which has a standard deviation of 5. Which of the following is a correct interpretation of her results?

A. Kayla earned a 72% on the exam.

B. Kayla scored as well as or better than 72% of all exam takers on this exam.

C. 72% of the exam takers scored as well as or better than Kayla on this exam.

D. Kayla scored 77% on the exam.

E. Kayla scored within one standard deviation of the mean on the exam.

28. David agreed to distribute at least 10,000 advertisement flyers for a new company. The number of flyers that he has already delivered to homes in his city is noted in the table below. How many more flyers does David need to deliver to reach his goal?

Day	Number of advertisements distributed
Monday	1,645
Tuesday	2,787
Wednesday	946
Thursday	1,104
Friday	1,702

A. 816

B. 1816

C. 2816

D. 7184

E. 8184

29. Justin ordered forty-five t-shirts online for $9 each. He then sold 36 of them for $16 each and then returned the unsold t-shirts but receives only $7.50 for each returned t-shirt. How much profit did Justin make selling these t-shirts?

A. $315.00

B. $301.50

C. $252.50

D. $238.50

E. $207.00

30. Read the problem below, then answer the question that follows.

> Nick drove his car 546 miles from college to his parents' house. On the trip he spent $15 on tolls, $60.25 on gasoline, $24.20 on meals, and $40 when his car had a flat tire. How much money did Nick have left after his trip?

What single piece of additional information is required to solve this problem?

A. the miles per gallon his car gets

B. the total driving time

C. the type of gasoline Nick uses in his car

D. whether Nick paid for his costs by cash or credit card

E. the amount of money Nick began the trip with

31. Read the information below, then answer the question that follows.

    Frances sold 436 boxes of cookies. She only sold two types: mints and chocolate chips. She sold 16 more than twice as many mint cookies as chocolate chips. The boxes of cookies were sold for $1604.

    Which of the following facts can be determined from the information given above?

    A. the total number of people Frances sold cookies to
    B. the total amount of money Frances collected for selling mint cookies
    C. the profit she made in selling cookies
    D. where she sold the cookies
    E. how many boxes of each type of cookie Frances sold

32. Paul owes Jason $220. Paul gave Jason $30 last week and this week he paid Jason $56. Paul calculated what he still owed Jason using the following expression:

    $$220 - 30 - 56$$

    Which of the following expressions could Paul have also used?

    A. $220 - (30 - 56)$
    B. $220 - (30 + 56)$
    C. $30 + 56 - 220$
    D. $30 - (56 - 220)$
    E. $20 - 56 - 220$

33. This table represents a linear function with input value x and output value y.

x	y
0	126
1	119
2	112
3	
4	98
5	91

What is the missing value of y?

A.   110

B.   109

C.   107

D.   105

E.   102

34. Which of the following mathematical statements is correct?

A. $3.462 < 3.464 < 3.546$

B. $3.462 > 3.464 > 3.546$

C. $3.464 < 3.462 < 3.546$

D. $3.464 > 3.462 > 3.546$

E. $3.462 < 3.546 < 3.462$

35. Consider the inequality:

$$\frac{7}{12} < p < \frac{19}{30}$$

For which of the following values of p will the given inequality be true?

A. $p = \frac{7}{10}$

B. $p = \frac{9}{10}$

C. $p = \frac{1}{2}$

D. $p = \frac{3}{5}$

E. $p = \frac{2}{5}$

36. Allison ran a 5 mile charity race in 1 hour and 30 minutes. How much faster should Allison have run to finish in 1 hour 15 minutes?

A. $\frac{3}{5}$ mph

B. $\frac{3}{4}$ mph

C. $\frac{1}{2}$ mph

D. $\frac{2}{3}$ mph

E. 1 mph

37. Which of the following numbers is between $\frac{1}{4}$ and $\frac{1}{3}$?

    A. $\frac{5}{12}$

    B. $\frac{7}{12}$

    C. $\frac{7}{24}$

    D. $\frac{13}{24}$

    E. $\frac{19}{36}$

38. Sam wants to buy three bargain books at his local bookstore. The bargain prices are $7.48, $11.84, and $14.52, respectively. If each of the prices are rounded to the nearest dollar, what is the estimated total bargain price of the three books ?

    A. $32
    B. $33
    C. $34
    D. $35
    E. $36

39. On a recent car trip, Tamara drove for five days. The distance she drove each day is shown in the table below. What is the average number of miles per day that Tamara drove on her trip rounded to the nearest tenth of a mile?

Day	1	2	3	4	5
Total miles	363.4	401.75	377.5	221.8	533.1

    A. 379.5 miles per day
    B. 392.4 miles per day
    C. 398.4 miles per day
    D. 402.5 miles per day
    E. 411.2 miles per day

40. If the value of m is between 1,484,160 and 1,510,147, which of the following could be m?

    A. 1,398,327

    B. 1,466,790

    C. 1,488,981

    D. 1,510,902

    E. 1,568,060

41. Jack weighs 356 pounds. His football coach has asked Jack to lose 8% of his weight before football season begins. How much weight, to the nearest tenth of a pound, must Jack lose to satisfy his coach's request?

    A. 284.8 pounds

    B. 28.5 pounds

    C. 28.48 pounds

    D. 27.4 pounds

    E. 27.37 pounds

42. Use the table below to answer the question that follows.

Food expenses	Transportation expenses	Housing expenses
$495	$384	?

The table shows Jade's expenses for the month except for her housing costs which are equal to $100 less than two times the sum of her food and transportation expenses. Which of the following can be used to find Jade's housing expenses?

    A. $100 - 2 \times 495 - 384$

    B. $100 - 2 \times 495 + 384$

    C. $2 \times 495 + 384 - 100$

    D. $2 \times (495 + 384 - 100)$

    E. $2 \times (495 + 384) - 100$

43. Use the information below to answer the question that follows.

    • Mitchell has more pets than Tim.

    • Cora has fewer pets than Tim.

Which of the following statements is true?

A. Cora has more pets than Mitchell.
B. Mitchell has more pets than Cora.
C. Mitchell has no pets.
D. Tim has no pets.
E. Tim has the most pets.

44. Use the information below to answer the question that follows.

    • Tonya owns a large car

    • All owners of compact cars must park their cars in the blue parking lot.

From the given information, which of the following could be true?

A. Tonya must park her car in the blue lot.
B. The blue lot is a small parking lot.
C. The blue lot is full.
D. Tonya may park her car in the blue lot.
E. There is more than one blue lot.

45. Use the following pie chart to answer the question that follows.

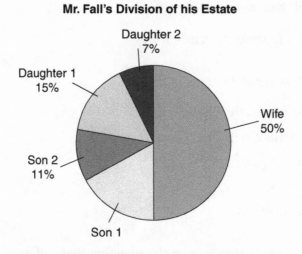

Mr. Fall's Division of his Estate

Mr. Fall's division of his estate after his death is shown in the chart. What percentage of his estate will his first son receive?

A. 11%

B. 13%

C. 15%

D. 17%

E. 19%

Use the graph below to answer questions 46–47.

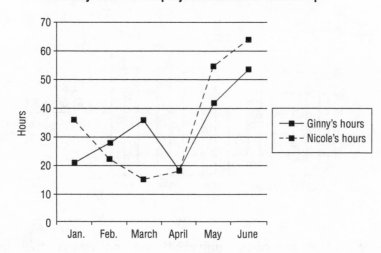

Monthly Hours of Employment at Bob's Patio Shop

46. According to the graph, in how many months did Ginny work more hours than Nicole at Bob's Patio Shop?

   A.   2
   B.   3
   C.   4
   D.   5
   E.   6

47. According to the graph, in what month was the sum of Ginny and Nicole's hours the least?

   A.   January
   B.   February
   C.   March
   D.   April
   E.   May

Use the graph below to answer the questions.

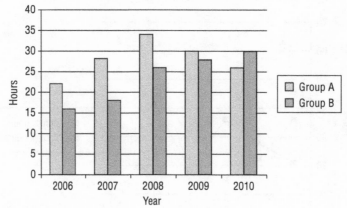

Average Weekly Study Time

Two groups of students at a certain university were polled over their five years at the university on their study habits, the results shown in the above graph.

48. In what year did the average study time for the two groups most differ?

A. 2006

B. 2007

C. 2008

D. 2009

E. 2010

49. In what period did Group B have the greatest percentage increase in average study time?

A. from 2006 to 2007

B. from 2007 to 2008

C. from 2008 to 2009

D. from 2009 to 2010

E. Group B's time did not always increase

50. The pictograph below represents how many of each color stuffed bear that Susan has in her collection. Each bear picture represents 2 bears in that category.

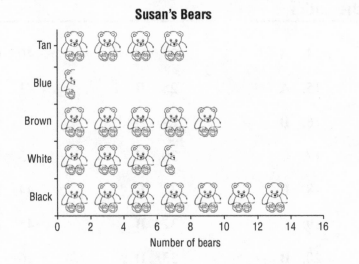

Susan's Bears

What is the total number of black, blue, and brown bears in Susan's collection?

A. 12

B. 19

C. 24

D. 25

E. 40

Answer Key

Section 2: Mathematics

1.	A	14.	A	27.	B	40.	C
2.	D	15.	A	28.	B	41.	B
3.	C	16.	D	29.	D	42.	E
4.	B	17.	C	30.	E	43.	B
5.	D	18.	E	31.	E	44.	D
6.	C	19.	C	32.	B	45.	D
7.	A	20.	B	33.	D	46.	A
8.	B	21.	E	34.	A	47.	D
9.	E	22.	C	35.	D	48.	B
10.	E	23.	D	36.	D	49.	B
11.	D	24.	E	37.	C	50.	D
12.	A	25.	A	38.	C		
13.	C	26.	A	39.	A		

PRACTICE TEST 2 – Detailed Explanations of Answers

Section 2: Mathematics

1. **A**

    Centimeters and yards are units of length and liters is a measure of liquid volume. An ounce is a small unit weight appropriate for light objects. Pounds is the appropriate unit of measure for a horse; the correct answer is (A).

2. **D**

    Lisa builds 3 birdfeeders every two days. There are 21 days in a three-week period. There are 10.5 blocks of 2 days in a three-week period. So 10.5 times 3 birdfeeders is 31.5 birdfeeders, so the correct answer is (D).

3. **C**

    The stop sign is about 1.75 inches on the ruler. Set up a proportion as follows: $\dfrac{1 \text{ inch}}{7.2 \text{ feet}} = \dfrac{1.75 \text{ inches}}{y \text{ feet}}$. To solve for the unknown y which represents the height of the sign, use the following property of proportions: $\dfrac{a}{b} = \dfrac{c}{d}$ is equivalent to $ad = bc$. Use this rule to get $1 \times y = 7.2 \times 1.75$ or $y = 12.6$. Thus, (C) is the correct answer.

4. **B**

    Eighty of the 180 spectators came to cheer on Team Angels. $\dfrac{80}{180} = \dfrac{4}{9} \approx 44.4\%$ so the correct answer is (B).

5. **D**

    The average weight of the four puppies is $\dfrac{8+14+16+22}{4} = \dfrac{60}{4} = 15$ pounds. The correct answer is (D).

6. **C**

    $9 \times (1 \text{ pound} + 5 \text{ ounces}) = 9 \text{ pounds} + 45 \text{ ounces}$. Since 1 pound = 16 ounces, 45 ounces = 2 pounds + 13 ounces. Hence, 9 pounds + 45 ounces = 9 pounds + 2 pounds + 13 ounces = 11 pounds 13 ounces. The correct answer is (C).

7. **A**

Round each number to its greatest digit place: $5762 \times 22 \approx 6000 \times 20 = 120{,}000$. Thus (A) is the correct answer.

8. **B**

$\frac{5}{7} \times (613) \approx 5 \times 87.5 = 437.5$, so (B) is the correct answer.

9. **E**

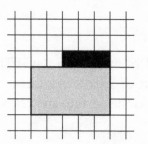

The shaded grey rectangle is 3 by 5 or 15 squares, and the shaded black rectangle is 3 by 1 or 3 rectangles. Thus, there is a total of 18 rectangles with scale 2 by 2 feet or 4 square feet. Then 18 times 4 is 72 square feet. The correct answer is (E).

10. **E**

The word "stanine" means STAndard NINE and is a method of scaling test scores so that the mean is five and standard deviation is two. The scale ranks scores from 1 to 9 with 1 being the lowest score and 9 being the highest. The lowest 4% of scores are assigned the stanine 1, the next 7% are assigned the stanine 2, the next 12% are assigned the stanine score 3, the next 17% are assigned a 4, the middle 20% are assigned a 5, and so on as shown in this table:

grouped ranking	4%	7%	12%	17%	20%	17%	12%	7%	4%
stanine score	1	2	3	4	5	6	7	8	9

A stanine score of 7 in a standardized reading test indicates that he scored in the third highest stanine group. The correct answer is (E).

11. **D**

Set up a proportion: $\dfrac{3 \text{ quarts}}{7 \text{ lemons}} = \dfrac{16 \text{ quarts}}{x \text{ lemons}}$. Use the following property of proportions: $\dfrac{a}{b} = \dfrac{c}{d}$ is equivalent to $ad = bc$ to arrive at $3x = 112 \;\Rightarrow\; x = \dfrac{112}{3} = 37\dfrac{1}{3}$. So, Cary will need 38 lemons. Therefore, (D) is the correct answer.

12. **A**

There are 28 marbles in the box. The probability that the randomly chosen marble is speckled is $\dfrac{\text{number of speckled marbles in box}}{\text{number of marbles in box}} = \dfrac{12}{28} = \dfrac{3}{7}$. The correct answer is (A)

13. **C**

Dana needs to use 9×3.5 or 31.5 feet of rope which is $\dfrac{31.5}{3} = 10.5$ yards of rope. She will have $12 - 10.5 = 1.5$ yards of rope left over. Therefore (C) is the correct answer.

14. **A**

The median value is the middle value. List the values from least to greatest: \$75, \$93, \$100, \$128, \$173, \$180, \$203. It is clear that \$128 is the middle value so it is the median and the correct answer is (A).

15. **A**

The probability that the first randomly chosen earring is a pearl earring is given by $\dfrac{6 \text{ pearl earrings}}{16 \text{ earrings}} = \dfrac{3}{8}$. Now there are 15 earrings left in the jewelry box with only five of them pearl earrings. The probability that the second randomly chosen earring is a pearl earring is $\dfrac{5 \text{ pearl earrings}}{15 \text{ earrings}} = \dfrac{1}{3}$. When making consecutive choices (called "events" in probability) use the Multiplication Principle which is to multiply these probabilities to get the probability of the second event following the first event. In this problem this is: $\dfrac{3}{8} \times \dfrac{1}{3} = \dfrac{1}{8}$. So, (A) is the correct answer.

16. **D**

Last week Tim earned $30 \times \$14.50 = \$435$. So he needs $\$800 - 435 = \$365$ more to buy the two motorcycles. The correct answer is (D).

17. **C**

The difference is $479.83 - 352.58 or approximately $480 - 353 = $127, so the correct answer is (C).

18. **E**

The order of operations rules indicate to simplify inside the parentheses first. Then do all multiplication and division from left to right, and perform all addition and subtraction from left to right last. This produces $16 - 20(5 + 7) = 16 - 20(12) = 16 - 240 = -224$ which gives (E) as the correct answer.

19. **C**

The correct answer is (C). The average number of tickets sold by each seller is $\dfrac{186 + 244 + 189}{3} = \dfrac{619}{3} = 206\dfrac{1}{3}$.

20. **B**

Using a Venn diagram to visualize this problem will help. Let A be the collection of all students who snack on pizza and let B be the students who eat popcorn. Let x be the number of who snack on both pizza and popcorn. Then the number of students who eat pizza but not popcorn is $188 - x$ and the number of students who snack on popcorn but not pizza is $162 - x$. See how this is shown in the Venn diagram where the left circle represents set A and the right circle represents B, while the intersection represents those who snack on both popcorn and pizza. Note that 240 students were interviewed and 25 said they ate neither pizza nor popcorn, so the number of students who are represented in the circles (Venn diagram) below is $240 - 25 = 215$. Thus it is true that $(188 - x) + (162 - x) + x = 215$. Simplify the left side of the equation: $350 - x = 215$. Solving this equation we arrive at $x = 135$. Therefore there are 135 students who eat both pizza and popcorn. Therefore, (B) is the correct answer.

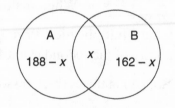

21. **E**

   The Remainder Theorem states that when $a \times b) + r = c$ then $c \div a = b$ with remainder r. For example, $(4 \times 3) + 2 = 14$ so $14 \div 4 = 3$ with remainder 2. Therefore our given division problem can be rewritten as a multiplication problem: $(21 \times 224) + 3 = 47m7$ where m represents the missing digit. So, $(21 \times 224) + 3 = 4704 + 3 = 4707$ so that m equals 0. So, (E) is the correct answer.

22. **C**

   To add the numbers we will need to use a common denominator to add the fractions: $3\frac{2}{5} + 2\frac{1}{4} + 5\frac{5}{8} = (3+2+5) + (\frac{2}{5} + \frac{1}{4} + \frac{5}{8}) = 10 + \left(\frac{2}{5} \cdot \frac{8}{8} + \frac{1}{4} \cdot \frac{10}{10} + \frac{5}{8} \cdot \frac{5}{5}\right) = 10 + \left(\frac{16}{40} + \frac{10}{40} + \frac{25}{40}\right) = 10 + \frac{51}{40} = 10 + \frac{40}{40} + \frac{11}{40} = 11\frac{11}{40}$. The correct answer is (C).

23. **D**

   Peter's highest score is 87 and his lowest score is 65; the difference is $87 - 65 = 22$. Thus (D) is the correct answer.

24. **E**

   Let x be the amount of money Tina had at the start of her shopping trip. She spent half of her money on the dress, leaving $\$\frac{1}{2}x$. Lisa next spent \$15 on a purse so that she then had $\$\frac{1}{2}x - 15$. Tina spent one fourth of this remaining money so that she was left with three fourths of this amount or $\$\frac{3}{4}(\frac{1}{2}x - 15)$ which must be \$12. Solving this equation: $\$\frac{3}{4}(\frac{1}{2}x - 15) = 12 \Rightarrow \frac{1}{2}x - 15 = \frac{4}{3}(12) = 16 \Rightarrow \frac{1}{2}x = 31 \Rightarrow x = 62$. Thus, (E) is the correct answer.

25. **A**

   Let p be the original price for all 20 boxes of pizza. Then 80% of this amount is equal to \$72. The equation for this is $.8p = 72$. Solve this equation: $0.8p = 72 \Rightarrow p = \frac{72}{0.8} = \frac{720}{8} = 90$. So if all 20 boxes originally cost \$90, then one box originally cost $\frac{90}{20} = \$4.50$. (A) is the correct answer.

26. **A**

   To solve the equation $16 - 2x = 110 - (4x - 2)$ for x, eliminate the parentheses on the right side of the equation. $16 - 2x = 110 - (4x - 2) \Rightarrow 16 - 2x = 110 - 4x + 2 \Rightarrow 16 - 2x = 112 - 4x$. Next gather all the terms with the variable x on the left side and those which are constant on the right by using the Addition Property of Equality: $16 - 2x = 112 - 4x \Rightarrow 4x - 2x = 112 - 16$ or $2x = 96$. Then divide both sides of the equation by 2 to arrive at $x = 48$. Thus, (A) is the correct answer.

27. **B**

   Kayla scored in the 72 percentile on an English Standardized Exam means that she scored as well as or better than 72% of all exam takers on this exam. (B) is the correct answer.

28. **B**

   The total number of advertisements that David has already distributed is: $1645 + 2787 + 946 + 1104 + 1702 = 8184$, so he still has $10000 - 8184 = 1816$ to deliver. The correct answer is (B).

29. **D**

   Justin made a profit of $7 on each of the 36 shirts he sold for a total of $7 \times 36 = \$252$. But for the 9 t-shirts he did not sell he lost $1.50 on each t-shirt for a total of $9 \times 1.50 = \$13.50$. Subtracting his losses from his gain gives $252 - 13.50 = \$238.50$ so the correct answer is (D).

30. **E**

   Nick's total expenses for the trip are listed so if the amount of money that Nick had at the beginning of his trip was given, the amount of money that he had when he ended his trip could be calculated. The correct answer is (E).

31. **E**

   Set x equal to the number of boxes of chocolate chip cookies Frances sold and then the number of boxes of mint cookies that she sold would be $2x + 16$. The equation $x + 2x + 16 = 436$ illustrates the total sales. The number of boxes sold of each type of cookie can be calculated from this equation. The correct answer is (E).

32. **B**

    $220 - 30 - 56$ is the same as $220 - (30 + 56)$ since subtracting 30 and then 56 is the same as first adding 30 and 56 and then subtracting the total from 220. Therefore, the correct answer is (B).

33. **D**

    According to the table, for every 1 unit increase in the x value there is a 7 unit decrease in the y value. So as x increases from 2 to 3, the y value must decrease from 112 to 105. The correct answer is (D).

34. **A**

    Each of the three numbers in each possible answer have the same units digit 3 (the place to the left of the decimal point) and two have the same tenths digit 4 (the place to the right of the decimal point) while the third number (3.546) has a larger tenths digit, so that number (3.546) must be the greatest of the three given numbers. Thus the only possible correct answers are (A) and (C). Now to compare 4.462 and 4.464 note that the hundredths digit (two places to the right of the decimal point) is the same but the thousandths digit in 4.462 is less than the thousandths digit in 4.464; hence 4.464 is greater than 4.462. Answer (A) is correct.

35. **D**

    To compare these fractions, find equivalent decimals. $\dfrac{7}{12} = 0.58\overline{3}$ and $\dfrac{19}{30} = 0.6\overline{3}$.

    Next considering the decimal equivalents of the possible answers: $\dfrac{7}{10} = 0.7$, $\dfrac{9}{10} = 0.9$,

    $\dfrac{1}{2} = 0.5$, $\dfrac{3}{5} = 0.6$, and $\dfrac{2}{5} = 0.4$, the only one of these numbers that is greater than $0.58\overline{3}$ and less than $0.6\overline{3}$ is 0.6. Hence the correct answer is (D).

36. **D**

    Rate x time = distance or rate = distance/time. So Allison's speed in the race was $\dfrac{5}{1.5} = \dfrac{50}{15} = \dfrac{10}{3} = 3\dfrac{1}{3}$ mph. If Allison had finished the race in 1 hour and 15 minutes her rate would have been $\dfrac{5}{1.25} = \dfrac{500}{125} = 4$ mph. Thus she would have to increase her speed by $\dfrac{2}{3}$ mph. Therefore (D) is the correct answer.

37. **C**

$\frac{1}{4}$ and $\frac{1}{3}$ are both less than $\frac{1}{2}=50\%$ which can be seen by looking at $\frac{1}{4}$ as "1 out of 4," and $\frac{1}{3}$ as "1 out of 3." Also $\frac{1}{4}<\frac{1}{3}$ since $\frac{1}{4}=0.25$ and $\frac{1}{3}=0.3333...$ Note that $\frac{7}{12}$ is greater than $\frac{6}{12}=\frac{1}{2}$; $\frac{13}{24}$ is greater than $\frac{12}{24}=\frac{1}{2}$, and $\frac{19}{36}$ is greater than $\frac{18}{36}=\frac{1}{2}$, so answers (B), (D), and (E) are eliminated. Looking at $\frac{5}{12}$ note that $\frac{5}{12}>\frac{4}{12}=\frac{1}{3}$ which leaves $\frac{7}{24}$ to examine: $\frac{1}{4}=\frac{6}{24}<\frac{7}{24}<\frac{8}{24}=\frac{1}{3}$, so (C) is the correct answer.

38. **C**

The three bargain prices rounded to the nearest dollar are: $7, $12, and $15, respectively. Thus, the estimated total bargain price of the three books is 7 + 12 + 15 = $34 and the correct answer is (C).

39. **A**

To find the average number of miles per day that Tamara drove we add the five day's driving miles and divide by 5: $\frac{363.4+401.75+377.5+221.8+533.1}{5}=\frac{1897.55}{5}=379.51$ and this rounds off to 379.5 miles per day. Thus, the correct answer is (A)

40. **C**

Note that 1,484,160 is less than 1,510,147 and that both numbers have "one million" as part of them; i.e., their millions place digits are the same. Their hundred thousands place digits are 4 and 5 respectively, so for *m* to be between 1,484,160 and 1,510,147 the hundred thousands digit must be 4 or 5; this eliminates answer (A). Also since *m* must be greater than 1,484,160 *m* cannot be (B) since although 1,484,160 and 1,466,790 agree in the millions and hundred thousand place digits, the ten thousands digit in (B) is less than the ten thousands digit in 1,484,160. Answer (C) (1,488,981) is greater than 1,484,160 since although the millions, hundred thousands and ten thousands digits are the same, the thousands place digit in answer (C) is greater than that of 1,484,160. Comparing answer (C) to 1,510,147 it is clear that (C) is less than 1,510,147 because they share the same millions place digit but the hundred thousands digit in answer (C) is less than that in 1,510,147. Thus (C) is the correct answer.

41. **B**

    To find 8% of Jacks weight multiply his weight by 0.08: $0.08 \times 356 = 28.48$; we then round off to the nearest tenth of a pound to get $28.48 \approx 28.5$ pounds. The correct answer is (B).

42. **E**

    Jade's housing expenses are $100 less than two times the sum of Jade's food and transportation expenses: First find the sum of the food and transportation expenses, then multiply by 2, and lastly subtract 100. This translates into the mathematical expression: $2 \times (495 + 384) - 100$ and (E) is the correct answer.

43. **B**

    "Cora has fewer pets than Tim" is the same as "Tim has more pets than Cora." Hence it follows from this and the first fact that *Mitchell has more pets than Tim* that Mitchell has the most pets and Cora the least number of pets. (B) is the correct answer.

44. **D**

    The statements in the box do not mention the size of the blue lot, how many blue lots there are, or whether the blue lot is full; this eliminates answers (B). (C), and (E). There is nothing that indicates that Tonya must park her car in the blue lot so (A) cannot be the correct answer. However nothing in the box indicates that she cannot park her car in the blue lot, thus (D) is the correct answer.

45. **D**

    The total of the percentages shown on the chart is $50 + 7 + 15 + 11 = 83\%$ so son 1 will receive $100 - 83 = 17\%$. (D) is the correct answer.

46. **A**

    Ginny's hours are indicated in blue. The blue graph is greater in only February and March; thus, the correct answer is (A).

47. **D**

    Clearly the sum of Ginny and Nicole's working hours is not least in May or June when their hours increased significantly. Their total hours in the other months are approximately: January = 60, February = 50, March = 50, April = 40 so (D) is the correct answer.

48. **B**

      Studying the differences in the heights of the pairs of bars, the greatest difference in the average weekly study hours occurred in 2007. The correct answer is (B).

49. **B**

Percentage increase is calculated using the formula: $\dfrac{\text{change in amount}}{\text{original amount}}$.

The percent increase from 2006 to 2007 is $\approx \dfrac{18-16}{16} = \dfrac{2}{16} = \dfrac{1}{8} = 12.5\%$

The percent increase from 2007 to 2008 is $\approx \dfrac{26-18}{18} = \dfrac{8}{18} = \dfrac{4}{9} \approx 44.\tilde{4}\%$

The percent increase from 2008 to 2009 is $\approx \dfrac{28-26}{26} = \dfrac{2}{26} = \dfrac{1}{13} \approx 7.7\%$

The percent increase from 2009 to 2010 is $\approx \dfrac{30-28}{28} = \dfrac{2}{28} = \dfrac{1}{14} \approx 7.1\%$

The correct answer is (B).

50. **D**

      Each picture of the bear is worth 2 bears. Susan has 14 black bears, 1 blue bear, and 10 brown bears. The total number of black, blue, and brown bears that Susan has is 25 so the correct answer is (D).

Section 3: Writing

DIRECTIONS: Carefully read the two writing topics below. Plan and write an essay on each, being sure to cover all aspects of each essay. Allow approximately 30 minutes per essay.

Topic 1

Ideologies or ways of looking at things, range from very liberal to very conservative views of how lives should be lived and what is good and bad for society. A controversial ideology in our culture holds that women's primary responsibilities are homemaking and child rearing; that men are primarily responsible for the financial support of the family; that women with children should ideally not work outside the home; and that a double standard in these social customs is acceptable.

You may not hold these views personally, but they have pervaded our culture for many years and have influenced everyone to some degree. What is your position on the issue of male and female roles in the home and society?

Topic 2

Sometimes you want something badly, but when you get it, it's not what you want.

PRACTICE TEST 2 – Detailed Explanations of Answers

Section 3: Writing

SAMPLE SCORED ESSAYS WITH EXPLANATIONS

Topic 1 Sample Answers

Essay #1—Pass (Score = 4)

The ideology that "anatomy is destiny" is completely false. There are, however, explanations for the gap between boys and girls as they take their place in the world as masculine and feminine beings. Different sex role experiences and socializing forces may contribute to the differences in sex in ways far more powerful than the biological ones. The question recognizes ideologies as either liberal or conservative, but doesn't label any as discrimination. There is an unfortunate tradition of women's primary responsibilities as homemaking and child rearing, while men are responsible for the financial support of the family. That is discrimination against both men and women.

The question fails to acknowledge the social changes that have been occurring in contemporary history which have brought about equality and opportunity for women. The ideology of "happy family" is a fast fading one, for in a society of rising divorce rates, single parents, and latchkey kids, women are assuming the roles of sole parent, sole provider, and professional career persons. Beginning with the Voting Rights Act in the 1920s, women have become more independent and more outspoken. Masculine and feminine have become adjectives of the past; fashion has introduced blazers and slacks as the attractive female apparel, rather than the traditional skirts and blouses; the media is introducing a society of "Mr. Mom's" (motherly fathers) on television shows. One final example that proves anatomy is not destiny is the sharp increase in woman professionals. More and more women are assuming managerial (rather than secretarial) positions.

Although I do not share the more traditional views about sex roles, I agree that they have pervaded our culture and influenced everyone to some extent. Thankfully, however, those views are quickly changing, and although women may always possess a certain "feminine" charm, hopefully they won't forever be labeled only mothers, wives, and homemakers, but have the ability and the right to be professional persons as well. And for the men who choose a homemaker's role, there won't be scorn but acceptance.

Scoring Explanation for Essay #1—Pass

This essay demonstrates an understanding of the question that is quite sophisticated, arguing that sex roles, largely determined by society, are, in fact, a form of discrimination. The body of the essay argues for this thesis by demonstrating the ways that both men and women have risen above the stereotypes that tradition has dictated. As evidence for its claim, it offers examples as diverse as style of dress, the depiction of gender roles on television, and changes in business management. The writer gives compelling evidence to support his/her thesis in a readable, reasonable fashion.

The writer's syntax is above average and demonstrates variety and complexity. Grammatical errors are few, the vocabulary is broad and intelligent, and the voice of the writer is compelling. Although the second-to-last sentence runs on in a meandering fashion, such stylistic slips do not detract greatly from the writer's message. Finally, both aspects of the question—sex roles in home and society—are addressed. For its overwhelmingly positive features, the essay earns a Pass.

Essay #2—Marginal Pass (Score = 3)

The society, in which we live, is filled with double standards, none so drastic or common as that between men and women. Throughout my growing up, I have witnessed these contradictions and I have come to find these standards to be unfair.

The programming that children receive, while growing up, is a major cause of established double standards. I have experienced times when my sister and I would be playing together and my father would scold one of us because either I shouldn't be playing with dolls, my sister shouldn't be playing with toy guns. I have also found that at a young age in school, society directs us into boy activities and girl activities. I remember that girls got in trouble for horsing around and boys would get in trouble for playing house. In school we learn that only daddies can be doctors, and that mommies must be nurses.

In high school years, this double standard first becomes challenged by the girls. As teenagers begin dating and going out with friends, I have noticed that guys have less restrictions and later curfews. However the most blatant and offensive double standard, to me, is that over sex. In plain terms, if a guy does it, he is a stud, but if a girl does it, she is a slut. I have observed this happen and have several times been guilty of this thinking myself. Besides the issue of sex, goals following high school also reveals this double standard. It is a common stereotype that guys should go to college or get a job, and that women should go out to raise a family. Despite the fact that increasing numbers of girls go to college and get a good job today, and that it's more common for a father to watch the kids, the double standard still exists.

In the workplace, there is a struggle by women and some men, to shatter the double standards and stereotypes. The typical image of a male boss with a female secretary is being toppled by the rising number of women executives and professionals. The question identifies the double standard of women raising families, and men working to support the family. This is beginning to be permanently altered with the huge efforts to fight that image seen in the business world and family situation every day.

Scoring Explanation for Essay #2—Marginal Pass

This essay largely draws on personal experience from childhood and school years to demonstrate that environmental conditioning in both home and school results in the double standard. While this essay offers a more simplistic treatment of the subject of sex roles than the previous essay, the writer is generally still clear. Although the essay lacks a firm and convincing conclusion, sufficient supporting information illustrates the writer's position and bolsters the authors generalizations of societal conditioning. This essay is a good example of one that takes no risks and relies on commonplace observations; though not exciting or particularly engaging, it is adequate.

The essay's syntax and vocabulary are rather ordinary, and the author has problems with punctuation. The first sentence, for example is over-punctuated; the second sentence of the second paragraph is awkward and ungainly. Despite these problems, the writer succeeds in communicating a message to the reader and, therefore, receives a Marginal Pass.

Essay #3—Marginal Fail (Score = 2)

Societies view points on the role of male and female are often caused by many standards and factors that are put on the male or the female upon birth.

At birth, the infant is placed in one of the categories, if it is a boy, or if it is a girl. Immediately after this is determined, the infant is wrapped in a blue blanket if it is a boy, and a pink blanket if it is a girl. Thus showing that one is taught at a very young age what he/she is expected to wear. Children learn early in the home what is right for them.

A point is that a women's primary responsibilities are homemaking and child rearing; that men are responsible for the financial support of the family; that women with children should ideally not work outside the home; and that a double standard in social customs is acceptable. I find that one generation ago this was true, but with todays generation I feel that this passage is not as accurate as it was one generation ago.

From my personal experiences I find the previous statement to be true. I was raised with my mother being a homemaker, my father being responsible for the financial support and there was definately a double standard present. These ideologies range from old customs and beliefs that women are inferior and they have their place in the home.

From my observations, however, I see that the women of today are more independant and defiant to the expectations that are sat upon them from birth. More women are proud to be women and there are not as many girls/women expressing dissatisfaction with the sex they are.

One issue in a family with one boy and one girl is the issue of the double standard. In most families I know, there is always a double standard present on certain issues. (i.e. going out, parties, curfues) The boy usually has more privileges than the girl and the girl is usually the one with the stricter rules. Even though women is trying to be more independent, old habit die hard and protection of their children, especially girls, is always on a parent mind.

The role of a male and a female in todays society is changing from their roles in the past. The female is becoming more independent and don't exactly live up to the expectations sat upon them.

Scoring Explanation for Essay #3—Marginal Fail

This essay draws on personal experience to demonstrate that male and female gender roles are the result of societal influences. The author has less control over organization than is desirable in a brief, analytic essay. The middle paragraphs repeat key points rather than developing them, and no clear transitions assist the reader from paragraph to paragraph. For example, the penultimate paragraph raises the issue of a sex-role double standard for teenagers that allows boys more privileges and less restrictions than girls, but this paragraph more properly belongs earlier in the essay to support the writer's claim that experiences in the home account for the double standard.

The author has inadequate control over punctuation, spelling, and verb tense to a degree that is quite distracting for the audience; these problems are evident in such sentences as "Even though women is trying to be more independent, old habit die hard and protection of their children, especially girls, is always on a parent mind" and "The female is becoming more independent and don't exactly live up to the expectations sat upon them." Sentence fragments also appear. Although the writer attempts to respond to the question put forth in the prompt, severe problems with the development of the thesis and numerous grammatical and punctuation errors earn this essay a score of Marginal Fail.

Essay #4—Fail (Score = 1)

The main point is that ideologies are more effective then the sex of an individual. For centuries traditions influence people more than the sex of a person does. People learn very young, what they think is right from wrong and what they think is sutable for the opposite sex.

Sex should not determine your future. But everyone has the right to their own opinion. Everyone should always do what they think is best for them regardless of what society is used too. Ideologies of many people, especially young people will grow with open minds to what society should be like if everyone does what best for them and work to their full ability.

Customs and traditions are now changing because every individuals are doing whats best for them. Traditions such as women homemaking and men supporting the family has totally changed in some household. Now women are going out and bringing home the bread and men are at home taking care of the home. People are finally starting to realize that customs and traditions are just ideologies.

The new generation is growing up with different views because of what they see is going on our present society. The new generation sees that the idea that man and women can do just about the same. For example, women are now fighting in wars and trying to do just about everything a man could be.

In conclusion, Ideologies are more effective then a persons' sex.

Scoring Explanation for Essay #4—Fail

This writer does not appear to have adequate control of language to communicate his/ her ideas. The opening sentence, "The main point is that ideologies are more effective then the sex of an individual," is an unclear and unsophisticated statement of the writer's thesis. This thesis—that tradition determines sex roles—gradually becomes clearer, but the reader must work hard to arrive at this assumption. Also, very little evidence is offered to support the writer's assertions. Without adequate support, the reader is left to wonder why they should see the writer's position as a reasonable response to the question at hand.

Too many errors in diction and spelling make the essay incomprehensible at key points, and several sentences are awkward and confusing, both syntactically and semantically. For example, in the next-to-the-last paragraph, we read: "The new generation sees that the idea that man and women can do just about the same." The reader is left wondering what exactly the writer means by this statement. The essay concludes with a restatement of the thesis ("Ideologies are more effective then a persons' sex") that has not been adequately argued. The many errors in logic and language are impossible to ignore, and the essay, therefore, receives a failing score.

Topic 2 Sample Answers

Essay #1—Pass (Score = 4)

Lee was the most attractive person that I had ever seen. He was tall and well-built, with dark brown hair and piercing hazel eyes. I had had my eye on him for a long, long time. In fact, everytime I went to the dance club, I went to see him. Although it seemed like it had taken forever, the momentous day finally arrived. Just when I least expected it, Lee came up from behind, tapped my shoulder, and asked me to dance. We swayed to the tune of "Take My Breath Away," exchanged telephone numbers, and then left for home. He called the following night at dinner time. Not only did Lee have a terrible sense of timing, but also a very boring personality. All he could talk about was his car. He was obviously not a conversationalist. Much to my disappointment, Lee and I had little in common and had trouble carrying on even a five-minute conversation. He was definitely not the guy that I had expected.

Many people claim that "sometimes when you want something badly and then when you get it, it's not what you expected." Obviously, in my situation, getting to know the "wondrous" Lee was definitely different than what I expected. He had represented a challenge for me and upon overcoming the challenge and actually talking with him, I found myself disappointed and regretful. Why did I feel this way after meeting this once-considered "dreamboat"? I can see two distinct reasons.

To begin with, Lee, after asking me to dance, no longer represented a challenge to me. The high-energy nights of watching and waiting and staring had come to an abrupt end. There was no longer an awe or a mystery to his character—he was a normal human being! The challenge was gone.

Another major reason for the disappointment was the fact that neither Lee, nor any other guy, could ever live up to the image that I had created in my mind of him. In my eyes, Lee could do no wrong. He had the looks of Mel Gibson, the personality of Chevy Chase, and the heart of Mother Theresa. After meeting him and realizing that he seriously lacked in all three areas, it is only obvious that I would be disappointed. True, Lee really did not have a chance, but I was still disappointed.

Disappointment is definitely a factor in wanting something badly and then finally getting it. Maybe because the challenge is gone, maybe because the expectations were too high or maybe because you really thought you would never get it to begin with—whatever the reason, more often than not, finally getting something that was previously desired can definitely be a letdown.

Scoring Explanation for Essay #1—Pass

This personal essay recounts, with much relevant detail, the anticipation of meeting a "dream date" and the subsequent disappointment the writer feels once she knows him better. The writer begins with a very descriptive anecdote of her first interaction with Lee and his failure to live up to her expectations. The writer withholds her thesis until the second paragraph; this approach is atypical, yet effective in this context, and demonstrates a more sophisticated approach than the usual five-paragraph essay structure.

This essay is both well-written and interesting. The writer not only offers a well-developed narrative of her disappointment, but also analyzes her sense of letdown as she speculates that she herself may have caused it by expecting too much. Finally, she uses this specific incident to speculate on the nature of expectation and disappointment in general. Throughout the entire essay, the writing is exceptionally competent, exhibiting sentence variety and a unique overall structure. For these many positive and striking features, the essay merits a Pass.

Essay #2—Marginal Pass (Score = 3)

If anyone where to ask me what my biggest dream in life was, I would have to say it was the hope for a perfect family. When I was young, I lived with only my mom because my father had left my Mom, before I was born.

Together, Mom and I, struggled to find enough money for food, and even a little peace of mind. I had always thought that the answer to our problems would be found in a complete family. By this I mean, I thought a family must consist of a father, mother, brother, and sister. I even included a family dog that would run in the yard that was enclosed by the white picket fence.

As a result of my Mom having to work and worry so hard, we didn't have sufficient time to develop a good relationship. She was having a difficult providing for me, so I had to move in with another family. This family was friends of my mother, so I felt comfortable with them. I thought that this would be the perfect home. It included everything I had ever dreamed of. It had the room, dad, siblings, and pets. I was sure that this family was perfect.

It was not soon before I realized how wrong I really was. This family had their share of problems to. For example, they found it hard to find adequate time together. They were always doing their own thing. I have to admit that initially I was shocked. However, I soon realized that there are many types of families and each of them has their own problems. The families protrayed on T.V. were not how family life really was. Of course it was sometimes difficult, but I now know that what constituts a family is love. It is not always having enough time for each other, or having a white-picket fence. It is not always being understood, or having all members present. It is about love. That love is demonstrated by the family trying to do the best they can.

Scoring Explanation for Essay #2—Marginal Pass

This essay, which focuses on the author's desire for a "perfect" family, is reasonably well-organized and competently written. The writer helps the reader to understand the author's hopes for a perfect family and how these hopes were disappointed, but surprisingly little detail fortifies the narrative. The writer offers a limited description of the problems of living with the author's mother ("my mom having to work and worry so hard") and an equally inadequate discussion of the disappointing new situation ("They were always doing their own thing"). The writer ignores important opportunities to move from the general to the specific, to enliven the essay, and to make it more engaging.

Although some minor grammatical errors distract the reader from the writer's narrative, they do not prohibit the reader from following the writer's message. However, many of the sentences are quite simple in structure, and this dulling simplicity limits the essay to a minimal success. Despite its problems with detail, development, and punctuation, the essay successfully communicates an interesting narrative in response to the essay prompt; it warrants a Marginal Pass.

Essay #3—Marginal Fail (Score = 2)

Growing up, I always wanted to be older. This had a lot to do with my older brothers and sisters. They never would let me play with them. I always looked forward to the following grade. It seemed like that being older had so much more freedom. And excitement.

That is why, after about the age of eight or nine, I couldn't wait til my sweet sixteenth birthday. I would have all the freedom I wanted. I never wanted something so much. I even wanted it more than my cabbage patch kid. When I was six.

I would go to extremes because I wanted my license. When I was fourteen I got caught one evening taking my brother's car for a little spin. Nothing major just a little ride to Carl's Jr. and back. Well the car got a flat on the way back and their was no way of avoiding the inevitable, but to call my parents. I wasn't intellectual enough to call triple A. I got an extreme punishment; that fit my crime perfect.

I was the oldest out of all my classmates because I was held back a year. So out of all my friends I was the luckiest because I would receive—my gold card to freedom—my driver's license.

I turned fifteen and you can bet that I was first in line to getting my permit that foggy cold morning at the DMV. After receiving this I was taxi service everywhere. I had to practice and practice because I wasn't going to fail my driver's test. Everytime I got behind the wheel, shivers tickled across my back. I was so excited be behind the wheel.

Finally, my sixteenth birthday rolled around. I took my drivers test—Passed with a 97. I already had a car waiting in the driveway when I came home. My little Jetta was crying out my name. The first month, I loved it. I could drive anywhere, anytime.

This got old real fast. I was soon driving friends home — home meaning an hour away. Picking up things for the family. I was basically, "slaves incorporated." The worse was having to drive to parties. I sat around watching everybody get drunk. It was not fun. Boy, was I wrong. Two years later, I still won't drive unless its' unavoidable. My friends know that. Now its' there turn to pay the piper.

Scoring Explanation for Essay #3—Marginal Fail

This essay contains many short, choppy sentences and an overwhelming number of errors in grammar and syntax. The writer's sassy and conversational style would be quite engaging if he/she could correctly construct sentences; unfortunately, the many errors frustrate the reader's attempts to comprehend the writer's message. Also, the essay's chronology, which the writer uses as an organizational scheme, confuses rather than assists the reader. Much is made of the author's sixteenth birthday and the subsequent acquisition of a driver's license. But other ages (fourteen and fifteen) are described as "driving years" without needed clarification. This error results in confusion for the reader and the necessity of several readings to achieve coherence. In short, the writer makes the reader work too hard. Although the essay might have been quite effective, since many amusing details pique the reader's interest, the writer's inability to write clearly puts too many demands upon the reader.

The author concludes with the unexpected dismay he/she felt soon after obtaining a driver's license. This section has potential, but it is underdeveloped. As the prompt asks the writer to analyze why this event was so disappointing, the writer should address this key point in extensive detail. The final line ("Now its' there turn to pay the piper") is indicative of the author's lack of control, reliance on inappropriate clichés, and punctuation and spelling errors. The essay receives a Marginal Fail for these reasons.

Essay #4—Fail (Score = 1)

One time when I went to the store I had wanted to by a video cammra. So I went to the department where they were being sold and looked at the different types of cammra. I was surprised at the low prices they were asking. I picked out the one I wanted; and bought it.

When I got home I was messing around with the cammera to see what different type of things it could do. It had a zoom, it had a mic and had many other interesting function. When I was done playing around with it and finding out everything that it could do I went to the park with my little sister. She was only 3 years old I thought I could get some funny pictures. My older sister said that she wanted to go along also; just to watch. When we got to the park I had the cammera no more than 30 seconds and Kelly my older sister wanted to use my cammera. I let her but I said for only a couple. I went to get something to drink and when I came back I saw my cammera being passed around in a group of 15. I asked for it back but all I got was a black eye. Some guy didn't like the way I was trying to get my cammera. As it was being passed around some body dropped it. It broke into a thousand small pieces. I was very upset. I got to use my cammera for about 30 seconds; and I got a black eye.

As you could of told I was very dissapointed; with how much I got to use the cammera. One thing I did learn it if you ever buy a new "toy" than keep it to yourself; or let somebody you can trust.

Scoring Explanation for Essay #4—Fail

Lack of development and errors of many sorts (syntax, grammar, punctuation, and spelling) are, unfortunately, the most memorable features of this essay. The writer begins with an overly simplistic and pedestrian account of the purchase of a "video cammra." The sentences are elementary and surprisingly void of useful detail.

The longest, central paragraph in this too-brief personal essay is a narrative account of the "borrowing," misuse, and destruction of the camera. Although the reader may sympathize for the writer's plight, little effort has been made to make the camera a highly desired or valued object. The story of its untimely demise lacks relevant detail to engage the reader on a meaningful level. The author concludes with a typically awkward sentence: "As you could of told I was very dissapointed; with how much I got to use the cammera." The writer's disengaging style and many errors distance the reader, and the essay fails on these accounts.

Index

375

NOTES

NOTES

 **Available Titles for California Teacher Certification**

ISBN: 978-0-7386-1202-7   ISBN: 978-0-7386-1209-6